TIME LIFE ® BOOKS

Other Publications:

*This volume is one of a series that explains and demonstrates
how to prepare various types of food, and that offers in each
book an international anthology of great recipes.*

Beverages

BY
THE EDITORS OF TIME-LIFE BOOKS

TIME-LIFE BOOKS/ALEXANDRIA, VIRGINIA

Cover: Ice-cold water and finely crushed ice transform a thick black currant syrup into a thirst-quenching drink *(page 40).* The quartet of enticing beverages also includes iced Ceylon tea *(page 19)* flavored with slices of fresh lime, a martini *(page 88)* garnished with a green olive, and a cup of black coffee *(page 21).*

Time-Life Books Inc.
is a wholly owned subsidiary of
TIME INCORPORATED

Founder: Henry R. Luce 1898-1967

Editor-in-Chief: Henry Anatole Grunwald
President: J. Richard Munro
Chairman of the Board: Ralph P. Davidson
Executive Vice President: Clifford J. Grum
Editorial Director: Ralph Graves
Group Vice President, Books: Joan D. Manley
Vice Chairman: Arthur Temple

TIME-LIFE BOOKS INC.
Editor: George Constable. *Executive Editor:* George Daniels. *Director of Design:* Louis Klein. *Board of Editors:* Dale M. Brown, Thomas A. Lewis, Martin Mann, Robert G. Mason, John Paul Porter, Gerry Schremp, Gerald Simons, Rosalind Stubenberg, Kit van Tulleken. *Director of Administration:* David L. Harrison. *Director of Research:* Carolyn L. Sackett. *Director of Photography:* John Conrad Weiser. *Design:* Arnold C. Holeywell (assistant director), Anne B. Landry (art coordinator), James J. Cox (quality control). *Research:* Jane Edwin (assistant director), Louise D. Forstall. *Copy Room:* Susan Galloway Goldberg (director), Celia Beattie. *Production:* Feliciano Madrid (director), Gordon E. Buck, Peter Inchauteguiz

President: Reginald K. Brack Jr. *Executive Vice Presidents:* John Steven Maxwell, David J. Walsh. *Vice Presidents:* George Artandi, Stephen L. Bair, Peter G. Barnes, Nicholas Benton, John L. Canova, Beatrice T. Dobie, James L. Mercer, Paul R. Stewart

THE GOOD COOK
The original version of this book was created in London for Time-Life Books B.V.
European Editor: Kit van Tulleken. *Photography Director:* Pamela Marke. *Planning Director:* Alan Lothian. *Chief of Research:* Vanessa Kramer. *Chief Sub-Editor:* Ilse Gray. *Chief of Editorial Production:* Ellen Brush. *Quality Control:* Douglas Whitworth

Staff for Beverages: Editor: Ellen Galford. *Series Coordinator:* Liz Timothy. *Text Editor:* Jane Havell. *Anthology Editor:* Tokunbo Williams. *Staff Writers:* Alexandra Carlier, Sally Crawford, Thom Henvey. *Researchers:* Tim Fraser (principal), Caroline Baum, Deborah Litton. *Designer:* Cherry Doyle. *Sub-Editors:* Charles Boyle, Kate Cann, Frances Dixon, Sally Rowland. *Design Assistant:* David Mackersey. *Editorial Department:* Sarah Dawson, Judith Heaton, Lesley Kinahan, Stephanie Lee, Debra Lelliott, Jane Lillicrap, Linda Mallett, Janet Matthew, Sylvia Osborne, Debra Raad, Ros Smith, Molly Sutherland, Helen Whitehorn

U.S. Staff for Beverages: Editor: Gerry Schremp. *Designer:* Ellen Robling. *Chief Researcher:* Barbara Levitt. *Associate Editors:* Anne Horan (text), Christine Schuyler (pictures). *Text Editor:* Sarah Brash. *Staff Writer:* Rita Mullin. *Researchers:* Fran Moshos (techniques), Jane Hanna (anthology), Karin Kinney. *Assistant Designer:* Peg Schreiber. *Copy Coordinators:* Tonna Gibert, Nancy Lendved. *Art Assistant:* Mary L. Orr. *Picture Coordinator:* Rebecca Christoffersen. *Editorial Assistants:* Andrea Reynolds, Patricia Whiteford. *Special Contributor:* Christine B. Dove.

CHIEF SERIES CONSULTANT

Richard Olney, an American, has lived and worked for some three decades in France, where he is highly regarded as an authority on food and wine. Author of *The French Menu Cookbook* and of the award-winning *Simple French Food,* he has also contributed to numerous gastronomic magazines in France and the United States, including the influential journals *Cuisine et Vins de France* and *La Revue du Vin de France.* He has directed cooking courses in France and the United States and is a member of several distinguished gastronomic and oenological societies, including L'Académie Internationale du Vin, La Confrérie des Chevaliers du Tastevin and La Commanderie du Bontemps de Médoc et des Graves. Working in London with the series editorial staff, he has been basically responsible for the planning of this volume, and has supervised the final selection of recipes submitted by other consultants. The United States edition of The Good Cook has been revised by the Editors of Time-Life Books to bring it into complete accord with American customs and usage.

CHIEF AMERICAN CONSULTANT
Carol Cutler is the author of a number of cookbooks, including the award-winning *The Six-Minute Soufflé and Other Culinary Delights.* During the 12 years she lived in France, she studied at the Cordon Bleu and the École des Trois Gourmandes, and with private chefs. She is a member of the Cercle des Gourmettes, a long-established French food society limited to just 50 members, and is also a charter member of Les Dames d'Escoffier, Washington Chapter.

SPECIAL CONSULTANT
Richard Sax, who was responsible for many of the step-by-step demonstrations for this volume, was for two years Chef-Director of the test kitchens for *The International Review of Food and Wine.* Trained in New York and in Paris, where he served an apprenticeship at the Hotel Plaza-Athénée, he has run a restaurant on Martha's Vineyard, written articles for a number of publications and conducted cooking courses.

PHOTOGRAPHER
Bob Komar is a Londoner who trained at both the Hornsey and Manchester Schools of Art. He specializes in food photography and in portraiture.

INTERNATIONAL CONSULTANTS
GREAT BRITAIN: *Jane Grigson* has written a number of books about food and has been a cookery correspondent for the London *Observer* since 1968. *Alan Davidson* is the author of several cookbooks and the founder of Prospect Books, which specializes in scholarly publications about food and cookery. FRANCE: *Michel Lemonnier,* the cofounder and vice president of Les Amitiés Gastronomiques Internationales, is a frequent lecturer on wine and vineyards. GERMANY: *Jochen Kuchenbecker* trained as a chef, but worked for 10 years as a food photographer in several European countries before opening his own restaurant in Hamburg. *Anne Brakemeier* is the co-author of a number of cookbooks. ITALY: *Massimo Alberini* is a well-known food writer and journalist with a special interest in culinary history. His many books include *La Tavola all'Italiana, 4000 Anni a Tavola* and *100 Ricette Storiche.* THE NETHERLANDS: *Hugh Jans* has published cookbooks and his recipes appear in several Dutch magazines.

Correspondents: Elisabeth Kraemer (Bonn); Margot Hapgood, Dorothy Bacon (London); Miriam Hsia, Lucy T. Voulgaris (New York); Maria Vincenza Aloisi, Josephine du Brusle (Paris); Ann Natanson (Rome)
Valuable assistance was also provided by: Janny Hovinga (Amsterdam); Bona Schmid (Milan); Mimi Murphy (Rome)

First printing. Printed in U.S.A.
Published simultaneously in Canada.
School and library distribution by Silver Burdett Company, Morristown, New Jersey 07960.

TIME-LIFE is a trademark of Time Incorporated U.S.A.

For information about any Time-Life book, please write:
Reader Information, Time-Life Books
541 North Fairbanks Court, Chicago, Illinois 60611

Library of Congress CIP data, page 176.

CONTENTS

Comfort and Cheer from Cup and Glass

Almost everywhere in the world, the offering of a drink is an act of hospitality. The beverage itself may vary with the climate, the time of day and the customs of the particular country—cooling fruit syrups and sherbets under the hot Middle Eastern sun; a warming brew of tea, milk and yak butter in the chilly foothills of the Himalayas; an eminently soothing martini presented 50 stories above the noisy, frenzied traffic of a Manhattan thoroughfare.

This splendid variety, this vast range of hospitable beverages, is the subject of our volume. You will learn the techniques for preparing a full spectrum of drinks, from a simple cup of tea to a bartender's repertoire of cocktails. After an introduction to the main ingredients and the histories of some of the most popular drinks, a series of chapters takes up the preparation of beverages according to type. The first chapter deals with various preparations of teas, tisanes and coffees. Subsequent chapters illustrate how to make fruit, nut and vegetable juices; milk drinks; savory broths; and alcoholic drinks. The second half of the book consists of an anthology of more than 300 recipes gathered from all parts of the world.

Water

Water—after mother's milk, man's earliest drink—remains the basis of virtually all beverages. Despite its uniform appearance, water varies widely. It may be naturally hard (rich in mineral salts) or rain-water soft or anywhere in between. It may be drawn untreated directly from a country well; it may be conditioned by chemicals and conducted through a maze of city pipes to a kitchen faucet; or it may be commercially distilled and poured from a bottle. Depending on the beverage you are making, some waters will work better than others.

Hard water, which prevails in most parts of the United States, is of course widely used in making all household beverages, and in most instances there is no reason to avoid it. However, for a drink of crystal clarity and utmost purity—particularly when you are brewing coffee or steeping tea—try naturally soft water, if you can get it. Failing that, you might use bottled distilled water. There are, of course, chemical softeners on the market. But it is better not to use them because such chemicals produce a bitter-tasting drink. For wine making, avoid water that is extremely hard; it will adversely affect the taste and clarity of the finished beverage. You can use bottled distilled water if you live in a hard-water area.

Quite the opposite is true in the case of beer; unlike most beverages, it profits from hard water because the mineral salts help precipitate the starchy compounds present in the grains used to make beer. Indeed, there are times when chemical hardeners are well worth using (pages 70-71).

In the case of mixed drinks, let your palate be your guide; if the water tastes good it will be fine for such beverages. The same applies to the ice with which you will chill most mixed drinks since it will lend its taste to a beverage when it melts.

Tea

Tea is one of the best-known and most widely produced of hot beverages. Tea plants are known to have been cultivated in China as early as 350 A.D., and some references to tea in legend and lore go back more than 4,000 years. At first, tea was drunk as a cure for nervous and digestive disorders. But by 500 A.D. it was also being described as a "pleasing beverage" and valued as a stimulant, particularly by Buddhist monks who found it an aid to staying awake during their long hours of meditation.

Names such as Pure Delight, the Pearl and Precious Thunder reflected the esteem that tea enjoyed, as did the epicurean tournaments Chinese emperors held to appraise new varieties. The making of tea became a stylized ritual, codified by the Eighth Century poet and scholar Lu Yu, who wrote a compendium on the subject. The proper brewing of tea, Lu Yu wrote, required toasting cakes of compressed tea leaves over a fire until they were "as soft as a baby's arm"; these were to be put into water that was boiling so that "billows surge wildly in the kettle." Lu Yu favored teacups glazed in blue, which lent a jadelike greenness to the tea.

The mystique attached to tea drinking in China spread to Japan, where it evolved into the celebrated tea ceremony, which reached its apogee in the 15th and 16th Centuries. The rite took place in a teahouse specially constructed of fragile materials—a thatched grass roof, rough-hewn pillars and bamboo supports—that called to mind the temporality of human life. The entrance to the building was a mere three feet high, signifying humility: Those who would pass through had to bow down, and proud Samurai warlords had to remove their swords. Inside, the room was decorated with spare precision, with a painting and a flower arrangement by the place of honor. The gathering was limited to six men, who conversed sedately while the water was made ready—a fact that was signaled when pieces of iron that had been placed in the bottom of the kettle produced a sound like wind whispering in the trees.

In the 17th Century, tea was brought to the West by Dutch trading ships, and tea drinking soon became a symbol of status, particularly in England. There, tea drinking was not simply a social ritual, but a passion. Dr. Samuel Johnson, the 18th Century critic and lexicographer, wrote that he was "a hardened and shameless tea-drinker, who has for many years diluted his meals with only the infusion of this fascinating plant; whose kettle has scarcely time to cool; who with tea amuses the evening, with tea solaces the midnight, and with tea welcomes the morning." No one knows exactly when tea arrived in America, but lading records show that by the middle of the 17th Century the Dutch settlers in New Amsterdam were importing silver and porcelain tea services similar to those they had used at home.

In England, Europe and the New World, tea remained an expensive luxury until the 19th Century, when English and Dutch colonists began to cultivate tea in India and Indonesia. Then Ceylon (now Sri Lanka) and Formosa (now Taiwan) followed suit, and today tea is commonly exported from those countries to others all over the world.

The delicate leaves that produce tea all belong to the species *Camellia sinensis,* which flourishes in tropical and subtropical countries. All varieties contain natural oils that give the tea flavor; caffeine, which acts as a mild stimulant; and tannin, which provides the tea with its pungency, color and body. The different characteristics of the finished teas result from differences in the soils and climates in which the plants are grown and from the different ways in which the leaves are harvested and processed. Plucking the leaves is a delicate task that is carried out manually on most plantations, and the most highly esteemed tea is made with tender young leaves, especially those that are still unopened.

For black teas, which produce dark liquids with strong flavor, the plucked leaves of the plant are treated by fermentation. (Tea-leaf fermentation is quite different from the better known yeast-induced fermentation used to make alcoholic beverages, but falls within the broad meaning of the word, which refers to the transformation of organic material by enzymes.) First, the leaves are spread out thin and left uncovered to dry—a process known as withering—which makes the leaves pliable and easier to treat evenly. Next, the withered leaves are rolled in a drum; rolling bruises them and breaks open their cells, releasing the essential oils that carry the tea's flavor. The leaves are then spread out again and left uncovered: At this stage, the enzymes that were also released by rolling oxidize the tannin in the leaves, reducing their pungency and darkening their color; at the same time, the flavor in the leaves' natural oils develops further. The whole process is stopped by firing the leaves with a blast of hot air. Firing also dries the leaves; drying, in turn, helps to preserve them.

The same process is modified to produce oolong teas, which have a smoother taste and a paler color than most black varieties. For green teas—known as unfermented teas—the leaves are steamed to make them pliable, then rolled and fired; because their tannin has not been oxidized, green teas have a pleasantly bitter flavor and yield a very light-colored liquid.

Tisanes—teas made from dried herbs, roots, seeds or flower blossoms—offer further scope for experiment. A wide range of such tisanes is available commercially, but it is a simple matter to preserve freshly picked herbs or flowers at home *(pages 14-15).* Linden, rose hips, camomile, mint, sage and rosemary are just a few of the garden sources of fragrant and delicately flavored beverages.

Coffee

Like tea, coffee was first valued mainly for its medicinal and stimulating properties, and was used for religious purposes. The coffee tree is indigenous to Africa, and it was African tribesmen who prepared the first beverage from whole ripe coffee berries. Its popularity had spread through the Arab world by about 1200 A.D. Some time during the century that ensued, the practice of extracting the beans from the berries was introduced, as was the technique of roasting them to develop flavor. By the 16th Century, coffee was prepared by pulverizing the roasted beans and combining the powder with boiling water. This method is still widely used today in the Middle East; the drink that results is often called Turkish coffee *(page 25).*

When coffee was introduced to Europe by Venetian traders in the late 16th Century, fanatical priests in Rome tried to persuade Pope Clement VIII to ban it because of its association with Muslim infidels. The Pope surprised them; he decided to taste some coffee for himself and solemnly declared it to be a truly Christian drink.

For more than two centuries, coffee continued to cause controversy. In France, wine merchants objected to the new drink because it affected the sales of their vintages. In Prussia, Frederick the Great looked with a greedy eye on the large sums of money that were going into the pockets of foreign coffee merchants; to control the trade, he forbade the roasting of coffee beans to all but a select few and enforced the prohibition with the aid of coffee spies, who patrolled the streets literally sniffing out offenders. Coffeehouses also became meeting places for the disaffected in times of political unrest and were therefore viewed with hostility by those in power, though few rulers were as savage as the 17th Century Ottoman Grand Vizier who, it is said, punished persistent coffee drinkers by sewing them into leather bags and dropping them in the Bosphorus.

Until the end of the 17th Century, most coffee production remained in the hands of the Arabs, and during the next hundred years, theft, piracy and intrigue were employed in attempts to break the Arab monopoly. Dutch spies finally managed to steal some coffee seeds from Arabia; they planted the seeds in the Dutch colony of Java and from there sent coffee to Europe. In 1723, a French naval officer named Gabriel Mathieu de Clieu somehow stole a coffee tree that was nurtured as a curiosity in the Botanical Gardens in Paris; with this unusual cargo, he set sail for Martinique. Despite having to share his meager water rations with the tree, elude pursuit by pirate vessels and fend off sabotage attempts by a stowaway Dutch spy, de Clieu eventually planted his tree in Martinique and thus initiated the cultivation of coffee in the West Indies.

Four years later, in 1727, a Brazilian army officer won the heart of the Governor's wife in neighboring French Guiana; she made him a gift of some cuttings from a coffee tree. He duly smuggled the cuttings back to Brazil—thus begetting the most prodigious yield of all. Since then, Brazil has grown to be the largest coffee supplier in the world.

The coffee fruit, or berry, resembles a cherry in appearance. Inside most berries are two flattened oval beans: Some berries have only one round bean called a peaberry; from this the highly esteemed peaberry coffee *(page 16)* is made. Both types of berry are harvested by hand, then processed to free the beans, which are surrounded not only by the fruit pulp, but also by two thin, clinging skins. Most berries are spread on the ground to dry for several weeks so that enzymatic action—fermentation—can loosen the skins and pulp for milling. In areas where water is plentiful, however, the finest, ripest berries are often cleaned by washing. The berries are hulled, then the pulp-and-skin-covered beans are repeatedly washed to free them from the pulp

and briefly dried, after which the skins can be removed. Washed coffee beans tend to have better flavor—and higher prices—than those cured by drying.

Milk

Ever since wild sheep and goats were first domesticated, about 10,000 years ago, animal milk has been a staple of man's diet. Most of the milk consumed today is cow's milk, but sheep's milk and goat's milk are drunk in the Middle East and Southern Europe. About half of India's milk is supplied by the water buffalo, and the milk of the same animal is used in Italy. Milk from asses, yaks and reindeer is a common beverage in the remoter regions of the world.

Milk is rightly prized for versatility. It can be combined with eggs for thick and fluffy textures *(pages 48-49)*; and with coffee and fruit syrups for flavor. It has a particularly wonderful compatibility with cocoa and chocolate, which form a variety of sweet drinks, both sustaining and pleasantly rich in texture.

By another version of the process of fermentation, milk can be transformed into yogurt, which yields any number of refreshing drinks *(pages 50-51)*. The milk is inoculated with special strains of bacteria that both ferment and coagulate the liquid into thick, tangy curds. According to one theory, yogurt was first discovered accidentally by desert nomads who found that the milk in their saddlebags turned into curds after a day's riding, thanks to the natural bacteria contained in the leather.

Today yogurt is widely available commercially, but homemade yogurt is far superior in taste and texture to most manufactured varieties. Yogurt can be diluted and combined with sugar syrups, fruit, herbs and spices to make sweet and pungent drinks.

Savory broths

Perhaps even more than tea and coffee, broths figure as folk medicine. For centuries, people have believed that a liquid containing all the goodness of meat, poultry or vegetables, drawn out by gentle and prolonged simmering, is an effective preventive and cure-all. This faith crosses national boundaries: In Provence, an ancient and enduring maxim says that garlic broth *(pages 58-59)* "saves lives," and generations of anxious mothers the world over have relied on concentrated chicken broth *(pages 60-61)* as an infallible elixir. The method for making this essence has scarcely changed since the 16th Century, when the English writer Andrew Boorde advised cooks to seal up their meat in a glass or stone jar "so no air goes out, and seethe it with water in a cauldron." Needless to say, ill-health is not a prerequisite for any of these beverages; they are always welcome sources of both warmth and nourishment, especially when the weather is cold.

Beer, wine and spirits

Fruit and vegetable juices and grains become alcoholic when—by yet another variation on the principle of fermentation—their starch or sugar content is transformed by yeast into alcohol and carbon dioxide. Some fruits and grains contain natural yeast and may ferment spontaneously; the ancient Egyptians, Greeks and Chinese all had fermented beverages—wines from naturally fermented grapes and honey, and beers from naturally fermented cereal grains. But it required a bit of luck, for uncontrolled fermentation can result in sour liquid rather than good beer or wine. However, fermentation can be controlled, and once you understand the techniques, you will be able to brew a wide range of alcoholic beverages, including fizzy ginger beer, ready to drink in two days, longer-aged beer and homemade wine and even a fermentation of honey that needs months or even years to mature.

Mixed alcoholic drinks, such as punches and cocktails, combine wines, spirits or liqueurs with other ingredients or bring different types of alcohol together. Both punches and mixed drinks are essentially party drinks that not only will enhance a special occasion but also will do much to mitigate a dismal one. Attractively garnished, an iced sparkling punch is the perfect refreshment for a warm summer's day. And a hot punch warms a person chilled to the bone on a bitter winter's night.

Cocktails offer ample opportunity for the exercise of flair and imagination. You can perfect your own favorite techniques for preparing classic mixed drinks such as martinis and robust mixtures like Black Velvets, which contain equal parts of stout and Champagne. And once you understand the techniques of drink mixing you can indulge in the pleasant occupation of creating new mixtures: Cocktails—and most of the other beverages described in this volume—offer almost unlimited opportunities for improvisation.

Airtight Seals for Bottled Drinks

Although most homemade beverages are served immediately, some—such as fruit syrups *(pages 40-41)* and liqueurs *(pages 66-67)*—may be stored in sealed bottles for the sake of convenience. And beers, ciders and wines *(pages 70-77)* must be stored in bottles so that they ferment properly, developing full flavor without the risk of contamination from the air.

Liqueurs and syrups may be kept in bottles of almost any type. However, fermented beverages require bottles made of fortified glass that will withstand pressure that might build inside: Bottles that have previously held the same kind of fermented beverage are ideal.

To prevent spoilage, the bottles must be scrubbed thoroughly. For liqueurs or syrups, use a bottle brush and plain hot water: Soap might leave a residue that would flavor the liquid inside. For fermented beverages, the bottles must be sterilized to destroy any contaminating microorganisms. Putting the scrubbed bottles through the rinse and dry cycles of a dishwasher will heat the bottles enough to kill any bacteria on them. Alternatively, the bottles can be scrubbed and sterilized simultaneously in a solution of hot tap water and sodium metabisulfite, a sterilizing agent available from brewing-supply stores in loose powder form or as Campden tablets. Once the bottles have been sterilized, they must be rinsed well in hot water.

Tight covers are essential for bottles. Metal caps, which clamp over the rim of a bottle to seal it, will resist the pressure exerted by beers or sparkling wines. The caps are available in a standard size that fits most bottles. Corks should be slightly larger than the opening to prevent leakage. Corks are available in a range of sizes and may be tapered, for easy insertion, or straight-sided.

Before use, caps and corks should be sterilized in a solution of hot water and sodium metabisulfite, then rinsed well. Caps can be left to dry, but corks should be used while still damp enough to be squeezed into the bottles.

Attaching caps requires special tools. One of the simplest is the twin-levered capper shown below. Tapered corks can be inserted partway by hand, then hammered in with a wooden mallet *(opposite, left)*. Straight-sided corks are inserted with a simple corking tool *(opposite, center)* or with a levered device *(opposite, right)* that works like the capper.

Sterilizing Bottles

Scrubbing bottles. Crush Campden tablets and dissolve them in hot water, using a ratio of seven tablets to each quart [1 liter] of water. Soak bottles in the solution for several minutes before scrubbing them with a bottle brush. Rinse them well under hot running water and invert them in a towel-lined rack to dry.

Anchoring Metal Caps

1 **Loading the capper.** Extend the two levers of a bottle capper as high as possible. Place the flat side of a sterilized and rinsed metal cap on the magnet head at the base of the capper's chamber; make sure that the cap is secure.

2 **Sealing.** Invert the capper over the neck of a beer bottle, centering the cap. Applying equal pressure on each side, press the levers down. When the levers cannot be moved further, the bottle is sealed. Lift the capper away.

Hammering In Corks

1 **Softening corks.** Dissolve crushed Campden tablets in hot water. Place tapered corks in the water; put a plate over them to submerge them. After 20 minutes, remove the corks, rinse them in hot water and dry them slightly.

2 **Corking bottles.** Push a damp tapered cork partway into the neck of a bottle. Grasp the neck firmly and, with a wooden mallet, gently hammer the cork until its top is flush with the rim of the bottle.

Using a Wooden Corker

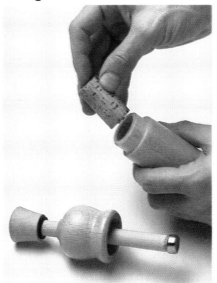

1 **Loading a cork.** Sterilize straight-sided corks in a bowl of crushed Campden tablets and hot water *(left)*. Separate the parts of a corking tool. Push a damp cork partway into the wide end of the tube section of the tool.

2 **Corking.** Place the narrow end of the tube over the bottle. Fit the extended plunger into the top of the tube to cover the cork. Holding the plunger casing and the tube together, hammer gently until the plunger is fully depressed.

Levering Corks into Place

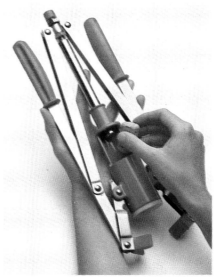

1 **Filling the chamber.** Sterilize straight-sided corks in a solution of crushed Campden tablets and hot water *(far left)*. Extend the levers of the corking device upward, and place a damp cork in the hollow chamber of the tool.

2 **Corking the bottle.** Center the corking tool on the bottle. Press the levers down evenly until the orange fingers surround the neck to steady the bottle. To insert the cork, pull the levers down as far as possible. Lift the corking device.

1
Teas, Tisanes and Coffees
Brews of Strength and Subtlety

Choosing and brewing tea
Roasting and grinding coffees
Infusing coffee for mellowness
Exploiting coffee's bitterness
Chilled and frozen beverages

Tea and coffee—those ubiquitous, revivifying beverages—are both very simple to make: The ingredients are brought into contact with water so that their flavors are drawn out into the liquid. They are usually served hot, but they need not always be; chilled, they make such cooling summer drinks as the iced coffee shown opposite. Coffee can even be semi-frozen, making a delicious drink with the texture of a water ice *(page 26)*.

The dried leaves of the tea plant are processed in many different ways to make a range of teas, from the strong, astringent Japanese green tea to the smoky Chinese lapsang souchong. A selection of teas is illustrated and described on pages 12-13. In addition to tea, many other leaves, flowers and herbs make delicious drinks—they are called tisanes or herb teas *(pages 14-15)*. Tea leaves are bought dried and ready for use; herbs and flowers for tisanes, however, can easily be dried at home. Both beverages are usually made simply by pouring boiling water over the leaves or flowers, leaving them to infuse, then straining the liquid *(pages 18-19)*.

Coffee is always made from the ground roasted beans of the coffee tree, but subtle differences in color and flavor are achieved by varying the way the beans are roasted and the way the drink is made. Roasting develops the flavor and aroma of the beans; they are then ground to allow maximum contact with the water. Many coffee enthusiasts buy fresh, unroasted beans and prepare them at home *(pages 16-17 and 20)*.

One method of making coffee works in the same manner as for tea: The ground coffee is steeped in hot water and the liquid is then strained *(page 21)*. Another depends on allowing the hot water to drip through the coffee at a controlled rate *(page 22)*. Both these methods produce coffee with an excellent aroma and a mellow flavor. A third technique produces a more bitter, austere drink by forcing boiling water or even steam through ground coffee *(page 23)*. The taste of coffee is sufficiently assertive to take strong flavorings—spices, fruits and spirits, for example—to create sharp and potent after-dinner drinks *(pages 28-29)*.

Dry ingredients for tea, tisanes and coffee should be stored in tightly covered jars in a cool place. Herbs, flowers and scented teas will keep for up to six months; plain teas for one year. Unroasted beans will keep for a year or longer. Whole roasted beans should be used within three weeks; once ground, they begin to lose their flavor in a matter of days.

A dash of light cream enriches and marbles a tall glass of iced coffee. Very strong black coffee—cooled to room temperature and then refrigerated—has been poured over ice cubes to make the beverage refreshingly cold *(page 27)*.

A Guide to Teas

The broad range of teas—indicated by the sampling shown below and described at far right—belies the fact that all come from a single species, the *Camellia sinensis*. The diversity of tea leaves, and of the drinks they produce, reflects the many places where the plant is grown and the different ways it is processed.

Though usually associated with Asia, teas also grow in the Middle East, the Soviet Union, Africa and South America: The plants flourish in tropical and subtropical climates. Ironically, the leaves that are prized the most usually come from mountainous regions; the plants grow more slowly, but develop richer flavor. Because many teas are identified by their country, district or city of origin—Ceylon or Darjeeling, for example—their names often give a clue to their characteristics.

After they are harvested, the leaves may simply be heat-dried *(page 6)*, keeping them green in color and preserving their slightly bitter taste; these green teas yield a pale astringent drink. Alternatively, the leaves may be subjected to more complicated treatments that oxidize them, darkening their color to brown or black and mellowing their flavor. Depending on the extent of such processing, they become partly oxidized oolong teas or fully oxidized black teas. Oolong teas produce amber drinks with a mild taste; black teas—forming by far the largest category—yield drinks with a deep golden red or brown color and a rich flavor.

The leaves of both green and oolong teas usually are left whole and rolled tightly into cylinders or pellets. Those of black teas, which are often broken in processing, are sifted and graded according to size. Since large leaves and pieces infuse more slowly than small ones, this grading helps ensure that leaves sold together will infuse at the same rate.

In many cases, size designations form part of a tea's name. Souchong, for example, indicates large leaves. Medium-sized leaves are pekoe—the Chinese word for "white hair" and a reference to the white tips such leaves once had. The smallest whole leaves are called orange pekoe; the name derives from a Chinese custom, long since abandoned, of mixing these leaves with orange blossoms. This grade of tea may include leaf tips and buds.

Moyune gunpowder

Green Japanese

Formosa oolong

Lapsang souchong

Ichang

Ceylon

Assam

Darjeeling

Broken leaves, used primarily in tea bags, also are graded. The largest pieces are designated broken pekoe souchong; the smallest are tiny particles of leaves referred to as fines.

Individual teas of all varieties and sizes are easiest to find at specialty tea stores and where Asian foods are sold. Even there, the most popular teas are blends of two or more varieties, combined because they complement or balance one another. For additional fragrance, both individual teas and blends also are frequently flavored with citrus peel, flower blossoms or such spices as cloves.

Once purchased, teas may be stored for up to a year. Keep them in airtight containers away from light or moisture that might oxidize the leaves or cause mildew.

Assam. A black Indian tea grown at a low altitude, yielding a pungent, malty beverage.
Ceylon. A popular black tea with a brisk, sweet flavor.
Darjeeling. A black Indian tea grown in the foothills of the Himalayas; the penetrating flavor is suggestive of muscat grapes.
Earl Grey. A blend of Indian and Chinese black teas flavored with oils from the peel of the bergamot, a small citrus fruit.
Formosa oolong. An oolong tea with a pungent, peachlike flavor.
Green Japanese. A green tea producing a delicately scented, astringent liquid.
Ichang. A black Chinese tea with a slightly smoky flavor.
Jasmine. A Chinese oolong tea, scented with jasmine flowers.
Java. A black tea with a slightly astringent flavor; commonly used in blends.
Keemun. A black Chinese tea with a flowery aroma and a winelike taste.

Kenyan. A black tea with a rich, sweet flavor similar to that of Ceylon tea.
Lapsang souchong. A black tea from China or Taiwan with a smoky flavor.
Moyune gunpowder. A green tea from China yielding a fragrant, subtly fruity liquid. The name "gunpowder" derives from the pellet-like appearance of the treated leaves.
Rose pouchong. An oolong tea from Taiwan, scented with rose petals; a Chinese black tea is also sold under this name.
Russian. A black tea from the Caucasus Mountains of the Soviet Union. Because it is harvested mechanically, it contains bits of twig that impart an earthy flavor. It should not be confused with Russian-style tea, which is a blend of Indian and Chinese black teas.
Scented orange pekoe. A Chinese oolong tea that is made with leaf tips; it yields a flowery infusion.
Yunnan. A black tea from China with a sweet smell and a smoky taste.

Jasmine

Rose pouchong

Scented orange pekoe

Yunnan

Keemun

Earl Grey

Kenyan

Java

Russian

A Guide to Tisanes

Tisanes are fragrant infusions that may be based on any substance from culinary herbs to tree leaves and shrub flowers. In fact, any edible plant material is usable. The ingredients illustrated below and described at right represent only a sampling of the choices available.

Leaves and flowers are the most commonly used plant materials, although the fruits, seeds, bark and roots of some plants are also prized. In season, leaves and flowers can be infused fresh. Drying preserves them for use year-round *(box, far right)*; enclosed in airtight containers and stored in a cool, dark place, they will keep for at least six months.

Ingredients for tisanes may be homegrown or bought at a supermarket, if common, or at an herbalist or health-food store, if exotic. Whole or roughly broken forms will hold flavor longest, but will infuse more slowly. To make tisanes, chop, crush or crumble the materials.

Depending on the content, tisanes vary from pale and delicate to rich and robust. Usually they are served hot, but some—especially those with a fruity taste, such as rose hip and lemon verbena—are also delicious cold. They can be sweetened with sugar or honey and accented by lemon juice or lemon or orange peel.

Bitter orange. The flowers of the tree produce a delicate-tasting infusion that has a fruity scent.

Boldo. The tree's leaves yield an invigorating tisane with a bitter flavor and a strong scent.
Camomile. A beverage made from the herb's flowers has an apple-like scent and an earthy, slightly bitter flavor.
Elder. The shrub's flowers produce a highly scented, slightly bitter, honey-flavored tisane.
Hibiscus. The flowers of the shrub yield a cherry-colored tisane with a bold, fruity taste and a sweet, full-blown scent.
Lemon verbena. The leaves of the shrub make a tisane with a lemon-scented bouquet and a pronounced lemon flavor.
Linden. The flowers and leaves of the tree produce a brew of exceptional sweetness and fragrance.
Meadowsweet. The young leaves, branch tips and flower buds of the herb produce a sweet-smelling tisane with a delicate taste.
Nettle. A tisane made from the young

Sage

Yerba maté

Thyme

Linden

Elder flower

Bitter orange

Meadowsweet

shoots and leaves of the herb has an almost imperceptible scent, but a full flavor.

Peppermint. The cool, pungent flavor of this sweet-smelling leaf has made peppermint the most popular of the mint plants for tisanes.

Raspberry leaf. Delicately scented, raspberry-leaf tisane has an astringent taste.

Rose hip. The fruit of the wild rose yields a tisane with a light scent and a sweet taste.

Sage. A refreshing, peppery-tasting, aromatic infusion is made from sage leaves.

Thyme. The pungent, aromatic infusion prepared from the herb's leaves has an earthy flavor with an astringent edge.

Vervain. A tisane made from the herb's leaves has a woody, slightly minty flavor.

Yerba maté. The leaves of the shrub are also called Paraguay or Brazil tea. They produce a high-caffeine tisane with a strong, smoky flavor.

Drying Herbs to Conserve Flavor

1 **Tying sprigs.** Gather herb sprigs— here, rosemary—into a loose bundle. Using raffia or string, tie the sprigs at their cut ends. Finish the knot with a loop.

2 **Removing leaves.** Hang the bundle in a dark, airy place for several weeks. When the leaves are crisp, pull them off. Store them in an airtight container.

Boldo

Raspberry leaf

Nettle

Lemon verbena

Hibiscus

Peppermint

Camomile

Vervain

Rose hip

A Guide to Coffees

Unroasted

Pale roast

Like fine tea leaves, the best coffee beans are grown at high altitudes in the tropics and subtropics; the beans are categorized by their countries or regions of origin. Although their characteristics vary widely, all such beans come from trees of the *Coffea arabica* species. The other major species, *Coffea robusta,* flourishes at lower altitudes and yields the less delicately flavored beans upon which most commercial blends are based.

The inherent flavor and aroma of coffee beans are developed by roasting. Simultaneously, their natural sugars caramelize so that the green beans darken.

The degree of roasting determines the taste of the drink. For example, a pale roast—also called a light city roast—gives coffee beans a delicate, acidic taste. A medium, or full city, roast imparts stronger character and mellower flavor. Dark roasts—known as French, continental or Viennese roasts—and the very dark Italian or espresso roasts produce a distinctive bittersweet coffee.

To ensure freshness, quality-conscious coffee dealers roast the beans they sell. Ideally, however, the beans should be roasted at home *(box, far right)* just before the drink is brewed. Although it is possible to roast coffee in an open pan, stirring the beans continuously, a rotating roaster such as the one shown will yield more evenly roasted beans.

Before the roasted beans are used, they are ground so that they will release their flavors when exposed to water. Because grinding increases the surface area of the beans, water passes through coarse grinds faster than fine ones. Each pot or coffee machine works best with a specific grind *(below)*. Only professional equipment can pulverize beans for Turkish coffee, but other grinds can be made at home *(page 20)* to ensure aromatic brews.

Coffees can be used singly or blended —before the beans are ground—to yield balanced mixtures bringing out the best in each variety. Bright acidic beans— such as those from Colombia or Kenya— may be contrasted with rich Java or Sumatran Mandheling coffee.

How long coffee can be stored depends on its form. Although raw beans keep for more than a year in a tightly covered container, roasted beans maintain quality for only about three weeks at room temperature—or about four months in the freezer. Ground beans—still more fragile—should be used within a week.

Angola. The best coffees grown here are pungent but lack smoothness; they make good bases for blends.
Brazil. Most of this country's wide range of coffees are used in blends. The best individual variety is Bourbon Santos, which has a sweet, clear, neutral flavor; Parana is harsher, but with good acidity; Rio has a heavy, pungent taste.
Burundi. Coffees from this northeast African nation have a rich, strong flavor and high acidity.
Cameroon. Beans produced here yield a fine, sweet, mellow brew.
Colombia. Generally regarded as South America's finest, the coffees of Colombia are flavorful, aromatic and delicately acidic. They blend well with other beans. Among the best are Medellíns, Armenias and Manizales.
Costa Rica. Coffees from the Pacific slopes of this Central American land have a fine, mild flavor, a fragrant aroma and sharp acidity. They blend well.
Cuba. Coffees grown on this Caribbean island have a sweet, full flavor.
Dominican Republic. Coffees grown here, sold as Santo Domingos, are pleasantly sweet and strong.
Ecuador. Beans produced here have a sharp, woody flavor that is best appreciated in blends.
El Salvador. Coffees grown on high ground here have good acidity and mild flavor. Low-grown coffees are lighter,

Coarse grind
For ceramic drip pots

Medium grind
For plain infusion pots, plunger infusion pots and coffee concentrate

Medium-fine gr
For Italian drip pots and filter coffee machine

Medium roast

Dark roast

Very dark roast

pleasantly acidic and winelike in taste.

Ethiopia. Harrar coffees—the finest grown in Ethiopia—have a piquant aroma, a rich, winey taste and high acidity.

Guatemala. Beans produced here yield an acidic, rich brew. High-grown Cobans and Antiguans have a full flavor and a fragrant, spicy bouquet.

Haiti. The best Haitian coffees, like those of the neighboring Dominican Republic, are mildly sweet, very mellow, rich in flavor and slightly acidic.

Hawaii. Kona, the only coffee grown here, has a smooth, pungent flavor, slight acidity and rich aroma.

India. The bulk of the coffee crop comes from Karnataka, formerly Mysore, which produces beans with a deep color and distinctive full, soft flavor that blend well with Ethiopian beans. Coffees from Nilgiris are rich and delicately acidic.

Jamaica. The prized Blue Mountain variety is aromatic with an extremely mellow, sweet, rich flavor. The more acidic High Mountain Supreme coffee has good body, and Prime Jamaican Washed has medium acidity and less body.

Java. The best Javanese beans are rich and slightly spicy with low acidity and full body. They blend well with Mocha, Ethiopian or Colombian beans.

Kenya. The tart, aromatic coffees grown here have an excellent mild flavor that blends well. Peaberry beans from Kenya are popular for home roasting.

Mexico. The best Mexican coffee, Coatepec, is rich, mellow and subtly acidic. A favorite for Turkish coffee, it blends well with Javanese or Kenyan coffees.

Nicaragua. The mild coffees that are grown here have good acidity and are useful in blends.

Papua New Guinea. Coffees produced here have a full, smooth flavor.

Peru. The finest Peruvian coffees are delicate in flavor and have good acidity.

Puerto Rico. The beans grown here produce sweet, rich, high-quality coffees.

Rwanda. The best coffees from this northeast African country have high acidity and a rich flavor.

Sumatra. Mandheling and Ankola are rich, heavy coffees; nearly acid-free, like the coffees of Java, they are excellent in blends with the more acidic Ethiopian or Jamaican High Mountain Supreme coffees.

Tanzania. Coffee produced here, sold as Kilimanjaro, is rich and mellow with delicate acidity. Peaberry beans from Tanzania are popular for home roasting.

Venezuela. The excellent coffees grown here on high ground are mild and mellow, with a delicate, winelike flavor.

Yemen. Mocha, the prize coffee of this country, has a distinctive winelike flavor and high acidity.

Zaire. Strongly flavored coffees, grown largely in the Kivu and Ituri regions, have a rich, highly acidic flavor. They blend well with milder coffees.

Roasting Raw Beans

Using a roaster. Place the stand of a rotating roaster over a burner. Pour raw beans into the roaster globe, cover it and set it in the stand. Turning the handle slowly, rotate the globe over medium heat until the beans crackle— about five minutes. Reduce the heat and rotate the globe quickly for two minutes, or until the beans reach the desired color. Lift off the globe, shake out a bean and crack it to be sure it is evenly browned inside. Spread the beans on a baking sheet to cool.

Fine grind
For steam-
pressure pots
and espresso
machines

Very fine grind
For paper-filter
drip pots

Pulverized
For Turkish
coffeepots

Basic Tactics for Perfect Potions

There is no mystery about making a perfect cup of hot tea. Whether you want a conventional tea or a tisane, you need only ensure that the leaves and flowers are of good quality and that the water poured over them is fresh and boiling fiercely so it brings out their aroma and flavor to the full.

When preparing a potful, use a teapot that retains heat well—china or glazed earthenware is an ideal choice (top demonstration). To prevent the water from cooling prematurely, warm the teapot a few moments in advance. Then place the dry ingredients in it, allowing 1 teaspoon [5 ml.] of leaves or flowers for each ¾ cup [175 ml.] of water—enough to fill a standard 6-ounce teacup. When making a single serving, warm the cup and use an infuser—a perforated spoon or ball that will hold enough loosely packed leaves or flowers for the drink (right, below).

In either case, well-aerated water is essential. Begin with water drawn straight from the cold-water tap and bring it to a boil quickly. Infusing tea takes three to six minutes, depending on how strong you want the drink; tisane needs eight to 12 minutes. Taste the drink to determine its intensity. Many teas—especially the black ones—color the water well before the flavor of the drink develops.

For an especially fragrant drink, robust black tea can be infused in water flavored with whole or crushed spices—cloves, cinnamon, allspice or the cardamom shown in the demonstration opposite, below (recipe, page 92). Because spice changes the character of the tea, freshly drawn water is not necessary.

For iced tea or tisane, you can simply chill the hot drink before pouring it over ice. However, boiling water extracts compounds from the leaves or flowers, and these will precipitate when the drink is chilled, thus clouding it. The problem can be solved by infusing the dry ingredients in cold water instead (box, opposite). Because cold water draws out flavors slowly, double the proportion of leaves or flowers to water and increase the infusion time to at least six hours.

All teas and tisanes can be spiked with lemon and sweetened with sugar or honey. Milk can be added to mellow a tea, but cream will mask the tea's flavor.

An Everyday Ceremony Carefully Performed

1 Warming the pot. In a kettle, boil fresh cold water for the tea—allowing ¾ cup [175 ml.] for each serving. Meanwhile, boil water in a pan and pour it into a teapot. After a minute or so, swirl the water around inside the teapot. Then discard this water.

2 Adding tea. Measure tea leaves—Formosa oolong is shown—or tisane leaves or flowers into the warmed teapot. Allow 1 teaspoon [5 ml.] of leaves or flowers for each serving.

A Foolproof Method for a Single Cup

1 Filling an infuser. Place tea leaves, or tisane leaves or flowers—here, equal proportions of rose hips and hibiscus flowers—in a section of an infuser spoon or ball. Close the infuser.

2 Stirring the drink. Place the infuser in a warmed cup and pour in freshly boiling water. Let tisane infuse for 10 minutes; tea, for five. Stir the drink with the infuser to distribute the flavor evenly, then remove the infuser and serve the beverage.

A Cold-Water Infusion

3 **Adding boiling water.** As soon as the water in the kettle comes to a rolling boil, pour it into the teapot. Place the lid on the pot and let the leaves or flowers steep. If you like, cover the pot with a tea cozy.

4 **Pouring the drink.** For a medium-strength drink, allow tea to infuse for five minutes, tisane for 10. Half a minute before serving, stir the drink once. To serve, pour the tea or tisane into cups through a strainer. Accompany it with lemon, sugar or honey, and milk.

1 **Mixing the drink.** In a tall jar or other glass container, combine 3 heaping tablespoons [45 ml.] of tea leaves—Ceylon is used in this demonstration—or tisane leaves or flowers with 1 quart [1 liter] of cold water. Cover the container and refrigerate it for six to nine hours.

An Enhancement of Spice

1 **Spicing water.** In a saucepan, bring whole cardamoms and cold water to a boil. Cover, simmer for five minutes, then set the pan aside for 10 minutes. Put black tea—Darjeeling is used here—and a strip of orange peel in a warmed teapot. Return the spiced water to a boil and pour it, with the cardamoms, into the pot.

2 **Serving the tea.** Cover the teapot and let the spiced tea infuse for five minutes. Stir it once and pour, through a strainer, into cups. Offer lemon wedges, sugar and milk separately, so they can be added to taste.

2 **Serving.** Strain the infusion into a pitcher. Fill tall glasses with ice cubes and a few thin slices of lemon. Pour the tea or tisane over the ice up to the rim of each glass. Serve accompanied by sugar.

Releasing Flavor and Aroma

The plethora of coffeepots and coffee machines available can be daunting. However, the best all operate by one of three methods: infusion, drip or filter drip, and steam pressure. The kind of equipment you should choose depends chiefly on the sort of drink you want to brew. Infusion and drip devices yield mellow drinks whereas steam-pressure systems produce astringent brews.

The simplest devices are infusion pots. With a plain pot *(right)*, the ground coffee is merely steeped in hot water, then strained. Some infusion pots are fitted with plungers that strain the drink as it is poured *(opposite, bottom)*.

Drip coffee is made by placing ground coffee in the perforated filter section of the pot or machine, then letting hot water trickle through the coffee into the decanter. For the clearest possible drink, the perforated section of many drip pots is lined with a paper filter *(page 22, top)*.

Coffee concentrate *(page 22, bottom)* is made by a combination of methods: Ground coffee is infused in cold water, then the resulting liquid is dripped into a decanter through a filter.

Brewing coffee by steam pressure requires more complicated devices. Among these is the well-known percolator, disliked by coffee lovers because in it the coffee itself boils and becomes bitter. An inexpensive and better steam-pressure coffee maker is a three-part pot *(page 23, top)*. Water is boiled in the bottom of the pot and steam forces water upward through the ground coffee into the top of the pot. Elegant espresso machines work on the same principle, although in these machines steam is controlled with valves and levers *(page 23, bottom)*.

Whatever the method, perfect coffee starts with quality beans that are roasted and ground just prior to use. Any of the grinders shown below will enable you to grind beans to suit your equipment *(pages 16-17)*. A hand-cranked mill grinds the beans between spiked wheels that are adjusted manually to produce grinds of varying fineness. An electric blade grinder chops the beans rather than milling them; the fineness depends on how long the machine runs. An electric mill grinder can be adjusted by dials to produce the fineness desired.

How much ground coffee you need will vary with the brewing method and how strong you want the drink to be. In general, 2 tablespoons [30 ml.] of ground coffee to each ¾ cup [175 ml.] of water will yield a medium-strong infused or drip coffee. Double the amount of ground coffee if you use a steam-pressure device.

The best coffee is made with fresh cold water. For infused or drip coffee, mellowness is ensured by heating the water to just below boiling. If the water is much hotter than 200° F. [93° C.], it will extract bitter flavors. To achieve the correct temperature, let the water come to a boil, then cool for 10 seconds before using.

A Hand-cranked Mill

Grinding by hand. Adjust the wheels of a hand-cranked mill grinder: The closer the wheels, the finer the grind. Put coffee beans in the bowl, but do not fill it to the top lest the beans spill over during grinding. Crank the handle until all of the beans are ground; remove the ground coffee from the drawer in the base.

An Electric Coffee Chopper

Using an electric blade grinder. Fill the top of a grinder with up to ½ cup [125 ml.] of coffee beans. Put on the lid and run the machine for a few seconds, then check its progress. Continue to run the grinder until the coffee is as fine as you want.

An Electric Mill

Grinding with an electric mill. Pour up to ½ pound [¼ kg.] of coffee beans into the upper receptacle and cover it. Set the dial next to the receptacle for the grind desired. To start the machine, adjust the dial on the side to the number of cups required. When the machine stops, remove the lower receptacle holding the ground beans.

Steeping in a Pot

1 **Putting coffee in the pot.** Warm the coffeepot by rinsing it out with boiling water. Spoon medium-ground coffee—here, Colombian coffee beans ground by hand—into the warmed pot.

2 **Stirring the coffee.** Bring cold water to a boil. Remove the water from the heat, and let it stand until it stops bubbling—about 10 seconds. Pour the water immediately into the pot and stir the mixture once with a spoon. Put the lid on the pot to keep the mixture hot.

3 **Straining the coffee.** Let the coffee infuse for five minutes. Most of the grounds will have settled on the bottom of the pot. Nonetheless, for a perfectly clear beverage, pour the coffee into cups through a strainer.

Straining inside a Pot

1 **Spooning in coffee.** Pour boiling water into a coffeepot fitted with a plunger attachment. Swirl the water around inside the pot, then discard it. Spoon medium-ground coffee—dark-roasted Costa Rican is used in this case—into the warmed pot.

2 **Pouring in water.** Bring cold water to a boil, then let it cool for 10 seconds, or until it stops bubbling. Pour the water into the pot and stir the mixture once. Set the lid—with its plunger raised—on the pot.

3 **Filtering the coffee.** After five minutes, gently press the plunger down to the bottom of the pot: The filter will trap all the grounds underneath it as it descends. Serve the coffee at once.

Filtering Coffee through Paper

1 **Placing coffee in the filter.** Fit a paper filter inside the cone of a filter coffeepot, and set the cone over the pot. Spoon very finely ground coffee into the paper-lined cone.

2 **Moistening the coffee.** Bring fresh cold water to a boil. Let the water cool for about 10 seconds. Place the coffeepot on a heat-diffusing pad set over low heat. Immediately pour a little of the hot water into the cone to moisten the coffee. Let the coffee infuse and swell for about 30 seconds.

3 **Filling the cone.** Slowly pour the remaining hot water into the cone until it is filled. Leave the pot over the heat until all of the liquid has filtered through the cone into the pot. Remove the cone containing the grounds, stir the coffee once and serve it immediately.

Filtering a Cold-Water Concentrate

1 **Inserting the stopper.** Secure the rubber stopper in the opening at the bottom of the brewing container. Set the container upright, wet the filter disk and fit it into the base of the container. Fill the container with 1 pound [½ kg.] of medium-ground coffee.

2 **Adding cold water.** Pour 2 quarts [2 liters] of cold water into the container. Using the back of a spoon, gently submerge any dry coffee that floats to the top. Cover the container and refrigerate it for 12 hours to produce medium-strength coffee—24 hours for stronger coffee.

3 **Draining the concentrate.** Hold the brewing container over the decanter and remove the stopper. Set the container on the decanter, then let the concentrate drain into it. Cover and refrigerate. For each serving, mix 2 tablespoons [30 ml.] of concentrate with ¾ cup [175 ml.] of boiling water.

Forcing Steam through a Fine Grind

1 **Inserting the filter.** Pour enough fresh cold water into the base of a steam-pressure coffeepot to fill it to just below the steam vent. Put finely ground coffee into the filter section of the pot. Place the filter in the base. Screw on the top section of the pot.

2 **Making the coffee.** Set the pot over medium heat. When the coffee begins to bubble through the central funnel into the top of the pot, reduce the heat to low. As soon as the bubbling stops, remove the pot from the heat. Serve the coffee immediately.

Using Steam Pressure to Extract Full Flavor

1 **Pouring in water.** Measure out a little more water than the volume of coffee you want. Unscrew the cap from the water tank of an espresso machine and pour in the water. Screw the cap back on. Make sure that the steam valve and the two outlet taps are closed tight. Then turn the machine on at its highest setting.

2 **Filling the filter section.** After steam has begun to appear through the safety valve, begin timing: Let steam escape for one minute, then turn the machine to low. Place finely ground coffee in the filter—in this case, enough for two servings. Pack down the coffee using either the plunger provided (*above*) or the back of a spoon.

3 **Extracting the coffee.** Place two cups on the drainage tray under the outlet taps. Lift the lever, hold it up for two to three seconds and then press it firmly down, forcing coffee through the taps. Continue to lift and press the lever down until both cups are full. Serve the coffee immediately.

Classic Counterpoints to Coffee

Part of the appeal of coffee lies in its compatability with a spectrum of flavoring elements. Spices ranging from nutmeg, cinnamon and cardamom to white or black pepper can be introduced singly or in combination. Cocoa powder, grated chocolate or a lemon twist can garnish a finished drink. White or brown sugar, even honey can be used to sweeten coffee; milk or cream—plain or whipped—can enrich and lighten it.

The demonstrations here show four classic tactics for producing flavored coffee. The simplest and most familiar is to blend equal portions of brewed coffee and hot milk *(right, top)*. Called café au lait in France, café con leche in Spain and kaffee milch in Germany, the drink is traditionally served at breakfast from small, deep bowls rather than cups. For best results, the coffee and milk should be at the same temperature and poured simultaneously into the bowl.

Italy's cappuccino *(right, bottom)* marries espresso coffee with milk that has been frothed with the steam pipe of an espresso machine. The name of the drink comes, it is said, from the similarity between its color and that of the garb worn by Capuchin monks.

More exotic—and more intensely flavored—are Turkish coffee *(opposite, top; recipe, page 96)* and Mexican coffee *(opposite, bottom; recipe, page 97)*. Both coffees are made potent and astringent by bringing the brew repeatedly to a quick boil; both are presweetened. Despite its name, Turkish coffee is popular in the Middle East and the Soviet Union as well as in southeastern Europe. Made by boiling pulverized beans in sweetened water, it is served unstrained and black. The traditional pot, obtainable from specialty food stores, is narrowed at the top to trap the foam that forms on the surface of the liquid as it boils.

By contrast, Mexican coffee starts with coarsely ground, dark-roasted coffee that is combined with water flavored by stick cinnamon and brown sugar. Traditionally the sugar is a chunk of *piloncillo*—an unrefined sugar with a molasses-like flavor, sold in cone form at Mexican food stores. In Mexico, the coffee is prepared in an earthenware pot, but any small saucepan is suitable.

Simultaneous Pouring for Café au Lait

1 **Blending coffee and milk.** Make coffee from dark-roasted beans. Meanwhile, heat an equal amount of milk in a pot until bubbles form at the edges; put the milk in a warmed pitcher. Pour the coffee and milk together into a cup or—as here—a small bowl.

2 **Serving the coffee.** To prevent the hot milk from forming a skin on the surface of the coffee, serve the drink at once. Accompany the coffee, if you like, with sugar to be added to taste.

Frothing Milk for a Foamy Topping

1 **Frothing milk.** Make espresso *(page 23, bottom)* and pour it into cups, filling each halfway. Add cold water to the espresso machine and turn to its highest setting. Hold a pitcher half-full of cold milk under the steam pipe. To froth the milk, move the pitcher up and down as you release steam.

2 **Serving cappuccino.** When the milk is frothy, turn off the machine. Pour the milk at once into the cups of espresso. If you like, sprinkle a little grated chocolate on top before serving the coffee.

Incorporating Sugar for a Thick Brew

1 **Adding coffee to syrup.** Put sugar to taste and cold water in a small saucepan or—as here—in a Turkish coffeepot. Set the pan over medium heat. Stir constantly until the sugar is dissolved, then stop stirring and bring the syrup to a boil. Remove the pot from the heat; add pulverized coffee.

2 **Boiling the coffee.** Stir the mixture; return the pot to the heat and bring the coffee to a boil. As soon as froth rises to the surface of the liquid, take the pot off the heat. Let the froth settle, then return the coffee to the heat. Bring it to a boil and let it settle twice more.

3 **Serving the coffee.** As soon as the grounds settle for the last time, pour the coffee into demitasses or other small cups. Serve immediately.

Spicing and Sweetening the Brew

1 **Dissolving the sugar.** In a small saucepan, bring fresh cold water to a boil. Add a cinnamon stick and dark brown sugar—in this case, sliced from a cone of Mexican *piloncillo*. Stir until the sugar dissolves completely.

2 **Adding ground coffee.** Spoon coarsely ground, dark-roasted coffee into the sweetened, spiced water. Stir once and bring the mixture to a boil. As soon as it boils vigorously, remove it from the heat. Let the grounds settle for 10 seconds. Then return the pan to the heat and bring the coffee to a boil again.

3 **Serving the coffee.** As soon as the coffee begins to boil, pour it through a strainer into a cup or coffee mug. Serve the coffee at once, accompanied by additional brown sugar.

Coffee and Ice: A Refreshing Partnership

Coffee yields delicious and refreshing cold drinks, whether simply chilled and served over ice *(box, far right)* or partly frozen to create the crunchy water ice known as a granita *(right; recipe, page 99).* The starting point for both drinks is a fresh pot of coffee, made by any of the methods shown on pages 20-23. Because coffee's taste is diminished by chilling or freezing, a dark roast will produce a drink with the most flavor.

For iced coffee, the liquid is cooled, then refrigerated until it is thoroughly chilled—three hours or so—before being poured over ice cubes for serving. Even in a covered container, coffee should not be kept for more than a day lest it lose its fresh flavor and become bitter.

For sweetness, sugar may be added to the pot or individual glasses. For a sharp accent, garnish the coffee with lemon or mint or add a dash of rum. The coffee can be enriched with cream or—for a thicker drink—with ice cream in place of ice.

Granita requires only slightly more preparation. The coffee must be made extra strong by doubling the amount of ground coffee or coffee concentrate. To ensure that the sugar is evenly distributed throughout the ice, dissolve it in water to form a syrup *(Steps 1 and 2, right).*

After the syrup and hot coffee are combined and cooled, the mixture can be flavored with vanilla extract or a little brandy or rum before it is frozen. The time the mixture will take to freeze depends on its sweetness. Sugar lowers the freezing point of a liquid, so the more sugar used in the syrup, the longer the freezing time will be. To hasten the freezing as much as possible, pour the cooled mixture into ice trays or a shallow metal baking pan, rather than into a deep bowl.

During freezing, stir the mixture occasionally to distribute the ice crystals that form around the edges. When the mixture has become uniformly icy, transfer it to a bowl and crush the crystals just enough to make the granita fluffy. At this stage it can be served immediately or returned to the freezer for up to half an hour; to keep it longer, stir it every half hour or so to prevent it from freezing solid. The finished granita can be presented plain, but a topping of whipped cream will complement its bittersweet flavor.

1 **Dissolving sugar.** Put sugar and water in a heavy saucepan and set it over medium heat. Stir the mixture to help dissolve the sugar. Dip a pastry brush in hot water and brush down the sides of the saucepan to dissolve sugar crystals; or cover the saucepan until steam washes the crystals down.

2 **Boiling the syrup.** When the sugar has dissolved and the syrup is clear, stop stirring. Increase the heat, bring the syrup to a boil and boil it for one minute. Remove the pan from the heat.

5 **Stirring the mixture.** When the coffee has begun to freeze at the edges but is still soft in the center—after about an hour—remove it from the freezer. Stir the mixture well with a wooden spatula. When the mixture is uniformly slushy, return it to the freezer.

6 **Crushing the granita.** Freeze the mixture for another two hours, or until it has become a mass of coarse ice crystals, but is not frozen solid. Empty the mixture out of the trays or pan into a chilled bowl. Crush the mixture with a spatula to break it into small crystals.

3 **Pouring in the coffee.** Prepare strong coffee—here, made in a steam-pressure pot *(page 23)*. Pour the coffee into the sugar syrup. Stir the mixture and set it aside until it cools to room temperature.

4 **Filling ice trays.** Pour the sweetened coffee into ice trays or a shallow pan. Then place the uncovered trays or pan in the freezer.

1 **Assembling.** Prepare strong coffee and, if you like, add sugar. Let the coffee cool, then chill it. Put ice cubes in a tall glass and pour the chilled coffee over them.

7 **Topping with cream.** For serving, spoon the granita into chilled parfait glasses or wineglasses. Whip heavy cream and add a spoonful to each glass.

2 **Serving.** Pour in a little cream, stir and serve the drink at once. If you prefer, present sugar and cream separately so that each diner can add them to taste.

Spirited Treatments for Coffee

A Spicy Blend of Brandy and Liqueur

The assertive flavor and aroma of coffee marry well with spirits to create hearty beverages to top off a meal. Creole café brûlot *(right; recipe, page 98)* and Irish coffee *(opposite, bottom; recipe, page 98)* are classic examples.

Literally translated, café brûlot means "coffee with burnt brandy." Outside New Orleans, similar concoctions go by such names as café diable, café royale and café flambé. By any name, the drink is made by pouring hot coffee over flaming brandy or other liquor that has been blended with enrichments such as liqueur, sugar, citrus peel and spices. The flavorings are crushed together and heated with the spirits. Igniting the mixture then burns off most of the alcohol, caramelizes the sugar and concentrates the flavors.

Irish coffee is a simple concoction of coffee laced with spirits and sugar and finished with a layer of heavy cream. Irish whiskey is traditionally used, although rum, brandy or coffee liqueur could be used instead.

1 **Peeling citrus fruit.** Prepare a pot of coffee using one of the methods shown on pages 20-23; keep it warm on a heat-diffusing pad set over low heat. With a small, sharp knife, pare the colored peel from oranges and lemons, leaving the bitter white pith on the fruits. Slice the peel into thin julienne.

2 **Releasing the oils.** Put the orange and lemon julienne into a shallow pan or the pan of a chafing dish. Add sugar cubes, a cinnamon stick and whole cloves. Crush all the ingredients with the back of a heavy spoon or a ladle to release the oil from the citrus peels.

5 **Serving the coffee.** After a few seconds, begin to pour the coffee into the pan in a thin stream, stirring until the flames have died *(left)*. Ladle the spiced coffee immediately into small cups for serving *(above)*.

3 **Stirring the flavorings.** Add brandy and Curaçao to the peels, sugar and spices in the pan. Set the pan over low heat—using a heat-diffusing pad, if necessary, to keep the heat gentle and thus prevent the alcohol from igniting spontaneously. Stir the ingredients with the spoon or ladle for a few minutes, pressing down on the sugar to help dissolve it. Stop stirring when the flavorings are thoroughly blended and the sugar is dissolved.

4 **Flaming the alcohol.** Light a long kitchen match and pass its flame over the edge of the pan, close to the surface of the liquid. Keep your head out of the way: The alcohol will ignite suddenly and its flames may leap high.

A Lacing of Whiskey and a Blanket of Cream

1 **Pouring in whiskey.** Prepare a pot of coffee and keep it hot. Put a spoonful of sugar—or more to taste—into a stemmed heatproof glass with a wide bowl. Then pour Irish whiskey over the sugar.

2 **Adding the coffee.** Pour the hot coffee into the glass to within about ½ inch [1 cm.] of the rim. Stir gently until the sugar dissolves.

3 **Garnishing the drink.** To keep the cream from sinking into the coffee, rest the neck of an inverted spoon on the rim of the glass so that the tip of the spoon's bowl barely touches the liquid. Gradually pour enough heavy cream over the back of the spoon to form a layer about ¼ inch [6 mm.] thick on the coffee. Serve at once.

2
Juices and Syrups
Capturing the Freshness of Fruits and Vegetables

Puréeing by hand and machine
Barley water: an old-fashioned treat
How to open a coconut
Preserving juices as syrups
Unlocking the flavors of nuts and herbs

The natural flavor of any fruit, vegetable, herb, nut or edible flower can be enjoyed in its purest form when drawn out as a juice. Such a juice can be presented freshly prepared *(pages 32-39)* or preserved in a syrup and diluted with plain or soda water for serving *(pages 40-43)*.

The method of obtaining a juice depends on the nature of the ingredient. Soft and semisoft fruits and vegetables—berries, citrus fruits and tomatoes, for example—can simply be squeezed and strained or puréed. Fibrous produce—such as rhubarb or celery—yields copious juices if simmered in water. Firm fruits and vegetables—apples, pears and carrots among them—can be sliced or chopped, then infused in water for a delicately flavored liquid. Infusion is also most suitable for extracting the essence from naturally dry ingredients such as nuts or citrus peel.

To remove any impurities that might otherwise contaminate the juice, wash fruits, vegetables and herbs thoroughly under cold running water. Cut away and discard any blemished sections. Remove the stems and leaves of soft fruits and the pits of such fruits as plums, apricots or cherries. Trim and peel root vegetables, and remove both the shells and skins of nuts. All fruits and most vegetables contain acid, so be sure that neither the whole ingredient nor its juice comes into contact with any utensils made from iron, copper or aluminum. These metals would react with the natural acid, causing discoloration and an impaired flavor.

Cooking a juice with sugar intensifies its flavor and transforms it into a syrup. In this strong concentration, the sugar has a dehydrating effect—depriving microorganisms of the moisture they need to develop—and thus acts as a preservative. Usually made from fruits, syrups also can be prepared with nuts, herbs and flowers. Besides creating deliciously refreshing drinks, syrups also serve as flavorings for cocktails and milk drinks such as shakes and ice-cream sodas *(page 53)*.

Syrup-based drinks will need no sweetening, but fruit or nut juices may. Sugar or honey will quickly permeate an infusion while it is still hot, but will dissolve slowly in a cold juice. For this reason, the best sweetener for cold drinks is sugar syrup *(page 26, Steps 1 and 2)*. Once prepared, the drinks can be served at room temperature or refrigerated until well chilled. To keep them chilled at the table, pack the glasses with ice cubes or crushed ice before the juice or syrup drink is poured.

A translucent rhubarb juice, sweetened with sugar and chilled *(page 35),* is poured into a glass. The fruit was cut up and simmered in water until it was reduced to a soft pulp, then strained through a fine sieve.

A Medley of Methods for Making Juices

Juices prepared at home from fruits and vegetables have fresher, purer flavors than anything you can buy ready-made. In devising them you can experiment with unusual ingredients or combinations—barley water, for example, provides a mellow contrast to lemon juice *(opposite, bottom)*.

Most important, making juices lets you take full advantage of seasonal produce at its cheapest and most plentiful, even using fruits or vegetables that have surface blemishes or have become soft and overripe: In fact, the riper the produce, the more juice it will yield.

Depending on the fruit or vegetable and the way you handle it, the drinks can range from delicate liquids, such as the three demonstrated here, through rich juices *(pages 34-35)* to thick but pourable purées *(pages 36-37)*.

Hard raw ingredients—carrots, fennel, pears or the apples shown at right—need only be sliced or chopped and infused in water to create a clear, fragrant drink. Sieving liquefies melons and, after the liquid rests, any traces of pulp fall to the bottom to leave the juice transparent. Equally easy to use, barley and such whole grains as wheat, rice or oats require only boiling and straining to become a base for the juice of citrus fruit.

Squeezers extract juice quickly from citrus fruits; for maximum yield, bring the fruits to room temperature. A juicing attachment for a food processor expresses clear liquid from hard, as well as soft and juicy, ingredients.

Crushing and sieving turns soft, ripe grapes, cherries or plums into drinks; stewing and sieving draws juice from firm rhubarb, celery or peas.

Soft fruits—peaches and berries, for example—and tomatoes are simply puréed through a food mill or sieve. The purées can be presented as is, diluted with water or strained into clear juice.

Sweetening or seasoning the juices is a matter of taste, as is the addition of ice. Keep fresh juices tightly covered and refrigerated, and serve them within a week lest their flavors deteriorate.

Infusing Hard Fruit

1 **Slicing apples.** Wash apples under cold running water. Halve each apple and cut it into ⅛-inch [3-mm.] slices. As you work, drop the slices into a bowl and toss them with lemon juice.

Sieving Tender Melon

1 **Sieving.** Cut watermelon into chunks and slice off the peel. Place a few chunks at a time in a stainless-steel or nylon sieve set over a bowl and use a pestle to extract the juice; discard the seeds. Cover the bowl with plastic wrap and refrigerate it overnight.

2 **Straining the juice.** Line a nonreactive sieve with cheesecloth or muslin and place it over a pitcher. Ladle the clear watermelon juice into the sieve, leaving behind the pulp that has settled in the bottom of the bowl. Discard the watermelon pulp.

3 **Serving.** Pour the juice into a chilled glass, adding crushed ice or ice cubes if you like. For a flourish, you can garnish the drink with a twist of lemon peel.

2 **Infusing.** Sprinkle sugar over the slices and add enough boiling water to cover them completely. With a spoon, toss the slices gently to distribute and dissolve the sugar.

3 **Straining.** Cover the bowl and let the flavors infuse for at least one hour. Strain the juice through a stainless-steel or nylon sieve into another bowl; discard the slices.

4 **Serving.** Transfer the apple juice to a pitcher for easier pouring. Serve the juice at room temperature or chilled, according to taste.

Blending Barley with Citrus Fruit

1 **Infusing barley.** Wash pearl barley and add it to a pan of cold water. Bring it to a boil, then simmer for 10 minutes. Strain the infusion into a large bowl; sweeten it with sugar to taste.

2 **Using a lemon squeezer.** One at a time, place lemon halves in the cup of a squeezer. Pull the handles of the squeezer together to extract the juice. Stir the lemon juice into the barley water.

3 **Serving the drink.** Refrigerate the barley water for about three hours, or until it is well chilled. To serve, pour the juice into a tall, chilled glass partly filled with crushed ice or ice cubes. Garnish the drink with a slice of lemon.

Getting Full Flavor from Citrus

1 **Extracting juice.** Peel oranges and a lemon; reserve the peels. Halve the fruits. Place each half in a squeezer. Then pull down the handle to squeeze the juice into a bowl.

2 **Straining the infusion.** In a pan, combine the peels with sugar and cold water. Bring to a boil over low heat, stirring to dissolve the sugar. Cool, then strain the infusion into the juice.

3 **Serving.** Transfer the juice to a pitcher and refrigerate it for about three hours, or until well chilled. To serve, pour the juice into a tall, chilled glass partly filled with cracked ice.

Crushing to Make the Juice Flow

1 **Crushing fruit.** Wash small, soft fruit—red grapes are used here—and remove any stems. Place the prepared fruit in a wide bowl and use a pestle to crush it into a coarse purée.

2 **Straining the juice.** Let the purée steep for about two hours to develop its flavor and to let the grape skins color it. Drain off the juice, a small batch at a time, by ladling the purée into a nonreactive sieve set over a pitcher.

3 **Serving the juice.** Put the juice in the refrigerator to chill it. To serve, pour the juice into chilled glasses. For a sweeter juice, stir in cooled sugar syrup (page 26, Steps 1 and 2). If you like, add a little lemon juice.

Extracting Juice with a Processor Attachment

1 **Preparing.** Peel carrots; peel and halve oranges. Fit a juicing extractor onto a food processor and set a bowl under the pulp ejector. Feed the carrots and oranges into the juicer in batches.

2 **Serving.** Transfer the juice to a pitcher and put it in the refrigerator to chill for about three hours. When serving the juice, you can add a pinch of salt to each glassful to bring out the flavors.

Simmering for Softness

1 **Chopping rhubarb.** Wash the fruit; cut off the poisonous leaves and the woody ends of the stalks. Slice the stalks into ¼-inch [6-mm.] pieces. Place the rhubarb in a nonreactive pan, add enough water to cover it completely and bring the mixture to a boil.

2 **Straining the juice.** Cover the pan and cook the fruit over medium heat until it is soft—about 20 minutes. Set a stainless-steel or nylon sieve over a large bowl; pour the rhubarb mixture gradually into the sieve and let the juice drain through. Discard the pulp.

3 **Serving the drink.** Sweeten the juice with sugar to taste and let it cool. Refrigerate the juice until it is chilled— about three hours. Serve the drink from a chilled glass, adding crushed ice or ice cubes if you like.

Grinding Fibrous Fruit to a Pulp

1 **Peeling the pineapple.** Cut off the stem and base from a firm, ripe pineapple. Stand the pineapple upright and slice off the skin. Use the tip of the knife or a vegetable peeler to dig out the tough brownish "eyes."

2 **Removing the core.** Quarter the pineapple lengthwise. Stand one quarter at a time on end and hold it firmly. Slice off the triangular section of pale, fibrous core. Cut the cored fruit into 1-inch [2½-cm.] chunks.

3 **Puréeing the pineapple.** Put the chunks of pineapple in a food processor. Operating the machine in short bursts and scraping down the sides of the container with a rubber spatula, process the fruit until it is puréed.

Puréeing Soft Fruit in a Food Mill

1 **Puréeing tomatoes.** Wash ripe tomatoes under cold running water and cut them into wedges. Set a food mill fitted with a fine disk over a bowl. Purée the tomato wedges a handful at a time; discard the skins and seeds.

2 **Flavoring the purée.** Season the purée with salt, pepper, a little lemon juice and some finely chopped fresh herbs—in this case, chervil. Stir with a wooden spoon to blend the ingredients.

3 **Serving the juice.** Dilute the purée to taste with water. Refrigerate the juice for about three hours, or until it is chilled, then serve it garnished with fresh herbs—a sprig of chervil is used here.

4 **Sweetening the purée.** Prepare a sugar syrup *(page 26, Steps 1 and 2).* Pour the purée into a bowl and mix in the sugar syrup to taste. Let the mixture stand at room temperature for two hours to allow its flavor to develop.

5 **Straining the purée.** Place a nylon or stainless-steel sieve over a pitcher. A little at a time, ladle the purée into the sieve. Press down on the solids to extract the maximum juice.

6 **Serving the juice.** Refrigerate the juice until it is chilled—about three hours. To serve the juice, pour it into tall, chilled glasses partly filled with ice cubes. If desired, dilute the juice with water or with soda water.

Gentle Pressing for Berries

1 **Puréeing fruit.** Wash small, soft fruit—raspberries, black currants and strawberries are shown—and remove leaves and stems. Using a pestle, push the fruit through a nonreactive sieve.

2 **Thinning the purée.** Prepare a sugar syrup *(page 26, Steps 1 and 2)* and add it to the fruit purée to taste. Stir well. Dilute the purée with water and add the juice of a lemon.

3 **Serving the juice.** Pour the juice into a pitcher and refrigerate it until chilled—about three hours. Serve it in a chilled glass, adding crushed ice or ice cubes if you like.

Nut Milk: A Versatile Mixer for Fruit Drinks

Nut milk—a thick, rich liquid made by infusing the meat of nuts in hot water—is ideal for flavoring fruit drinks. Any kind of nut—almonds, walnuts or the coconut here—is suitable: The technique of producing nut milk remains essentially the same for all of them.

To avoid any tinge of bitterness, the nuts must be peeled before they are infused, and the water must be boiling hot to draw out their flavorful oils. For the water to absorb maximum flavor, the nuts should first be ground, pounded or grated—with a food processor, mortar or hand grater.

Fresh coconuts—those that are covered by husk or that gurgle when shaken—contain a sweet liquid of their own that can strengthen the infusion.

Coconut's full flavor marries best with fruit juices or purées that have an assertive taste: citrus, rhubarb, pineapple or the papaya shown in this demonstration (recipe, page 103). Coconut milk goes especially well with mashed bananas, diluting the purée into a light beverage.

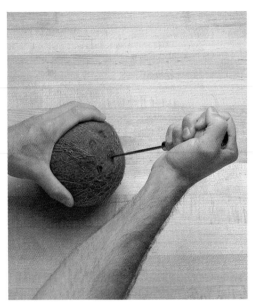

1 **Piercing a coconut.** Set the coconut on a work surface and turn it so that the three dark indentations—or the "eyes"—face toward you. Grasp the coconut firmly and pierce each of the eyes with a skewer or ice pick.

2 **Draining the juice.** Invert the coconut over a bowl; the milky juice will drain out through the three holes. Shake the coconut well to extract all its liquid. Taste the liquid and, if it is sweet, reserve it. Otherwise, discard the liquid.

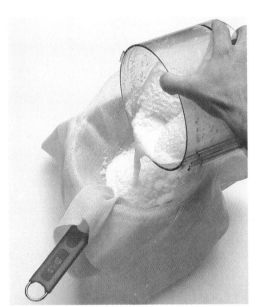

6 **Straining the pulp.** Let the coconut flesh infuse for one hour. Then line a sieve with a double layer of cheesecloth or muslin and set the sieve over a bowl. Slowly pour the coconut mixture into the sieve, allowing the liquid to drain through before you add more.

7 **Extracting all the milk.** When the liquid has drained through the sieve, twist the edges of the cloth together and squeeze it tightly to extract the maximum amount of milk. Discard the meat. The coconut milk may be bottled (page 40) and stored in the refrigerator for up to three days, or mixed at once with fruit juice or purée.

8 **Preparing papaya.** Peel each papaya with a small, sharp knife. Cut the fruit in half lengthwise. Using a spoon, scoop out and discard the black seeds in the center of each half. Cut the meat into 1-inch [2½-cm.] cubes.

3 **Opening the coconut.** With the dull side of a cleaver, hammer around the midsection of the coconut until a crack encircles it. Strike the crack: The coconut will split in half. Break the halves into pieces with the cleaver.

4 **Peeling the flesh.** With a sharp knife, pry each piece of coconut meat from its outer shell. Peel the brown skin off each piece so that only the pure white meat of the coconut remains.

5 **Grinding the meat.** Grind small portions of coconut in a food processor, turning the machine on and off in short bursts. Pour in the coconut liquid if you are using it, then add enough boiling water to cover the coconut completely. Grind the mixture together for a few seconds.

10 **Serving the drink.** Transfer the nut-and-fruit purée to a pitcher. To serve, pour the drink into chilled glasses. If you like, garnish each drink with a thinly sliced round of lime.

9 **Puréeing the ingredients.** Put the papaya cubes in a food processor or blender with sugar and crushed ice. Using a very sharp knife or—as here—a zester, scrape shavings of lime peel over the mixture. Add the coconut milk and the juice of the lime. Process until the ingredients form a smooth purée.

Fragrant Concentrations of Ripe Fruit

Fruit syrups are concentrated fruit juices preserved with sugar. When diluted, the syrups create refreshing warm or chilled drinks *(right; recipes, pages 111-113)*. The name "syrup," in fact, comes from an Arabic word that means drink.

Any fresh fruit juice made by the techniques shown on pages 32-39 may be strained through a cloth to form a pure, clear base for a syrup. Soft fruit that can be puréed whole—berries, grapes or the black currants shown here—will yield especially rich syrup if the purée is first left to stand overnight so that the natural enzymes of the fruit break down its cells, thus releasing more flavor elements.

Heating the juice with sugar transforms it into a syrup. As a rule, use 2 cups [½ liter] of sugar for each cup [¼ liter] of juice to ensure a thick syrup that stores well. Prepare the syrup in a nonreactive vessel such as the enameled pot used opposite. Aluminum, iron or copper might taint the flavor of the syrup.

All the sugar must be dissolved before the mixture boils lest crystals of sugar remaining in the pan cause all the syrup to crystallize. To help the sugar dissolve, stir the liquid very gently as it heats and dissolve any stray crystals with a wet pastry brush *(Step 5)*.

Once cooled and bottled, fruit syrup keeps for a month or so in the refrigerator. For longer storage, the syrup can be funneled into canning bottles, leaving a ½-inch [1-cm.] headspace. Cover the bottles and set them on a rack in a waterbath canner filled with enough simmering water to cover them by 1 inch [2½ cm.]. Cover the canner, bring the water to a boil and process the syrup for 15 minutes. Remove the bottles and let them cool undisturbed for at least 12 hours.

Syrups can be diluted in many ways to make both light and filling drinks. They can be thinned with water or soda water and served over ice, used to flavor ice-cream sodas *(page 53)* or mixed with hot or cold milk. To prevent the milk from curdling, pour it into the syrup very gradually and stir the mixture briskly.

1 **Crushing soft fruit.** Remove any leaves or stems from fruit—here, black currants. Wash the fruit and put it in a bowl. With a wide pestle, crush the fruit until it forms a coarse purée. Cover the purée and leave it overnight in a cool place, not the refrigerator.

2 **Straining the purée.** Line a nonreactive sieve with cheesecloth or muslin and place the sieve over a bowl. Pour the fruit purée into the sieve. You can hasten the straining process by stirring the purée with a wooden spoon.

6 **Skimming the syrup.** Increase the heat and bring the mixture to a boil. Reduce the heat to low and set the pot halfway off the burner. Simmer the syrup for about five minutes, skimming away the scum that forms repeatedly on the cooler side of the liquid. When scum has stopped rising, remove the pot from the heat and let the syrup cool.

7 **Bottling the syrup.** Position a nonreactive funnel in the neck of a clean, dry bottle. Ladle the cooled syrup through the funnel into the bottle. Fill the bottle completely, then close it securely with a cork.

3 **Measuring the juice.** Gather the four corners of the cloth and twist them tightly together to squeeze the juice out of the purée. Measure the juice to determine how much sugar will be needed for the syrup, then pour the juice into a heavy, nonreactive pot.

4 **Adding sugar.** Measure out the desired amount of sugar and add it to the juice in the pot. The proportions that are used here are 2 cups [½ liter] of sugar to each cup [¼ liter] of juice.

5 **Dissolving the sugar.** Place the pot over low heat and gently stir the mixture with a wooden spoon. When the sugar has dissolved—after about five minutes—brush down the inside of the pot with a pastry brush that has been dipped in hot water to dissolve any hardened crystals.

8 **Serving a syrup drink.** To make a simple syrup drink, half-fill a glass with crushed ice. Add syrup (above) and dilute it to taste with chilled soda water or plain cold water. Stir the drink and serve it with a straw (right).

Sumptuous Syrups from Unexpected Ingredients

A Delicate Extract from Almonds

To make syrups out of ingredients with little or no juice of their own—nuts, flowers and herbs, for example—you must first infuse them in water. The resulting flavored liquid can then be strained and boiled with sugar in the same way that fruit juice is *(pages 40-41)*.

Nuts pounded or ground with water release their oils to create a milky liquid when steeped. With coconuts the flavor of the milk is emphatic *(pages 38-39)*. The milk from small nuts such as the almonds used in this demonstration *(recipe, page 114)* has a delicate taste that may be intensified by adding a few drops of almond or vanilla extract to the syrup.

To draw the fragrance from flowers and herbs such as mint *(opposite, bottom; recipe, page 114)*, crush them with sugar, which acts as an abrasive and helps break down the fibers to extract the oils.

Like fruit syrups, those made from nuts, flowers or herbs will keep, tightly covered, for up to a month in the refrigerator. Once a bottle is opened, the syrup should be consumed within two weeks.

1 **Blanching almonds.** Bring a pan of water to a boil. Add shelled almonds to the water. Boil them for one minute, then drain the almonds in a colander.

2 **Removing skins.** Lay the hot nuts between two towels and rub hard on the top towel to remove the almond skins. If any skins still adhere, pinch each almond between your thumb and forefinger to ease off its skin. Soak the peeled nuts in a bowl of cold water for a few hours to soften them a little.

6 **Dissolving sugar.** Pour the almond milk into a pan with sugar and strips of lemon peel. Stir the mixture over medium heat until all the sugar has dissolved. Bring the liquid to a boil, then remove it from the heat. Take out the lemon peel with a slotted spoon; allow the syrup to cool.

7 **Bottling the syrup.** When the syrup is cool, set a funnel in a clean, dry bottle *(page 40)* and carefully ladle the mixture from the pan into the funnel. Close the bottles securely, with seals that clamp shut, as here, or with corks.

8 **Serving a syrup drink.** Put ice—here, cubes—into a tall glass, half-fill it with syrup and dilute with chilled soda water or plain cold water to taste. Stir the drink and garnish it, if you like, with a twist of lemon peel.

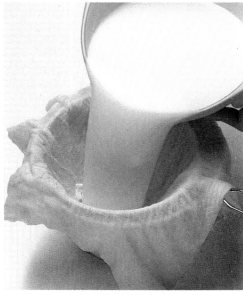

3 **Crushing the almonds.** Strain the almonds, reserving the water. In a mortar, pound the almonds with a pestle until they begin to break. Then gradually add the soaking water and continue pounding until the nuts form a paste. Or grind the almonds with the water in a food processor, operating it in short bursts.

4 **Infusing the nuts.** Pour boiling water into a large bowl and spoon the almond paste into it. Stir the mixture, cover it and leave it for at least one hour. For stronger flavor, leave it overnight.

5 **Straining the milk.** Line a sieve with a double thickness of muslin or cheesecloth. Set the sieve over a bowl. Pour the almond mixture into the sieve. Gather the four corners of the cloth together and squeeze tightly and repeatedly to extract all of the liquid. Discard the almond pulp.

An Essence Pounded from Leaves

1 **Crushing mint.** Put sugar and mint leaves in a mortar. Pound the leaves until they are crushed and their oils have absorbed the sugar. Transfer the pulp to a pan; add boiling water. Stir over low heat until the sugar dissolves.

2 **Making syrup.** Bring the mixture to a boil; simmer it for a few minutes. Remove the mixture from the heat and allow it to cool. Strain the syrup into clean, dry bottles (page 40) through a funnel lined with cheesecloth or muslin. Cork the bottles.

3 **Serving a mint drink.** To serve, fill a tumbler with ice—in this case, coarsely crushed ice. Pour in syrup to taste and top it with cold water or, as here, sparkling mineral water. Garnish with a few fresh mint leaves.

3

Milk Drinks
The Perfect Food in a Diversity of Guises

Dissolving cocoa powder and chocolate
Eggs for enrichment
Making yogurt at home
Sweet and tangy yogurt drinks
Creating ice-cream shakes and sodas

Served on its own, hot or cold, milk is both a thirst-quenching drink and a perfect food. Because its flavor is unassertive, milk also harmonizes with diverse flavorings and enrichments to create a wide variety of beverages. You can sweeten and flavor milk with syrups and purées, thicken it with eggs, incubate it to create yogurt and freeze it to form ice cream. In all of these guises, whole milk ensures the most luxurious effects, but low-fat and skim milk, which are lower both in calories and cholesterol, are suitable alternatives.

A flavoring for milk can be as simple as honey or a fruit syrup *(pages 40-41)* stirred straight into the liquid. Cocoa powder and block chocolate should first be smoothly dissolved in water before hot milk is poured over them; whisking the mixture then incorporates air to yield drinks that are frothy and light *(page 47)*. To enrich such a drink, you can fold· lightly whipped cream into the liquid or spoon the cream over the top of it just before serving.

Whole eggs or egg yolks alone transform hot milk into a creamy, custard-like drink. By contrast, egg whites whisked to a soft meringue will turn chilled milk into a light, foamy drink *(opposite; pages 48-49)*.

Making yogurt requires only warm milk and a bacterial culture, or starter *(page 50)*. The starter can be as easily obtained as a few spoonfuls of unpasteurized commercial yogurt. The *Lactobacillus bulgaricus* bacteria it contains coagulate milk while *Streptococcus thermophilus* ferments the milk sugar into lactic acid that in turn curdles the milk protein and acts as a preservative. The resulting yogurt has a fresh tanginess welcome in both sweet and savory beverages. Yogurt can be diluted merely with water or with such ingredients as pourable purées and juices that will flavor it at the same time.

Although yogurt can be produced without special equipment, an ice-cream maker is essential for forming velvety ice cream to use for the base of such soda-fountain drinks as milk shakes and ice-cream sodas. Despite its name, the richest ice cream starts with milk, egg yolks and sugar *(page 52)*. Once churned, ice cream can be thinned for drinking by blending it with milk and syrup, or enveloped in a syrup bubbled with soda water. A layer of whipped cream and a colorful garnish of fresh fruit will add a luxurious touch to such drinks.

A stemmed glass of frothy meringue milk *(page 48)* is topped with a final ladleful. For flavor, whole milk was infused with lemon peel and cinnamon, then it was strained and chilled. For a foamy consistency, whisked egg whites were folded into the liquid shortly before serving time.

Luxurious Drinks from Cacao Beans

Of the many flavorings that blend well with the mild taste of milk, cocoa and chocolate are among the most popular. Mixed with hot milk as shown here, they produce drinks that are filling as well as warming *(recipes, pages 115-116).*

Both cocoa and chocolate are made from the cacao bean, but they are processed differently and therefore yield subtly different beverages. In the manufacturing of cocoa, the roasted beans are pulverized to a paste and most of the natural fat is removed. The result is a soluble powder with a slightly bitter flavor. In chocolate manufacture, all the fat is retained—indeed, it is augmented—and the paste is molded into blocks that are frequently scored so they break easily into ½- or 1-ounce [15- or 30-g.] chunks. Melted chocolate yields a thicker, more velvety drink than cocoa.

Cocoa always needs sweetening with sugar or honey. So does unsweetened chocolate. However, chocolate paste is often mixed with sugar before molding to form bittersweet, semisweet or sweet chocolate that, used alone, may produce drinks of sufficient sweetness, depending on individual taste.

Both flavorings, and any sweetener, must first be dissolved in water, then cooked until smooth. The amount of cocoa or chocolate can be varied, but a general rule is to allow 1 ounce [30 g.] of chocolate or 1 tablespoon [15 ml.] of cocoa powder for each cup [¼ liter] of milk.

The milk should be heated separately and then poured slowly into the chocolate or cocoa. Continuous whisking while the flavoring and the milk are being blended will incorporate air to make the drink as light as possible. Whisking also prevents a skin from forming on the surface of the liquid as it heats.

Both cocoa and chocolate should be served while they are still frothy. The drinks can be further enriched with a topping of whipped cream and a spice such as ground cinnamon or grated nutmeg. An unusual way to give the drinks a suggestion of spiciness is to stir them with a cinnamon stick.

Whisking Cocoa for Lightness

Dissolving cocoa powder. Put cocoa powder and sugar in a saucepan. Dribble in 1 tablespoon [15 ml.] of water for each tablespoon of cocoa powder, stirring all the time with a wire whisk *(above, left)*. Place the pan over medium heat and bring the mixture to a boil, stirring continuously with the whisk *(right)*. Then reduce the heat to low.

Melting Chocolate for a Rich, Smooth Texture

Melting chocolate. Break a block of semisweet chocolate into pieces and put the pieces in a heavy saucepan. Add 2 tablespoons [30 ml.] of water for each ounce [30 g.] of chocolate and, if you like, sprinkle in some sugar. Place the pan over low heat and stir the ingredients together with a wooden spoon *(above, left)*. Continue to stir until the chocolate melts and the mixture is smooth *(right)*.

2 **Adding milk.** In a separate pan, heat milk until it is hot but not boiling. Add the milk to the dissolved cocoa powder and sugar—slowly at first— whisking all the time to blend the ingredients. Heat the mixture gently without letting it boil.

3 **Frothing the drink.** Remove the pan from the heat and place it on a trivet set on a firm surface. Holding the pan steady with one hand, whisk the cocoa briskly for about 15 seconds, or until the mixture is smooth and a light foam has formed on the surface.

4 **Serving the cocoa.** Rinse out serving mugs with hot water to warm them. When the hot cocoa is foamy, pour it into the mugs. If you like, spoon a layer of whipped cream onto the top. Serve the drinks immediately.

2 **Adding milk.** In another pan, heat milk until it is hot but not boiling. A little at a time, pour the milk into the melted chocolate, stirring continuously with a wire whisk. Heat the mixture well but do not let it boil. Continue whisking until the drink becomes frothy.

3 **Serving the chocolate.** When the chocolate is hot, pour it into warmed cups or mugs. Whip cream with a whisk (inset) and spoon it on top of each serving (above). The cream can be sweetened and flavored with a few drops of vanilla extract before you whip it. If you like, you can garnish the whipped cream with grated nutmeg or ground cinnamon.

Frothy Blends of Eggs and Milk

Chilled Foam from Beaten Whites

Eggs in any form—whole or just the yolks or the whites—contribute nourishment, flavor and textural interest to milk drinks. Beaten whites will give milk a frothy lightness; yolks and whole eggs will impart a rich creaminess. Drinks containing egg yolks are usually served warm, but those made with beaten egg whites can be served warm or cold.

For the airy, cold drink known as meringue milk *(right; recipe, page 117)*, the milk is first infused with lemon and cinnamon, then chilled and finally lightened with egg whites that have been beaten into soft peaks. Because the purpose of beating the whites is to incorporate the maximum amount of air into the drink, they must be folded into the milk very gently so that they do not deflate. The drink will be fluffiest if served immediately, although it can safely be kept in the refrigerator for up to half an hour—or frozen to create a delicate milk ice.

A warm, filling drink with a smooth, custard-like texture is fashioned by mixing whole eggs—or just yolks—with hot milk *(opposite, bottom; recipe, page 117)*. A dash of sherry or brandy can be beaten into the egg to give the drink extra flavor. The traditional way to aerate this drink is to combine the eggs and milk, and then pour the mixture back and forth between the pan and a pitcher, as demonstrated here. For an even foamier effect, the drink also can be aerated by separating the eggs, mixing the hot milk with the yolks, then lightly beating the whites and folding them in just before serving.

The delicacy of drinks made with eggs and milk dictates using the lightest of garnishes. Spices such as cinnamon and grated nutmeg will add piquancy and color; so will a sprinkling of cocoa powder.

1 **Flavoring the milk.** Put cold milk in a saucepan. With a sharp knife, peel a lemon, leaving all the white pith on the fruit. Drop the peel into the milk. Add sugar and a cinnamon stick. Place the saucepan over medium heat and stir the mixture until the sugar dissolves. Remove the saucepan from the heat before the liquid comes to a boil.

2 **Straining the milk.** Cover the pan and let the flavorings infuse the milk for about 15 minutes. Stir the mixture, then strain the milk through a sieve into a bowl. Refrigerate the flavored milk until it is thoroughly chilled—this will take approximately three hours.

5 **Folding in whites.** Remove the milk from the refrigerator. To lighten it, carefully stir in a spoonful of the beaten whites. Then tip in the rest of the whites and, with a spatula, gently fold them into the milk *(above)*. To serve, ladle the mixture into chilled glasses and dust the surface of each drink with a little ground cinnamon *(right)*.

3 **Separating eggs.** To avoid breaking yolks into the whites, crack one egg at a time on the rim of a small bowl. Upend the egg and pull off the top of the shell, leaving the yolk in the bottom. Pass the yolk from one shell section to the other several times, letting the white drop into the bowl. Put the yolk aside and place the white in a large bowl.

4 **Beating egg whites.** If you like, add a little sugar and a few drops of lemon juice to the egg whites for extra flavor. Using a wire whisk, begin to beat the whites—slowly, at first *(above, left)*. As the whites increase in volume, beat faster. Continue beating for about five minutes, or until the egg whites hold soft peaks when the whisk is lifted from them *(right)*.

Warmth and Nourishment from Whole Eggs

1 **Adding milk to eggs.** Break eggs into a bowl. Add sugar, and beat the mixture with a wire whisk until it is smooth. In a saucepan, heat milk without letting it boil. Pour the hot milk slowly onto the egg mixture, while you beat it constantly with the whisk.

2 **Aerating the drink.** Warm a pitcher by rinsing it out with hot water. Pour the milk drink into the saucepan. Then pour the milk drink back and forth between the pan and the pitcher until it is frothy—at least one minute.

3 **Serving the drink.** Pour the frothy drink immediately into a warmed mug. To add flavor and color, dust the top of the drink with a little spice—here, grated nutmeg is used.

Tangy Drinks from Fermented Milk

Yogurt is liquid milk transformed into a semisolid. Its piquant taste makes it a fine foundation for drinks both sweet and savory (recipes, pages 121-122).

To give yogurt a drinkable consistency, it need merely be thinned with liquid—water, soda water, cream, fruit or vegetable juice, or syrup. The diluted yogurt can be enhanced with pulverized or ground spices—nutmeg, ginger or cinnamon among them—or with chopped fresh herbs such as parsley, tarragon or dill. Chopped or puréed fruits and berries are welcome additions; so are tomatoes, cucumbers and scallions. In the demonstrations on the opposite page, a sweet yogurt drink combines diced mango with honey and lemon juice, and a savory drink derives its tanginess from chopped mint and crushed cumin seeds.

Although yogurt is sold in supermarkets everywhere, preparing it at home is both easy (box, right; recipe, page 165) and economical: A quart [1 liter] of milk produces a quart of yogurt. To provide the starter for the first batch, use a dried culture—available at health-food stores—or a fresh but not pasteurized commercial yogurt. Allow 1 tablespoon [15 ml.] of dried culture or 2 tablespoons [30 ml.] of fresh yogurt for each quart of milk. (Once you have made yogurt, save some to start the next batch.)

To prepare yogurt, heat milk just to the boiling point to sterilize it and kill any undesirable bacteria it may contain. Then cool the milk to about 110° F. [43° C.]. At 120° F. [49° C.] the starter will die; at 90° F. [32° C.] or less it will fail to react. Stir the starter into the milk and incubate the mixture—in a pot, bowl or individual custard cups as shown here—in a place where the temperature is between 90° F. and 120° F. An electric yogurt-making machine will control the temperature thermostatically. But such a machine is not necessary if you cover the mixture tightly.

As soon as the yogurt has thickened enough to hold its shape in a spoon, it is ready. In small containers the yogurt may be ready in four hours. In a large container, the incubation may take six hours or more. Yogurt tastes best when freshly made, but if tightly covered it will keep for up to a week in the refrigerator.

Simple Steps for Making Yogurt

1 **Preparing the milk.** In a saucepan, bring milk to a boil over medium heat. Remove it from the heat immediately. Place a cooking thermometer, warmed under hot water to prevent breakage, in the pan; let the milk cool to 110° F. [43° C.].

2 **Incorporating the starter.** In a large bowl, whisk plain unpasteurized yogurt until it is smooth. Skim the skin from the warm milk. Whisking gently, pour the milk over the yogurt. Then ladle the mixture into custard cups.

3 **Pouring in water.** Place the cups in a deep pot. Using a funnel, pour tepid tap water into the pot. Set the lid on the pot or wrap the pot with a cloth that covers the cups completely. Then set the pot in a warm place to allow the yogurt to incubate.

4 **Testing the consistency.** After about four hours, test the yogurt with a spoon; if it is still liquid, let it incubate for another hour. When the yogurt is firm, use it at once, or cover the cups tightly with plastic wrap and foil, and store them in the refrigerator for up to a week.

Sweetening with Fruit and Honey

1 **Preparing flavorings.** With a small knife, quarter a mango lengthwise; peel off the skin and cut away the pit. Slice the quarters lengthwise, then cut them crosswise into dice. Measure out clear honey and cold water and squeeze the juice from a lemon. Then pour fresh yogurt into a large bowl and stir it until it is smooth.

2 **Mixing the ingredients.** Add the mango, honey, water and lemon juice to the yogurt. Blend the ingredients thoroughly by stirring until the diced fruit is well distributed.

3 **Serving.** Refrigerate the mixture until it is well chilled—about three hours. To serve, ladle the drink into chilled glasses. If you like, decorate each drink with a few pieces of fresh mango.

A Savory Blend of Spices and Herbs

1 **Blending the yogurt.** Toast cumin seeds in a skillet over low heat, stirring them until they brown and begin to release aroma—one to two minutes. In a mortar, crush the cumin seeds to a powder. Place mint leaves, water and yogurt in a blender or processor and blend them until the mint is chopped fine.

2 **Adding the cumin.** Add the crushed cumin and a little coarse salt to the yogurt mixture. Drop in ice cubes. Blend the mixture until the ice cubes are crushed and the drink is foamy.

3 **Serving the drink.** Pour the yogurt drink immediately into tall, chilled glasses. If you like, garnish each drink with a few whole mint leaves.

Ice Cream: Eggs and Milk Churned and Chilled

A scoop of ice cream will transform a plain drink into a sumptuous one—especially if the ice cream is homemade. Luckily, producing ice cream becomes easy when you use an ice-cream maker: a hand- or electric-powered device consisting of a metal canister that is fitted with a churning paddle, or dasher, and set inside a large bucket.

The simplest ice cream is just what the name suggests: sweetened and frozen cream *(recipe, page 165)*. A richer and smoother version is based, as demonstrated here, on egg yolks, sugar and milk cooked together to form a custard. For vanilla ice cream, you can infuse a vanilla bean in the milk before making the custard. For a fruit, coffee or chocolate ice cream, add the flavoring after straining the custard *(recipe, page 166)*.

Before churning the custard, let it cool completely and chill both the canister and dasher: Warm ingredients or equipment would slow the freezing process.

After pouring the cooled custard into the canister, fill the bucket with alternate layers of lightly crushed ice cubes and rock salt. The salt will raise the melting point of the ice, making it melt faster. The melting ice will draw heat from the custard in the canister, causing it to freeze. Meanwhile, the motion of the dasher will prevent the custard from crystallizing, and ensure that the result is a velvety-textured ice-cold cream.

1 **Whisking yolks and sugar.** In a saucepan, bring milk and a vanilla bean almost to a boil; set aside. Whisk egg yolks and sugar until they thicken enough to form a broad ribbon.

2 **Adding milk.** Remove any skin from the hot milk, then ladle the milk—a little at a time—into the egg-yolk mixture. Whisk in each addition well. Pour this custard into the saucepan.

3 **Straining the custard.** With a wooden spoon, stir the custard over low heat until it is thick enough to coat the spoon. Strain the custard into a metal bowl. Discard the vanilla bean.

4 **Cooling the custard.** Set the custard in a bowl of ice cubes and water. Stir until the custard is cool—about 20 minutes. Meanwhile, chill the canister and dasher of an ice-cream maker.

5 **Filling the canister.** Set the canister and dasher in the ice-cream maker. Pack the bucket half-full with crushed ice and rock salt. Pour the custard into the canister and cover it with its lid.

6 **Freezing the custard.** Fill the bucket with ice and rock salt. Add a cupful of water to start the freezing. Adding ice regularly, churn the custard for 30 minutes, or until it is frozen.

7 **Removing the dasher.** Uncover the canister, lift out the dasher and scrape the ice cream off it. Lift out the canister. Use the ice cream at once or cover the canister and set it in a freezer.

Cool Concoctions Plain and Fancy

The uses of ice cream in beverages are many and marvelous. Ice cream can simply be spooned into a glass of iced coffee or floated on top of a fruit-syrup drink. It can be blended with milk and syrup to make a thick, foaming milk shake *(right; recipe, page 122)*. Adding a spoonful of malted milk powder to the shake mixture produces a malted. Combining syrup with ice cream and aerating the syrup with soda water yields an ice-cream soda *(below; recipe, page 166)*.

Shakes, malteds and sodas can be concocted from syrups of any flavor. You can use ice cream of the same flavor as the syrup, or experiment with different flavors in combination. If you prefer, you can replace the syrup with fresh fruit—peeled peach segments, banana slices or whole soft fruit such as strawberries or raspberries. Fresh fruit also makes an appropriate garnish for a fruit-flavored drink. Chopped nuts and grated chocolate enhance chocolate and coffee sodas.

A Creamy Milk Shake Swiftly Made

1 **Blending the ingredients.** Put slightly softened ice cream and cold syrup—chocolate syrup is shown—in a blender. Pour in chilled milk. Blend the mixture until it is smooth.

2 **Serving the milk shake.** Pour the milk shake into a tall, chilled glass and serve with straws. If you like, sprinkle a little cocoa powder over the shake, as here, or top it with whipped cream.

A Flourish of Ice Cream and Soda

1 **Diluting the syrup.** Pour cold syrup—here, a fruit syrup *(pages 40-41)* made from strawberry purée—into a tall, chilled glass. Add a dash of soda water; in this case, the soda water is sprayed from a soda siphon.

2 **Adding the ice cream.** Put two scoops of slightly softened ice cream—strawberry ice cream is shown here—in the glass. Fill the glass with soda water.

3 **Serving the soda.** Spoon whipped cream onto the top of the soda and garnish it, if you like, with fresh fruit—in this instance, a strawberry. Serve the soda with straws and a long spoon.

4
Broths
Coaxing Forth Savory Goodness

Centuries of folk medicine have invested the humble cup of broth with powers that border on the miraculous. According to legend, a few sips of a garlic broth or a beef tea are enough to dispel colds, chills, fits, fevers and even the pains of childbirth. Such beliefs may strain credulity today, but the fact remains that warm broth is highly nourishing, easily digestible and soothing to the spirit. A little care in its preparation will guarantee that it is also fragrant and delicious.

The techniques and ingredients for broth are similar to those used in soup-making; only the emphasis is different. Meat or vegetables—and sometimes both—are simmered gently in a liquid. But while the cooked meat and vegetables are likely to be an important part of the finished soup, in a broth they are usually strained off and set aside to leave a radiantly clear liquid.

In most cases, the meat can be reserved and presented cold in salads and sandwiches; the vegetables, however, will have given up almost all their flavor and should be discarded. There are, of course, some exceptions. Garlic, for example, is sometimes puréed into its own cooking liquid to create a savory drink with a velvety texture. Furthermore, light broths of any kind can be given creamy smoothness by the addition of a paste of egg yolks and grated cheese (pages 58-59).

For even the simplest broths, cooking usually begins in cold water. Slowly increasing heat ensures a gentle cooking that extracts every nutritive element from the ingredients without clouding the broth by disintegrating them. When beef, veal, lamb or chicken are included (pages 60-61), a cold-water start is essential. As the temperature of the liquid rises, the meats release albuminous proteins that form a scum on the surface of the liquid. Gentle heating allows the cook to skim off these particles, whereas rapid heating would disperse them into the liquid and cloud it irretrievably.

Such gentle cooking is carried to an extreme in the making of beef tea, perhaps the most concentrated of all broths (pages 62-63). Finely chopped beef is sealed in a pot and enveloped in the warmth of a water bath for at least three hours. After the resulting juices are strained through several layers of cloth and carefully reheated, they produce a pellucid brew of remarkably intense flavor.

A light vegetable broth is ladled into a warmed cup. Celery, turnips, leeks, onions, carrots, tomatoes, garlic, parsley and a bay leaf were simmered gently in water, then strained through cheesecloth or muslin (pages 56-57).

Fine Chopping for Maximum Flavor

For a particularly light and tangy broth, fresh vegetables can be induced to give up their flavors quickly by being chopped fine, then simmered in water with herbs and other seasonings. When strained, the liquid becomes translucent and has a delicate tint.

Such a broth can include as few or as many vegetables as you like, the selection varied according to taste and season. In this demonstration, turnips, carrots, celery, leeks, onions and garlic are combined with tomatoes, which provide valuable color as well as flavor (recipe, page 126). Vegetables that could be added or substituted include celeriac, parsnips, cabbage, spinach and zucchini.

In the same way, a wide range of herbs and spices can be used to contribute accents. Whole or only coarsely crushed forms will be more assertive than ground forms. Here, the herbs are bay leaf and parsley; other options include fresh dill, basil, chives and tarragon. Appropriate spices are cloves, coriander seeds, cardamom, ginger and cinnamon.

In the choice of seasonings, a little experimentation will reward you. If you are using an herb or spice for the first time, add only a small amount—no more than one or two whole cloves, for example, or five or six coriander seeds—to determine its nuances and how it blends with other ingredients. For the fullest flavor, place most seasonings in the water at the start. The notable exception is peppercorns, which become bitter if cooked with liquid and are best added when the broth is almost done.

A combination of timing and tasting will tell you when the broth is ready. Chopped vegetables will take an hour or so to render their essences into the simmering liquid. Taste it to find out if they have done so; when they have, discard them. Prolonged cooking will draw no more from them. The broth can then be strained through cheesecloth or muslin to remove all traces of solid and semisolid elements. To concentrate its flavors and nutrients, reduce the strained broth by rapid boiling. If you are not using the broth immediately, it will keep in the refrigerator for up to three days.

1 **Preparing the vegetables.** Peel and dice celery, turnips, leeks and onions; wash parsley. Slice carrots lengthwise into thin strips, then cut the strips crosswise into dice.

2 **Seeding tomatoes.** With a small knife, cut a conical plug out of the stem end of each tomato. Cut the tomatoes in half crosswise and use the tip of your finger to scoop out the seeds. Chop the tomatoes into chunks.

6 **Reducing the broth.** Rinse out the pot and return the broth to it. Set the pot, uncovered, over medium heat and bring the liquid to a boil. To concentrate the flavor of the broth, let it boil until it is about half its original volume.

7 **Adding lemon juice.** Take the broth off the heat and let it cool briefly. Then taste it and add more seasoning if necessary. For zest, add lemon juice. To emphasize the vegetables' sweetness, stir in a little sugar.

3 **Adding water.** Place all the vegetables in a large pot. Remove the outer husk of a garlic bulb but do not peel the cloves. Add the garlic bulb and a bay leaf to the vegetables. Pour in cold water to cover the ingredients by about 2 inches [5 cm.]. Bring the water slowly to a boil over medium heat.

4 **Removing scum.** When the water boils, reduce the heat and skim off scum from the surface with a ladle. Add a little salt. Place a lid slightly ajar on the pot: Letting steam escape will prevent the simmer from rising to a boil. Simmer the broth gently for at least one hour, adding peppercorns during the last five minutes of cooking.

5 **Straining the broth.** Line a colander with a double thickness of cheesecloth or muslin and set the colander over a bowl. Strain the broth into a bowl, pressing the vegetables lightly with a wooden spoon to extract all their liquid. Discard the vegetables.

8 **Serving the broth.** Pour the broth into warmed cups and serve it at once. If you prefer to drink it cold, let the broth cool, then chill it in the refrigerator. In either case, just before serving you can give it a colorful garnish of sliced scallions, chopped chervil leaves or finely cut chives.

Supplying Substance to a Light Broth

A rich paste, or *pommade*, of cheese, eggs and oil lends zest and creaminess to mild-flavored broths of all kinds: vegetable, chicken or the garlic broth demonstrated here *(recipe, page 127)*.

To those familiar only with the pungency of raw garlic, the delicate broth made from it may come as a revelation. Garlic softens and mellows as it cooks so that the resulting beverage is sweet—an effect that can be attenuated by simmering the garlic with assertive herbs such as rosemary, sage, tarragon, thyme and bay leaves. The garlic cloves need only be crushed, not peeled; during cooking the skins will come free, and when the broth is strained they will be left in the sieve.

For a smooth beverage, the eggs in the paste must be kept from curdling. To accomplish this, the broth is first cooled briefly and a few ladlefuls used to warm the paste before it is added to the remainder. Before serving, the broth is reheated—over the gentlest possible heat.

1 **Crushing garlic.** Remove the outer husks from garlic bulbs and separate the cloves. Place one or two cloves at a time under the side of a knife blade. Use one hand to steady the knife and press down on the blade with the heel of your other hand to crush the cloves.

2 **Boiling the garlic.** Bring water to a boil in a saucepan. Add herbs—in this case, sage, thyme and bay leaf—the crushed garlic cloves and a little salt. Cover the saucepan, reduce the heat to low and simmer gently for 40 minutes, or until the garlic is very soft.

4 **Making a paste.** Grate cheese—in this instance, Parmesan. Break an egg into a small bowl. Add egg yolks, the grated cheese and pepper. Blend the ingredients with a whisk *(above, left)*, beating until the mixture is smooth and creamy. Then add olive oil, pouring it slowly and whisking at the same time to ensure that the oil is thoroughly incorporated *(right)*.

5 **Adding broth.** When the olive oil is well combined with the eggs and flavorings, whisk a few ladlefuls of the cooled broth into the paste. Continue to whisk until the cheese is melted and the mixture of broth and paste is smooth.

3 **Straining the broth.** Pour the broth mixture into a sieve set over a bowl (above, left). Pick out the herbs and discard them. Use a pestle or wooden spoon to push the flesh of the garlic cloves through the sieve into the broth (right). Discard the skins from the sieve. Set the broth aside to cool a little.

6 **Finishing the broth.** Pour the rest of the cooled broth back into the pan, set it over low heat and add the broth-thinned paste all at once (above). Whisk the mixture gently to ensure that it thickens uniformly. Serve the finished broth in warmed bowls (right).

Gentle Treatment for Clear Results

Few beverages are more comforting than a strong and savory meat broth. Such a drink can be made by simmering almost any kind—or combination—of meat in water for several hours to extract its essence, then straining the liquid and boiling it briefly to concentrate its flavor.

Beef, veal, or the lamb and chicken used here are all suitable *(recipes, page 164)*. Lean muscular cuts such as beef or veal shank or lamb neck or shoulder result in the strongest broth; a stewing chicken imparts more flavor than a broiler or roasting chicken.

Most meats should be cut into chunks that will fit into the pot easily and release their juices rapidly. A bird can be cut into sections or, because it is less dense than meats, can be kept whole and trussed. The gizzard and heart—plus extra giblets and necks and wing tips—will enrich the liquid.

Any meat broth is tremendously enhanced by aromatic vegetables—onions, carrots, turnips and garlic, for example—and herbs. The herbs may be tossed loose into the pot or bundled into the fragrant package known as a bouquet garni. Here, a bouquet of fresh thyme, parsley and a bay leaf is tied with celery and leek.

No matter what its ingredients, the hallmark of a perfect broth is its clarity. To achieve this, first strip any excess fat from the meat or chicken so the broth will not be greasy. Then submerge the meat in cold water and bring it very gradually to the boiling point. The slow heating ensures that the albuminous proteins released by the meat collect as a scum on the surface where they can be removed by skimming. Add vegetables and herbs only after the liquid has been skimmed.

For the duration of cooking—from two to six hours—maintain the liquid at a gentle simmer to draw out the juices of the ingredients without agitating the broth. When cooking is complete, strain the liquid through cheesecloth or muslin to remove the solids and trap any particles of sediment. Let the broth settle, then skim it; if any traces of fat remain, cool the liquid and chill it for several hours until the fat solidifies on its surface and can be lifted off with a spoon. Once reheated and reduced, the broth should be served at once in warmed cups.

Slow Simmering for Meat and Aromatics

1 **Placing lamb in the pot.** Trim off the surface fat from lamb—in this instance, pieces of neck. Cut the meat into chunks and place these chunks on a rack in a large pot.

2 **Removing the scum.** Pour in enough cold water to cover the lamb. Bring the water slowly to a boil, skimming off the scum that rises to the surface. Add a little cold water occasionally to help draw out scum. Repeat the skimming until no more scum forms, but take care not to stir the liquid lest you disperse the scum.

Extra Strength from a Whole Bird

1 **Cleaning giblets.** Remove the giblets from a stewing chicken; reserve the liver for another use. Trim fat and blood vessels from the heart. Place the heart and gizzard on a rack in a pot. Add chicken necks and wings. Cover the meats with cold water and bring it to a boil over medium heat. Drain the meats, discard the water and rinse the pot.

2 **Adding the chicken.** Truss the chicken by looping a piece of string under the tail and around the drumsticks and wings, then knotting it across the neck end of the bird. Place the trussed chicken on the rack in the pot. Add the giblets and chicken trimmings. Cover the meats with fresh cold water and bring it slowly to a boil.

3 **Adding vegetables.** Peel an onion and stick two whole cloves into it. Peel turnips and slice them thin. Prepare a bouquet garni—here, thyme, parsley, celery, leek and a bay leaf. Add the vegetables and herbs to the pot.

4 **Straining the broth.** Set the pot lid slightly ajar and simmer the broth for several hours. Remove the lamb, onion and bouquet garni. Reserve the lamb, if you like; discard the onion and herbs. Line a sieve with a double thickness of cheesecloth or muslin and strain the broth into a clean pan.

5 **Finishing the broth.** Let the liquid settle for a minute or two, then skim any fat that rises to the surface. To concentrate the flavor, boil the broth in the uncovered pan until it is reduced by about a quarter. Season the broth to taste and serve it in cups that have been warmed in very hot water.

3 **Skimming the scum.** As the water approaches the boiling point, remove the scum from the surface with a ladle. Prepare a bouquet garni—in this case, thyme, parsley, bay leaf, celery and leek. Add the bouquet garni, carrots, onions and a whole unpeeled garlic bulb to the pot; set the lid ajar and simmer the broth over low heat.

4 **Removing the chicken.** When the chicken is tender—after about two and one half hours—lift it out with a slotted spoon and set it aside for serving at a meal. Continue simmering the giblets, chicken trimmings and aromatics for another hour or so.

5 **Serving the broth.** Line a colander with cheesecloth or muslin and strain the broth through it into a clean pan. Let the broth settle briefly, skim it, then set the uncovered pan over high heat. Boil the broth until it is reduced by about a quarter. Season the broth to taste and serve it hot in warmed cups.

Beef Tea: A Fragrant Concentrate

Enclosed with liquid in a tightly sealed vessel and subjected to very low heat, finely chopped lean beef will yield all its essential juices. The solid matter is then strained out and discarded, leaving behind a clear, flavorful, amber-colored beverage that is known as beef tea *(right; recipe, page 128)*.

The purest, lightest tea will be obtained from lean, muscular—and inexpensive—cuts. Shoulder is used here; round and tip are equally appropriate. Avoid gelatinous cuts such as shank— they would yield a heavier, more viscous liquid not suitable as a beverage.

The meat must be thoroughly trimmed of fat to prevent the tea from becoming greasy. Then, to ensure that the meat releases its juices readily during cooking, it should be chopped very fine. The chopping is best done with a matched pair of heavy, sharp knives *(Step 3)*. A food grinder or processor can be used instead, but will crush the fibers of the meat so that some of its juices are released prematurely.

Beef tea is traditionally made from meat alone, without seasonings or flavorings. But the addition of a few aromatic vegetables, as in this demonstration, will lend savory support to the meat without detracting from its taste. Like the meat, the vegetables must be cut very fine to cook evenly and give up their juices.

Because concentration of flavor is a prime consideration, the solid ingredients should be covered with the barest minimum of water. Choose a tall, narrow cooking vessel such as a bean pot or the marmite jar used here so that the surface area of the liquid will be small and its evaporation thus limited. Seal the vessel tightly and let the beef release its juices in the gentle heat of a water bath.

Once strained, the beef tea can either be drunk immediately or kept in the refrigerator for up to three days. To serve the refrigerated broth, either reheat it or present it cold in chilled cups.

1 Trimming beef. If the meat contains any bone, cut it away with a sharp knife. Trim off all fat. Divide the meat— a shoulder steak is shown in this demonstration—into sections along the muscle seams and pare away all traces of connective tissue and tendons.

2 Dicing the meat. Cut the meat into slices ½ inch [1 cm.] thick, then cut each slice into ½-inch strips. Gather a few strips of meat together at a time and cut across them to make small dice. Place all the dice together on the work surface.

5 Mixing the ingredients. Pour in just enough cold water to submerge the ingredients. Cover the jar and let it stand for 30 minutes, to allow the water to begin to draw out the meat's juices. Then stir the ingredients thoroughly. Cover the jar with a tight-fitting lid or with foil; if you use foil, tie it tightly into position around the rim.

6 Cooking. Set the jar on a rack inside a deep pot. Add cold water to come about three quarters of the way up the jar. Cover the pot and bring the water to a boil over medium heat. Reduce the heat until the water barely simmers. Cook for three hours, replacing the water as necessary to maintain its three-quarter level.

3 **Chopping the meat.** Choose two large knives of equal size and weight and hold them parallel. With a relaxed grip and a loose-wrist action, chop the meat rhythmically, alternating the blades and letting their weight do most of the work *(above, left)*. As chopping progresses, the meat will gradually spread out over your work surface. From time to time, slide one of the knife blades under the edge of the meat, flip the edge over and back onto the center so that you have a compact mass. Continue chopping until the meat is diced very fine *(right)*.

4 **Dicing vegetables.** Place the meat in a tall, narrow vessel—in this case, a glazed earthenware marmite jar. Cut aromatic vegetables—carrot, turnip and celery are used here—into ¼-inch [6-mm.] dice. Add them to the jar with salt, a blade of mace and a bouquet garni of parsley, thyme, bay leaf and a celery rib.

7 **Straining and serving.** Line a sieve with several thicknesses of muslin or cheesecloth; set the sieve over a saucepan. Ladle the contents of the jar into the sieve and let all the juice drain through *(above)*. Reheat the beef tea gently and serve it in warmed cups *(right)*. Alternatively, let the tea cool, then refrigerate it.

5

Homemade Alcoholic Beverages
Exhilarating Transformations

Appealing alcoholic drinks that can be made at home fall into two categories. One category consists of liqueurs—spirits or a combination of spirits and wines sweetened and flavored with fruit, herbs or spices and then aged for several weeks to absorb the tastes and aromas of the added flavorings (pages 66-67). The other category consists of beverages that you ferment yourself—beers, hard cider and wines—by combining flavored liquids with sugar and yeast. The yeast feeds on the sugar and converts it to carbon dioxide and alcohol, producing a light alcoholic beverage if fermentation continues a few days, or a more potent one if the process goes on for several weeks or months.

The equipment and ingredients you will need are available at stores that specialize in home wine making or brewing. A wine press helps to squeeze juice from firm fruits such as apples or pears for the making of cider (pages 72-73). No matter what you are fermenting, you will need a vessel with a capacity at least a third larger than the amount of liquid; during fermentation, the liquid will bubble and rise. Beer (pages 70-71) is made in a single fermenter—a large plastic bucket fitted with an airtight lid. Cider and wines, however, are first fermented in buckets and later transferred to glass fermentation jugs. All vessels are fitted with a device known as a fermentation lock—a small glass or plastic tube that fits into the bucket lid (for beer) or the neck of a jug (for cider and wine). The lock is filled with water, which prevents bacteria, molds and fungi from entering the fermenting liquid while allowing the carbon-dioxide gas produced during fermentation to escape. A siphoning tube is needed to transfer the liquid from one vessel to another without disturbing the sediment that always collects.

Every piece of equipment must be scrupulously clean; Campden tablets (page 8) are used as a sterilizing agent in the demonstrations in this chapter. They are also used in wines to rid the liquid of unwanted bacteria and yeasts that may spoil the beverage. Special strains of yeast are used to ferment beer and wine. Do not use baker's yeast—it will not ferment properly and gives alcoholic drinks a musty flavor.

During fermentation and storage, all alcoholic beverages should be kept in a dark place; yeast contains photosensitive bacteria that light can activate, changing the character and the taste of the beverage.

Orange-flavored liqueur (page 66) is poured into a tall stemmed glass. The drink was made by steeping fruit and other flavorings in white wine and vodka for several weeks, then straining out the solids to leave a clear, golden liquid; it is served slightly chilled.

Concocting Liqueurs

Liqueurs are simple infusions of sweet-ened spirits—or spirits and wine—that have been flavored with fruits, spices, herbs, coffee or even chocolate. Original-ly, liqueurs were based on wine alone and the resulting drinks were light. Today, homemade liqueurs are potent concoc-tions based either on spirits or on wines fortified with spirits—usually vodka or *eau de vie,* a colorless fruit brandy.

Of the possible flavorings for liqueurs, fruits are most popular. When the infu-sion is completed, the fruit may be re-moved and the liquid strained for a clear drink *(top demonstration; recipe, page 142).* Alternatively the fruit can be left in the liquid to be served with the drink *(bottom demonstration; recipe, page 136).*

All fruits carry bacteria that can spoil a liqueur, and for some preparations, you will have to take preventive measures. If you make a clear, strained liqueur based on spirits, the problem does not arise: Spirits are at least 40 per cent alcohol, a concentration strong enough to kill bac-teria. If you make a clear liqueur based on wine, you must blanch the fruit for three minutes to kill the bacteria be-cause the alcohol content will be too low to prevent spoilage. Soft fruits may disin-tegrate during blanching, but they will be strained out of the liqueur.

Fruits that are to remain in a liqueur should keep their shape and are prepared differently from fruits for strained li-queurs. The fruits should be given the briefest of blanchings to soften them so they will absorb flavor. Firmer fruits—peaches, plums, cherries and apricots—withstand blanching best. Because brief blanching does not kill the bacteria, the fruits must be preserved in spirits.

Sealed in crocks or jars, the fruit will mingle with the liquid. After a month or so, the liqueur can be strained and bot-tled or, if the fruit is to be kept, stored in jars. To keep liqueurs from discoloring, containers must be filled to the top. If the fruit is retained, the surface of the liquid must be sealed with paper. Liqueurs will be ready to drink after a second month of aging. Store wine-based liqueurs in the refrigerator; use them within two months of opening. Spirit-based liqueurs need not be refrigerated. Once opened, they will keep their flavor for two years.

A Wine Cordial Flavored with Orange

1 Squeezing juice. Blanch whole oranges and a lemon in boiling water for three minutes. Halve the fruits, squeeze out the juice and pour it into a glazed ceramic crock. Add the squeezed fruits, white wine, vodka, sugar and a vanilla bean.

2 Mixing the ingredients. Stir the ingredients well with a wooden spoon. Cover the crock tightly with plastic wrap, aluminum foil and a lid. Put the crock in the refrigerator and leave it undisturbed for about 30 days.

A Dividend of Preserved Fruit

1 Pricking fruit. Wash ripe apricots in cold water and drain them in a colander. With a skewer, prick each fruit through to the pit in three or four places to allow alcohol to penetrate the flesh. Bring a pan of water to a boil.

2 Blanching the fruit. Place a few apricots on a skimmer; lower them into the boiling water and keep them in the water for about 20 seconds. Put the blanched apricots into a bowl of cold water to arrest the cooking. Blanch the rest of the fruit in the same way.

3 **Straining the liquid.** Remove all of the fruits from the crock with a slotted spoon. Line a funnel with several thicknesses of muslin or cheesecloth. Using a ladle, strain the liqueur through the funnel into bottles.

4 **Corking the bottles.** Close the bottles by hammering in corks *(above and page 9)*. Refrigerate the bottles, upright and undisturbed, for at least a month. Sediment will settle to the bottom. Decant the liqueur into a clean carafe or bottle before serving it *(right)*.

3 **Sweetening a spirit.** Fill wide-necked jars two thirds full with the fruit. Make a sugar syrup *(page 26, Steps 1 and 2)*, cool it slightly and mix it with vodka. Ladling the sweetened vodka through a sieve lined with cheesecloth, fill the jars almost to the rims.

4 **Sealing the jars.** Using an empty jar as a guide, cut out circles of parchment paper to fit inside the necks of the jars. Place a circle of paper on the surface of the liquid in each jar; press the paper down gently to expel any air. Seal the jars tightly with lids.

5 **Serving the liqueur.** Leave the sealed jars in a cool, dark place for at least two—preferably six—months. To serve the liqueur, place an apricot in a glass and spoon the liquid over it.

Using Yeast for a Sparkling Effect

With the simple addition of a little yeast, a sweetened infusion of a plant's root or leaves can be fermented to acquire a mildly alcoholic and refreshing sparkle. During fermentation, the yeast feeds on the sugar in the liquid to produce alcohol and carbon dioxide gas, which normally escapes into the air. But since the liquid is bottled before fermentation is complete, some of the gas is trapped inside to yield a naturally effervescent drink.

A beverage made from such a liquid is known as a small beer because it is weaker in alcohol than a beer made from grains. Small beers were originally intended as substitutions for beers made from grains when grains were scarce or unavailable; today such drinks are enjoyed on their own. In the demonstration at right an infusion of ginger root *(recipe, page 130)* is fermented to produce ginger beer; sarsaparilla or licorice roots can be infused in the same way, as can the leaves of dandelion, burdock and nettle.

Before infusion, the roots should be peeled and finely chopped or ground in a mortar; leaves need no preparation other than washing. The subsequent steps are the same: infusing the roots or leaves in boiling water to which sugar has been added. (If you like, the peel of a citrus fruit can be included for extra flavor.) Beer yeast is activated in a little tepid water and then added to the liquid after it has cooled.

During fermentation, the liquid must be maintained at a temperature between 60° F. [15° C.] and 80° F. [25° C.]. Above that range the activated yeast will die; below it, the yeast will fail to work. The liquid is left to stand 12 hours, or until the vigorous bubbling action of the yeast has subsided. Then, after being strained to remove pulp, it is ready for bottling.

Use sterilized bottles made of fortified glass *(pages 8-9)* and leave at least a 2-inch [5-cm.] space in the neck of each bottle to allow for the build-up of pressure due to the continued release of carbon dioxide gas. Seal each bottle securely with a metal cap *(page 8)* so that the carbon dioxide will not dissipate.

Once it has been bottled, the beer will be ready to drink in two days. Serve it soon; if it stands any longer than three days, the flavor will be impaired.

1 Preparing ginger. With a small, sharp knife, peel fresh ginger root; then cut it into slices about ¼ inch [6 mm.] thick. Put the slices in a mortar.

2 Grinding the ginger. With a pestle, crush the pieces of ginger in the mortar until they approach the consistency of a purée. Alternatively, chop them fine with a heavy knife.

6 Fermenting. Pour the reserved lime juice into the bowl of steeped flavorings. Add the yeast mixture and stir. Cover the bowl and let the mixture ferment overnight or longer at a temperature between 60° and 80° F. [15° and 25° C.].

7 Straining the liquid. Uncover the bowl. Line a sieve with several thicknesses of cheesecloth. Strain the fermented liquid into a large bowl.

3 **Combining the flavorings.** Put sugar in a large bowl; add the crushed ginger. Peel fresh limes, taking care to leave the bitter white pith on the fruit, and put the peel in the bowl. Cut the peeled limes in half, then squeeze them and reserve their juice.

4 **Infusing the flavorings.** Bring water to a boil and pour it over the flavorings. Stir the mixture with a wooden spoon until the sugar has dissolved. Set the bowl aside and let the mixture stand until it is tepid.

5 **Preparing the yeast.** Sprinkle beer yeast into a small bowl of tepid water. Stir the liquid and let it stand until it is a little bubbly—about 10 minutes—showing that the yeast has been activated.

8 **Bottling the beer.** Set a funnel in a pressure-resistant bottle; ladle the liquid through the funnel into the bottle, leaving a 2-inch [5-cm.] headspace. Bottle all of the liquid this way. Seal the bottles with metal caps (page 8).

9 **Serving the ginger beer.** Store the bottled ginger beer for two days in a dark place where the temperature is from 60° to 80° F. Refrigerate the drink before serving it in chilled mugs, as here, or over ice in tall glasses.

Techniques for Brewing a Perfect Beer

Of all the world's fermented beverages, beer—made from grains and flavored with hops—is perhaps the most popular. A sparkling brew containing 3 to 6 per cent alcohol, beer is relatively easy to make at home, as is demonstrated at right *(recipe, page 166)*.

Beer is based on malt, which is made from barley that has been sprouted, dried and then mashed to produce a thick, sugary syrup known as malt extract. The malt used here is of medium strength, but light extracts and dark extracts can also be obtained.

Beer's distinctively bitter flavor comes from the flower of the hop vine. Hops are available dried or in pellets, and come in varying degrees of bitterness.

The other major ingredients in beer are corn sugar, or dextrose, which is more readily fermented than ordinary granulated sugar, and beer yeast and water. The water must be hard in order to help precipitate the starchy compounds of the malt and thus clarify the beer; if you live in an area where the water is soft, you will have to harden your water with calcium sulfate or another mineral salt.

After all of the ingredients have been strained into a fermentation tank, the liquid is cooled, yeast is added and the tank is set aside to ferment for about 12 days, or until there are no more bubbles in the fermentation lock. The beer is then tested to make sure that all of the sugars have been converted to alcohol. This is done with a hydrometer, a simple calibrated instrument that measures the sugar content—or specific gravity—of the liquid. Beer recipes vary widely, and each may have a different specific gravity depending on the ingredients used.

Before it is bottled, the beer is primed with the addition of more corn sugar. The liquid is then bottled and capped. As the yeast continues to feed on the added sugar, carbon dioxide is trapped in the bottle to create a naturally carbonated drink.

After two weeks the beer will be fully carbonated and drinkable—but not fully flavored; it will taste better if it matures for another four weeks, and it will keep for up to a year.

1 Preparing the malt mixture. Soak a can of malt extract in hot water for about five minutes; when the label has come loose, the syrup inside will have softened enough to pour. Bring water to a boil in a large pot. Add the malt extract to the water, scraping out the last little bit with a spatula. Add corn sugar, stirring well to dissolve it.

2 Heating the mixture. Add three quarters of the hop pellets and, if necessary, a water hardener—here, calcium sulfate—to the malt mixture. Bring to a boil and simmer for 30 minutes, stirring occasionally. Add the remaining hop pellets and simmer for 15 minutes to reinforce the hop aroma. Remove the pot from the heat and set it on a trivet.

5 Testing the specific gravity. Open the tank, remove a little of the brew and replace the lid. Pour the brew into a test tube, leaving a space at the top, and drop in a hydrometer. If the specific gravity that registers on the gauge does not correspond to the one called for in your recipe, let the beer ferment for another day, then test it again.

6 Siphoning the brew. Put the fermentation tank on a shelf or a table and put a clean pot below it. Put one end of a siphoning tube in the tank; take the other end in your mouth and inhale forcefully. As soon as liquid appears in the tube, remove the tube from your mouth and let all the liquid flow from the tank to the pot.

3 **Straining the liquid.** Measure 5 gallons [20 liters] of water into a fermentation tank. With a wax crayon mark the level on the outside of the tank; discard the water. Line a sieve with cheesecloth, place it over the tank and strain the liquid into the tank. Add cooled boiled water up to the 5-gallon mark. Cover; cool to 80° F. [25° C.].

4 **Fermenting the brew.** Mix a package of beer yeast in tepid water and let it stand for 10 minutes before stirring it into the malt mixture. Secure the lid on the tank. Half-fill the fermentation lock with water and fit the lock in the lid *(inset)*. Let the brew ferment at a temperature of 60° to 80° F. [15° to 25° C.] for about 12 days, or until bubbling in the fermentation lock has ceased.

7 **Priming the brew.** Put some of the siphoned liquid in a small saucepan and add corn sugar. Set the pan over medium heat. Stirring the mixture constantly, bring it to a boil. Let it boil for one minute and remove it from the heat. When the mixture has cooled, add it to the beer and stir well.

8 **Bottling the beer.** Place the pot on a shelf and arrange bottles below. Siphon the beer from the priming pot into the bottles, one at a time, leaving a 2-inch [5-cm.] headspace in each. Cap the bottles *(page 8)* and store them upright in a dark place where the temperature is between 60° and 65° F. [15° and 18° C.] for six weeks.

9 **Serving the beer.** Place the bottles in the refrigerator to chill. Open each bottle carefully to avoid dislodging the sediment. Gently pour the beer into a beer glass, taking care to avoid pouring in the sediment.

Exploiting the Natural Sweetness of Apples

Apples and pears contain plenty of sweet juice that will ferment easily to make delicious drinks with an alcohol content of about 7 per cent. In the demonstration at right, apples are used to produce hard cider *(recipe, page 130)*. Because both apples and pears are firm, they must first be broken down into a pulp to release their juices. For best results you will need a wine press, an instrument designed to extract juice from fruit pulp *(Step 4)*.

For every 3 pounds [1½ kg.] of fruit, you will extract about 1 quart [1 liter] of juice. Here, russets—an apple variety with a characteristic burnished appearance—were used for their subtle balance of aromatic oils, sugars and acids. But russets are difficult to find in many parts of the United States, and you can achieve a cider that is both tangy and sweet by blending different varieties together in the following proportions: Jonathans or Winesap (10 to 20 per cent) to provide tartness; McIntosh or Gravensteins (10 to 20 per cent) for their aromatic oils; Golden Delicious or Rome Beauty (40 to 60 per cent) for their sweetness; and a few crab apples (5 to 20 per cent) for astringency. You can also add lemon juice—as here—for extra tartness, and sugar syrup for added sweetness.

Whatever variety of apple you choose, use only fruit that has no blemishes. Brown spots contain bacteria that may turn your cider to vinegar. Unripe apples are too low in sugar and too high in starch to yield good cider.

The fruit should first be soaked in water to which a Campden tablet has been added; this will rid the fruit of unwanted yeast organisms. The fruit should then be sliced thin, mixed with wine yeast and sugar, and left to ferment for a week. During this period, you should assist the breakdown of the fruit into pulp by crushing it once a day with the end of a wooden rolling pin.

After the vigorous fermentation has subsided, the fruit is passed through a wine press to extract its juice. The liquid is then transferred to a large glass jug where it will continue to ferment for two weeks. Sediment will collect in the bottom of the fermentation jug; to remove it, the cider is both filtered *(Step 5)* and decanted *(Step 6)* before being served.

1 **Preparing the apples.** Dissolve a Campden tablet in a bucket of cold water. Immerse apples in the solution for two minutes to sterilize them, then drain, and rinse the apples and the bucket. Pour in lemon juice and cooled sugar syrup *(page 26, Steps 1 and 2)*. Halve the apples, slice them thin and add them to the ingredients in the bucket.

2 **Adding yeast.** In a small pitcher, sprinkle dried wine yeast on a little tepid water. Stir the yeast and let the mixture stand for 10 minutes. Then pour it into the bucket containing the apples, lemon juice and sugar syrup.

5 **Fermenting the liquid.** Half-fill a fermentation lock with water and fit it into the jug *(above)*. Store the jug at 70° F. [20° C.] for two weeks, or until the levels of water on each side of the lock's U bend are equal in depth, signifying that fermentation has ceased. Line a funnel with filter paper and siphon the cider into a clean jug *(right)*.

3 **Converting apples to pulp.** Crush the apples into coarse pieces with the end of a wooden rolling pin or a pestle. Cover the bucket and set it in a warm place—approximately 70° F. [20° C.]. Crush the apples with the rolling pin once a day for a week, or until they have broken down into a pulp.

4 **Pressing the pulp.** Set a funnel in the neck of a fermentation jug; position a wine press with its spout over the funnel. Fill the nylon bag inside the press with apple pulp *(left)*. Tie the bag, and fit the round plate, handle and support into position. Turn the handle so that the plate descends on the fruit and forces out the juice *(above)*.

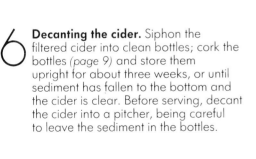

6 **Decanting the cider.** Siphon the filtered cider into clean bottles; cork the bottles *(page 9)* and store them upright for about three weeks, or until sediment has fallen to the bottom and the cider is clear. Before serving, decant the cider into a pitcher, being careful to leave the sediment in the bottles.

A Sure Approach to Wine Making

Homemade wine, rustic and full-bodied, is no more than the fermented juice of fruits such as grapes or berries, flowers such as dandelions or vegetables such as parsnips *(recipes, pages 130-135)*. Converting the juice into wine is not difficult, but it does require equipment and ingredients for monitoring and adjusting the acid and sugar in the juice, thus ensuring that the liquid ferments properly.

The first step after extracting juice *(pages 32-37)* is to determine its acid level: A juice low in acid will not ferment effectively. Most kits for testing acidity work on similar principles. An alkaline substance—sodium hydroxide—is combined with a juice sample to decrease the juice's acidity. As the acid reduces, the juice changes color, at which point a chemist's color indicator called phenolphthalein is added; this causes the juice to change color again, when it becomes fully alkaline. By measuring how much sodium hydroxide is needed to change the juice from acid to alkaline, you can determine how acid the juice was in the first place. If the acidity level is less than 5 per cent you will have to fortify the juice with tartaric, citric or malic acid.

The next test, made with a hydrometer *(page 70)*, is for sugar level, which should be between 20 and 28 per cent to yield a wine of 10 to 14 per cent alcohol. If the sugar level in the juice is too low, you must add sugar to ensure fermentation.

The rest of wine making is a matter of controlled fermentation and clarification. The prepared juice must be sterilized with a Campden tablet *(page 72)* to destroy unwanted yeasts and bacteria that might sour the wine. The juice must be treated with an enzyme that breaks down the pectins—carbohydrates that would cloud the wine. And it must be bolstered with nutrients to nourish the wine yeast that starts fermentation.

The wine yeast is added 12 hours after the Campden tablet; otherwise, the tablet might kill it. Several months of fermentation and clarification follow. During this time, the wine is strained to clarify it and siphoned to rid it of sediment. When it is clear, it may be bottled. Within six months of the start of the process, the wine will have matured enough to drink; it will be at its peak in a year.

1 Preparing juice. Rinse and drain blackberries. With a pestle, crush them in a bucket, then add water and stir. Line a sieve with cheesecloth, place it over a bowl and strain some juice through it. Fill the test-kit syringe with strained juice and put the juice in a test tube containing distilled water. Do the same with a second test tube.

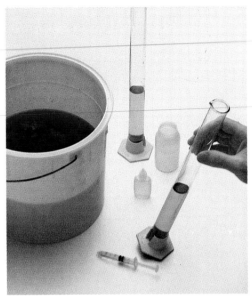

2 Testing the juice. Clean the syringe and fill it with the first testing agent—sodium hydroxide. Add a drop to one test tube (saving the other for color control) and shake. Carefully add more sodium hydroxide, one drop at a time, until the color suddenly turns—here, from pink to greenish brown.

6 Fermenting. Let wine yeast stand in tepid water for 10 minutes; add it to the juice. Cover the bucket and put it in a warm place—70° F. [20° C.]. Stir daily for a week, until foam has risen and subsided. Force the mixture through a cheesecloth-lined sieve into a bowl.

7 Filling the fermentation jug. Set a funnel in the neck of a jug. Carefully ladle the strained juice from the bowl into the funnel, and fill the fermentation jug to within 1 inch [2½ cm.] of the top.

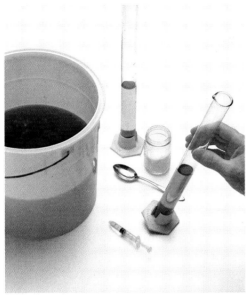

3 **Adjusting the acid level.** Add phenolphthalein; then add drops of sodium hydroxide until the liquid turns reddish brown. Note how much sodium hydroxide remains in the syringe and, by following the test-kit formula, determine the amount of acid needed to raise the acid level of the juice. Add the necessary powdered acid blend.

4 **Adding sugar.** Clean a test tube and put strained juice in it, leaving a 2-inch [5-cm.] headspace. Insert a hydrometer and read the scale that shows sugar content. If more sugar is needed, the addition of 3 tablespoons [45 ml.] of sugar for every gallon [4 liters] of liquid will raise the sugar level by one percentage point.

5 **Sterilizing the liquid.** Crush a Campden tablet in water and add it to the juice in the bucket. Add pectic enzyme and a yeast nutrient—here, food-grade urea and ammonium phosphate. Let the mixture stand, covered, overnight.

8 **Fermenting the juice.** Half-fill a fermentation lock with water and fit it into the jug. Let the jug stand, undisturbed, in a warm place—70° F. [20° C.]—for four weeks, or until the water has leveled out in the lock (page 72, Step 5), indicating the end of fermentation.

9 **Bottling.** Siphon the liquid into a clean jug, top it off with cooled boiled water, replace the lock and put the wine in a cool place—60° F. [15° C.]—for two or three months. When it is clear, siphon it into bottles (above); cork them (page 9). Serve chilled (right).

Liquid Gold from Molten Honey

If you have the patience to wait for two to five years to savor the fruits of your labor, you can make mead—one of the oldest alcoholic beverages known to man. A still wine that has an alcohol content of from 10 to 14 per cent, mead is a fermented solution of honey and water. The lengthy aging period of this venerable drink is necessary in order for the mead to become smooth and mellow.

For a delicate mead, choose a pure, pale-colored honey such as the clover honey used here *(recipe, page 136);* you might use a tupelo, basswood or orange-blossom honey instead—or a blend of several light honeys. Darker honeys will produce a stronger-tasting mead.

To prepare the ingredients for use, honey and water must first be boiled to rid them of any organisms that might spoil the taste of the fermented drink. Alternatively, you can dissolve a Campden tablet in hot water and add it to the honey without boiling the mixture; the Campden tablet will prevent the growth of microorganisms. Be sure to wait 12 hours before adding the yeast if you are following this procedure.

For tartness and astringency—honey contains no acids—you will want to add lemon juice, lemon peel and tea to the mixture. To ferment the honey, use a standard wine yeast activated in a small quantity of tepid boiled water. To be absolutely certain that the mixture will ferment properly, you can also add a yeast nutrient *(page 74)*. The honey, water, flavorings and yeast are then put in a fermentation jug and left to ferment for two to four weeks. The length of time will vary, depending on the sugar content of the honey and on the temperature at which you store the brew. The ideal temperature to maintain during fermentation is 70° F. [20° C.].

After fermentation has ceased, the liquid is siphoned into a clean jug and left to clear while the sediment falls to the bottom. If the wine has not become crystal clear in three months, repeat the siphoning process into another clean jug, and wait another two or three months. Once the liquid has cleared, the mead must be bottled and left to mature. It can be drunk in two years, but it will not reach its peak until five years have passed.

1 **Mixing flavorings.** Grate the peel of a lemon fine, avoiding the bitter white pith, and squeeze the juice from the lemon. Put water in a pan and set it over medium heat. Spoon honey—clover honey is used here—into the water. Add black tea leaves, the lemon juice and the grated lemon peel.

2 **Sterilizing the honey.** Stir the mixture until the honey has dissolved. Bring the liquid to a boil; then reduce the heat and simmer the honey and flavorings for 10 minutes. Remove the pan from the heat and allow the mixture to cool until it is tepid.

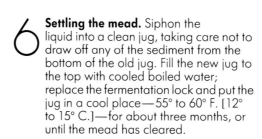

6 **Settling the mead.** Siphon the liquid into a clean jug, taking care not to draw off any of the sediment from the bottom of the old jug. Fill the new jug to the top with cooled boiled water; replace the fermentation lock and put the jug in a cool place—55° to 60° F. [12° to 15° C.]—for about three months, or until the mead has cleared.

3 **Straining the mixture.** Set a funnel in a narrow-necked fermentation jug; pour in tepid boiled water. Line a nonreactive sieve with a double layer of cheesecloth. Set the sieve over the funnel and strain the honey mixture through it into the fermentation jug.

4 **Adding yeast.** Sprinkle dried wine yeast in a little tepid boiled water and stir. Let it stand for 10 minutes to begin activating. Pour more tepid boiled water into the fermentation jug to bring the level to within 4 inches [10 cm.] of the top; then add the activated wine yeast.

5 **Fermenting the liquid.** Pour water into a fermentation lock, and fit the lock into the neck of the jug. Shake the jug vigorously to disperse the yeast and then let the jug stand, undisturbed, in a 70° F. [20° C.] place for four weeks, or until the water in the fermentation lock has leveled out *(page 72, Step 5)*, signifying the end of fermentation.

7 **Bottling the mead.** When the liquid is clear, siphon it into clean bottles *(inset)*, leaving a 2-inch [5-cm.] headspace in each bottle. Cork the bottles *(page 9)* and store them on their sides for at least two years. Serve the mead chilled *(right)*.

6

Punches and Mixed Drinks
Convivial Assemblies

Cold punches based on wines and spirits
Concentrating the flavor of wine
A classic blend of eggs and cream
Thickening a punch with yolks
Diverse techniques for mixing drinks
Assembling a layered drink

Combined with each other or with flavorings, alcoholic beverages produce a virtually limitless spectrum of punches, cocktails and after-dinner drinks. Beer, hard cider, wine, brandy, liquor or liqueurs of every variety are candidates for these concoctions. The potential flavorings run the gamut from fruit and vegetable juices and fruit syrups to eggs, cream, herbs and spices.

Punches are based principally on wines, spirits or a blend of the two. Traditionally dispensed from a decorative bowl, they can be cold or hot, according to the season. At its simplest, a cold punch may be no more than a mixture of still or sparkling wine and fresh fruit; for extra flavor, the fruit can be macerated ahead of time in brandy and liqueur *(pages 80-81)*. A savory, rather than sweet, punch results from blending spirits with such liquids as coffee or tea.

Hot punches, or mulled drinks as they are often called, generally start with a red wine enhanced by sweeteners and spices. Reducing the wine mixture by boiling concentrates its flavor, and any alcohol that evaporates in the process can be replaced by adding brandy or other spirits *(pages 82-83)*.

Blending eggs and sugar with wines and spirits yields a diversity of richer, more sustaining drinks. Whisked egg whites can transform a mixture of yolks, cream and spirits into a frothy cold eggnog. By contrast, cooking egg yolks gently with white wine creates a warm punch with the smooth texture of a custard *(page 85)*.

The cocktails and other mixed drinks that precede a meal can be based on almost any alcoholic liquid—sweet or tart, potent or mild. Most include such liquors as vodka, gin, rum or bourbon and are served chilled or with ice. They can be as simple as a martini *(opposite)* or as complex as a Margarita, in which citrus juice, orange liqueur and tequila are sipped from a glass rimmed with salt *(page 86)*.

Although liqueurs often feature in the composition of cocktails and punches, they come into their own as after-dinner drinks. Because these sweet spirits aid digestion, they are welcome when served plain or iced as a frappé. For a more dramatic effect, however, layers of different liqueurs can be amassed in a single glass with syrups and brandies to form a striped pousse-café as demonstrated on page 90.

A glacier-cold martini—gin with a suspicion of dry vermouth—is strained from a pitcher into a cocktail glass after being chilled and stirred with ice *(page 88)*. A garnish such as a green olive or a lemon twist will lend a pleasantly astringent edge to the drink.

Cold Punches, Bubbling and Still

Spirits, citrus, spices, sugar and water were the original five constituents of the drink known as punch—a name derived from the Sanskrit for "five." Hundreds of improvisations on this formula have transformed punch into an abundance of drinks, many nonalcoholic or based on wine rather than liquor, many with fruit incorporated in the blend or used for a garnish. In these demonstrations, brandy, orange liqueur, peaches and strawberries are mixed with sparkling wine to form a bubbling punch *(top demonstration)*, while rum, brandy, lemon juice and tea create a potent, still drink *(bottom demonstration; recipe, page 143)*.

Fruit for the punch bowl should be ready to be eaten. Small fruits—cherries, grapes and berries, for example—will need only to have their stems, seeds or pits removed. Large fruits—such as apples, pears, pineapple and peaches—must be peeled, cored or pitted, and cut into small pieces.

Once prepared, the fruit—sprinkled, if you like, with sugar—can be steeped in the wine or spirits that will be used for the punch in order to absorb their flavors. (Do not use sparkling wine at this stage; it would lose its zest during the maceration period.) A more pronounced citrus-fruit flavor can be obtained by infusing the peel in the juice and hot water, then removing the peel shortly before serving the punch.

Cold punch is traditionally served in a deep glass bowl that displays the drink's attractive color. The bowl should be well chilled beforehand. To preserve its coldness during mixing and serving, place a large block of ice in it. You can freeze water—decorated if you like by pieces of fruit—in a large mold or bowl for an attractive presentation, or chip a commercial block of ice down to size with a chisel or other sturdy, sharp implement.

To assemble the punch, arrange the fruits around the ice or pour them, with the liquids, over it. With sparkling wine, chill it separately and add it to the bowl just before serving.

A Union of Fruit and Sparkling Wine

1 **Peeling peaches.** Using a slotted spoon, dip peaches into boiling water for five seconds to loosen the skins. Put the fruit in cold water to stop the cooking. Peel the peaches and toss them in lemon juice to prevent discoloration.

2 **Macerating fruit.** Halve, pit and slice the peaches; put them in a shallow dish. Wash and hull strawberries; add them to the peaches. Pour in brandy and an orange-flavored liqueur. Let the fruit steep for one hour.

A Piquant Blend of Rum and Tea

1 **Preparing lemons.** With a sharp knife or a vegetable peeler, shave the peel from lemons, leaving the bitter white pith on the fruit. Halve the lemons and squeeze out the juice. Put the peel and juice into a heatproof bowl. Bring water to a boil and pour it in.

2 **Adding tea.** Make a pot of green or oolong tea *(pages 18-19)*; let it cool. Strain the cooled tea into the bowl containing the lemon juice and peel. Make a sugar syrup *(page 26, Steps 1 and 2)* and allow it to cool.

3 **Mixing the punch.** Chill a punch bowl and put a block of ice in it. Encircle the ice with the strawberries, peach slices and their macerating liquid. Refrigerate the bowl until you are ready to serve the punch.

4 **Completing the punch.** Just before serving, pour chilled sparkling wine into the punch bowl *(above)*. Ladle the drink immediately into chilled punch cups, including a few pieces of fruit in each cup *(inset)*.

3 **Pouring in spirits.** Pour white or— as here—dark rum into the bowl containing the lemon juice and tea. Add brandy. Sweeten the mixture to taste with the cooled sugar syrup. Stir the mixture to blend all the ingredients.

4 **Mixing the punch.** Chill a punch bowl and place a block of ice inside it. Using a ladle, pour the punch into the bowl through a sieve. Discard the peel.

5 **Serving the punch.** To provide color and extra flavor, add a few thin slices of cucumber and lemon to the punch. If you like, you may garnish the punch additionally with a few sprigs of mint or borage. Ladle the punch into chilled cups for serving.

Hot Wine and Spirits: A Happy Marriage

When wine, hard cider or ale is heated with sugar or honey and spices—in the process known as mulling—it mellows in flavor and becomes intensely aromatic. After straining to remove any solids, the mulled drink is served, as demonstrated here, as a hot punch.

Sweeteners balance the natural acidity of fermented beverages—a characteristic that is intensified when they are heated. Spices contribute their special flavors. Nutmeg, mace, ginger, cardamom, allspice, cinnamon or cloves are all appropriate; they are best used whole, for ground spices would muddy the drink. Both fresh and dried fruits—such as the combination of oranges, apples and figs used in this demonstration *(recipe, page 147)*—are welcome additions. Other possibilities include peaches, apricots, raisins and plums. To release their flavors quickly, the fruits should be cut into halves or quarters.

Mulling is simple. The wine, cider or ale is heated gently together with the sweetener and flavorings until the sugar or honey is dissolved. The conventional tactic is to preserve the alcoholic content of the fermented beverage by not allowing the temperature of the liquid to rise above 172° F. [78° C.]—the stage at which the alcohol begins to evaporate. In the technique shown here, however, the mixture is boiled briefly to concentrate its flavors, and set aside to infuse for five minutes or so. A measure of spirits then replaces the alcohol that evaporated.

Any still wine is suitable for mulling. Red wines are the most popular choice and even relatively inexpensive ones will produce a rich, colorful drink. Wines that are made from such fruits as blackberry or elderberry are delicious alternatives. White wines and rosés, being light in taste, yield more delicate mulled drinks and are better complemented by herbs—sweet woodruff or mint for example—than by spices.

The punch can be kept warm over low heat while you serve it. For more formal presentations, transfer the hot wine to a warmed punch bowl and garnish it with a few thin slices of orange or lemon.

1 **Cutting up the fruits.** Wash fruits under running water—here, oranges, apples and dried figs are used. To allow the fruits to release their juices, cut the oranges and apples into quarters and the figs into halves. There is no need to remove the skins or seeds; these will be discarded when the drink is strained.

5 **Straining the wine.** Place a nylon or stainless-steel sieve over a large bowl. Using a ladle, transfer the wine mixture to the sieve, a small batch at a time, and let the liquid drip through. Discard the solids remaining in the sieve. Return the strained wine to the pan.

6 **Pouring in brandy.** To fortify the wine, pour in a generous amount of brandy as shown here, or of fruit-flavored liqueur. Return the pan to low heat and warm the liquid until it just begins to bubble at the edges. Do not let it boil again, lest its flavor be impaired.

2 **Pouring in the wine.** Chop almonds into chunks. Put the fruit and nut pieces into a large, nonreactive pan. Add sugar and spices—in this instance, whole cloves and sticks of cinnamon are used. Pour in red wine to cover the ingredients generously.

3 **Stirring the mixture.** Place the pan over low heat. Using a wooden spoon, stir the mixture until all of the sugar has dissolved completely. Then increase the heat and bring the mixture to a boil.

4 **Simmering the wine.** Adjust the heat to maintain a simmer. Let the wine mixture cook, uncovered, for about 10 minutes. Remove the pan from the heat, cover with a lid and let the mixture infuse for another five minutes.

7 **Serving the punch.** Ladle the drink into warmed punch cups and serve it immediately. If you like, garnish each cup with thin slices of orange or lemon or with strips of citrus peel.

Eggs and Alcohol in Heady Unison

Beaten egg yolks and sugar provide a rich foundation for a wide range of alcoholic punches—both warm and cold. Depending on how the yolks are treated, and the ingredients with which they are blended, the finished drink can be as frothy as the cold eggnog in the top demonstration *(recipe, page 153)* or as custardy as the warm caudle in the bottom demonstration *(recipe, page 152)*.

For a cold punch of luxurious lightness the eggs are separated and the yolks beaten with the sugar until they incorporate enough air to double in volume—an operation that takes about 20 minutes with a whisk or rotary beater, or 10 minutes with an electric mixer. Liquids are blended in next, beginning with the flavoring elements. In this demonstration, rye and rum are used for the eggnog, but other spirits or combinations of spirits could be substituted; sherry or port would also be excellent. When these have been gently combined with the yolks, the cream and milk that provide most of the liquid for the drink are blended in. To lighten the eggnog further, the reserved whites are then beaten to the soft-peak stage and folded into the mixture.

For a warm punch such as the caudle—the name is derived from an Old French word for "warm"—the sweetened yolk mixture need not be beaten as thoroughly as it is for a cold punch because cooking will thicken it to a custard-like consistency. Both the flavoring and the liquid for warm egg punches are provided by fermented beverages—wine, hard cider or beer. Once mixed, the punch must be cooked gently over low heat, lest the yolks curdle. Set the pan either on a heat-diffusing pad as shown here or in a larger pan of simmering water.

Cold egg punches should be made an hour or so in advance so that they can be properly chilled in the refrigerator. Warm egg punches, on the other hand, should be served as soon as they have thickened. Both cold and warm versions can be garnished with ground cinnamon, grated nutmeg or finely grated orange or lemon peel.

Whiskey and Cream, Lightened and Chilled

1 **Adding sugar to yolks.** Separate eggs *(page 49, Step 3)*, putting the yolks in a large bowl. Set the egg whites aside. Whisk the egg yolks until they become pale in color. Little by little, add sugar, whisking after each addition.

2 **Incorporating spirits.** Continue to whisk until the mixture doubles in volume and falls in a slowly dissolving ribbon when the whisk is lifted from the bowl. Pour in rye in a slow, steady stream, whisking constantly to blend it in smoothly. Add rum in the same way.

A Warm and Winey Custard

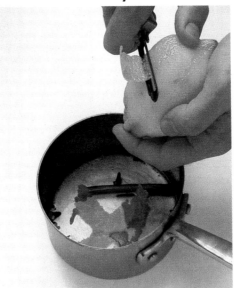

1 **Infusing flavorings.** Put whole cloves and a cinnamon stick into a pan; add the peel of a lemon. Pour in enough water to submerge the ingredients. Cover and simmer gently for 30 minutes. Remove the pan from the heat and let the infusion cool.

2 **Adding wine.** Separate eggs, dropping the yolks into a large bowl; reserve the whites for another use. Add sugar to the yolks and whisk them until the mixture is smooth and pale. While whisking continuously, pour in white wine in a slow, steady stream.

3 **Adding cream and milk.** Slowly pour in light cream, whisking at the same time. When the cream is incorporated, whisk in milk. Continue whisking until all the ingredients are smoothly blended.

4 **Adding whites.** Transfer the whites to a large bowl and whisk until they hold soft peaks *(page 49, Step 4)*. Stir a spoonful of the beaten whites into the yolk mixture. Then add the remaining whites and use a spatula to fold them in.

5 **Serving the punch.** When the whites are amalgamated, pour the mixture into a punch bowl and refrigerate it for about an hour. Just before serving the punch, grate a little nutmeg over the surface. Ladle the drink into chilled punch cups.

3 **Straining the infusion.** Pour the infusion of spices and peel into a sieve held over the yolk-and-wine mixture; discard the solids remaining in the sieve. Stir the mixture to distribute the spiced water through it evenly.

4 **Cooking the custard.** Pour the mixture into a heavy pan or, as shown here, a heatproof casserole. Place it on a heat-diffusing pad set over very low heat. Stir gently with a wooden spoon until the mixture coats the spoon lightly; remove it from the heat at once.

5 **Serving.** Pour the punch into a warmed bowl or, as shown here, dispense it directly from its cooking vessel. If you like, grate a little nutmeg over the punch. For serving, ladle the drink into warmed punch cups.

A Trio of Techniques for Mixing Drinks

The variety of mixed drinks that can be served before a meal verges on the infinite: A bar guide published in the late 1970s included more than 5,000 recipes.

Most cocktails, juleps, fizzes, collinses and other mixed drinks are based on distilled spirits, although some rely on wine, hard cider or beer. The mixers, or flavorings, include all manner of fruit and vegetable purées and juices, as well as eggs and cream. The demonstrations here and on the following pages show a sampling of the many options *(recipes, pages 154-163)*.

How ingredients should be mixed depends on their characteristics. Liquids of similar densities—liquors, wines and clear fruit juices, for example—can simply be stirred gently together, the technique used for the Tom Collins shown at right. Stirring is always the right tactic for combining transparent liquids: Too much agitation can make them cloudy.

Vigorous agitation is necessary, on the other hand, to mix liquids of different densities—liquors and liqueurs, for instance, as in a Margarita *(below)*. For these drinks, a cocktail shaker is essential; adding ice to the shaker chills and blends the liquids at the same time. With solid ingredients such as fruit, a blender forms a purée quickly and crushes ice into it to give drinks such as daiquiris a pleasantly granular texture *(opposite page, bottom)*.

Ice does more than simply cool a drink. Cubes melt slowly and are the best choice for maximum coldness and minimum dilution. Crushed ice imparts texture, but melts quickly to dilute a strong drink.

The glasses used for mixed drinks can vary as much as their contents. Stemmed glasses, or goblets, keep cold drinks away from warm hands. Tumblers—whether short old-fashioned glasses or tall collins glasses—and tankards provide capacious vessels for drinks served over ice. To ensure that the drinks will be cold when they are served, glasses should be chilled in the freezer for 15 minutes or so.

Stirring a Tom Collins

1 **Adding lemon juice.** Put sugar—superfine sugar, used here, dissolves most easily—in a chilled glass. Add lemon juice. Pour in gin.

Shaking a Margarita

1 **Filling the shaker.** Pack a cocktail shaker two thirds full with ice cubes. Pour tequila over the ice cubes. Add orange liqueur and lime juice.

2 **Shaking the cocktail.** Place the lid on the shaker. Hold the shaker firmly, keeping the lid in place with one hand. Shake vigorously for about 15 seconds to blend and chill the ingredients.

3 **Serving.** Rub the rim of a chilled glass with the cut surface of a lemon or lime, then invert the glass into a ⅛-inch [3-mm.] layer of coarse salt. Turn the glass upright and let the salt on its rim dry. Pour in the cocktail from the shaker.

2 **Stirring the liquids.** With a long-handled spoon, stir the ingredients together until they are thoroughly blended and the sugar is dissolved.

3 **Adding soda water.** Pack the glass to the rim with ice cubes. Fill the glass with soda water. Stir the drink briefly to blend in the soda water.

4 **Serving.** Impale a garnish—here, a quarter slice of orange and a cherry—on a cocktail stick. Lay the garnish on top of the ice; serve immediately.

Blending a Fruit Daiquiri

1 **Cutting up fruit.** Peel fruit—bananas, peaches, apricots or, as shown here, a honeydew melon—and remove any pits or seeds. Cut the fruit into medium-sized chunks.

2 **Mixing ingredients.** Put the fruit in a blender and add cracked ice. Pour in rum, lime juice and maraschino liqueur. Blend until the fruit is puréed and the ice crushed—about 30 seconds.

3 **Serving.** Pour the drink into a chilled tumbler, mounding it in the center of the glass. Garnish the drink with a quarter slice of orange and push two straws down the side of the glass.

Martini

Stirring a clear drink. Half-fill a chilled pitcher with ice cubes. Pour in gin *(above)*. Add a few drops of dry vermouth and, with a long spoon, gently stir the liquids together. Hold back the ice with the spoon while pouring the cocktail into a chilled glass. Twist a lemon peel over the drink, then drop it into the glass *(inset)*.

Silver Fizz

Foaming with egg white. Drop the white of an egg into a cocktail shaker *(above)*. Add lemon juice, superfine sugar and gin. Cover the shaker and mix the ingredients vigorously. Pour the drink into a tall, chilled glass containing ice cubes. Fill the glass with soda water. Garnish with a twist of lemon peel *(inset)*.

Sazerac

Swirling liqueur. Put a little anise liqueur in a chilled glass and swirl it to coat the inside of the glass *(above)*. Pour out any excess. Add a sugar cube to the glass and muddle it with water and bitters. Add ice, pour in bourbon and serve *(inset)*.

Bloody Mary

Shaking ingredients. Fill a cocktail shaker with ice cubes; pour in vodka *(above)*. Add tomato juice, lemon juice, Worcestershire sauce, Tabasco sauce and black pepper. Cover the shaker and mix vigorously. Strain into a chilled goblet *(inset)*.

Black Velvet

Pouring beer. Half-fill a chilled wineglass with cold stout or dark ale, tilting the glass and pouring the beer in a thin stream down the side of the glass *(above)* to prevent a deep head of foam. Slowly add chilled sparkling wine to fill the glass *(inset)*.

Champagne Cocktail

Dissolving a sugar cube. Chill a tall stemmed glass. Place a sugar cube in the bottom of the glass; shake in a few drops of Angostura bitters to flavor the sugar *(above)*. Add brandy, then fill the glass with chilled Champagne. Serve the cocktail while the sugar is still dissolving *(inset)*.

Mint Julep

Crushing mint. Put torn mint leaves, superfine sugar and cracked ice into a tall, chilled glass. Crush the ingredients to bruise the mint and dissolve the sugar *(above)*. Pack the glass with ice; fill it with bourbon. Serve the drink garnished with mint *(inset)*.

Wine Cobbler

Pouring over ice. Half-fill a chilled wineglass with cracked ice. Pour in table wine or a fortified wine such as port or the sherry shown here *(above)*. Add orange liqueur and superfine sugar. Stir the drink and garnish it with mint and an orange wedge *(inset)*.

Rainbow Stripes in a Single Glass

A smooth and flavorful liqueur ends the dinner with a flourish. Any single liqueur may be poured into a cocktail glass packed with crushed ice and presented as a simple frappé *(box, below)*. With a little extra effort, an array of liqueurs can be combined with brandies and fruit syrups in a tall narrow glass to create a pousse-café *(right; recipe, page 161)*—an elaborate presentation that takes advantage of the color of each ingredient by displaying it as a discrete stripe.

The secret of creating such a drink lies in the wide range of sugar contents—and therefore of densities—of its ingredients. Pour the heaviest liquid first, and be sure to add subsequent liquids in strict order by weight to ensure that each layer remains separate. The more alcoholic a liquid, the lighter it will tend to be, but a hydrometer *(Step 1)* will take the guesswork out of establishing densities.

Once prepared, a pousse-café can wait at room temperature for about an hour. Frappés can be stored in the freezer; the ice will solidify, but will melt in minutes.

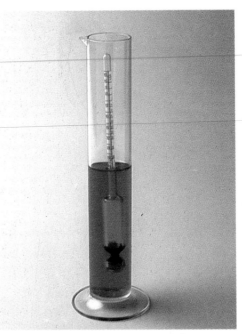

1 Measuring density. Pour a little liquid—here, crème de cacao—into a vial or narrow glass. Lower a hydrometer into the vial and let it float. When the hydrometer stops moving, note the reading at the liquid's surface. Measure each liquid in the same way.

2 Pouring the first liquid. Arrange the ingredients you intend to use in their order of density. Pour the heaviest—in this case, grenadine syrup—into the bottom of a tall liqueur glass, to a depth of about ½ inch [1 cm.].

Ice Drenched with Liqueur

Forming a frappé. Fill a cocktail glass with crushed ice. Pour in a liqueur—here, crème de menthe—until the ice is submerged. Serve with straws.

3 Adding layers. Put the tip of an inverted teaspoon just below the surface of the first layer. Slowly add the second heaviest liquid, letting it spread out over the back of the spoon as you pour. Add more layers—maraschino liqueur is shown—in order of weight.

4 Serving. Present the drink when the layers are complete; here, they consist—from bottom to top—of grenadine syrup, crème de cacao, *parfait amour*, crème de menthe, maraschino liqueur and Cognac. To drink a pousse-café, sip it, layer by layer, through a straw.

Anthology
of Recipes

Drawing upon the cooking literature of more than 30 countries, the editors and consultants for this volume have chosen 312 recipes for the Anthology that follows. The selections include simple drinks such as iced coffee as well as elaborate ones—for example, mead, a honey wine that must be strained, fermented, siphoned repeatedly and allowed to mature undisturbed for several years before it can be enjoyed.

Many of the recipes were written by world-renowned exponents of the culinary art, but the Anthology also includes selections from rare and out-of-print books and from works that have never been published in English. Whatever the sources, the emphasis in these recipes is always on fresh, natural ingredients that blend harmoniously and on techniques that are practical for the home cook.

Since many early recipe writers did not specify amounts of ingredients or cooking times, the missing information has been judiciously added. In some cases, clarifying introductory notes have also been supplied; they are printed in italics. Modern recipe terms have been substituted for archaic language and some instructions have been expanded. But to preserve the character of the original recipes and to create a true anthology, the authors' texts have been changed as little as possible. In any circumstance where the cooking directions seem abrupt, the reader need only refer to the appropriate demonstrations in the front of the book.

In keeping with the organization of the first half of the book, the recipes in the Anthology are categorized according to type of beverage. Standard preparations—syrups, broths and ice creams among them—appear at the end of the Anthology. Unfamiliar cooking terms and uncommon ingredients are explained in the combined General Index and Glossary.

All ingredients are listed within each recipe in order of use, with both the customary U.S. measurements and the metric measurements provided in separate columns. All quantities reflect the American practice of measuring such solid ingredients as sugar or flour by volume rather than by weight, as is generally done in Europe.

To make the quantities simpler to measure, many of the figures have been rounded off to correspond to the gradations on U.S. metric spoons and cups. (One cup, for example, equals 237 milliliters; however, wherever practicable in these recipes, the metric equivalent of 1 cup appears as a more readily measured 250 milliliters—¼ liter.) Similarly, the weight, temperature and linear metric equivalents have been rounded off slightly. Thus the American and metric figures do not exactly match, but using one set or the other will produce the same good results.

Teas and Tisanes

Mongolian Tea

Mongolski Chay

To make about 3 cups [¾ liter]

1 tbsp.	black tea leaves, crushed to a powder	15 ml.
2 cups	water	½ liter
1½ tbsp.	butter	22 ml.
2 tbsp.	flour	30 ml.
½ to 1 cup	milk	125 to 250 ml.
½ cup	cooked rice	125 ml.
	salt	

Place the tea leaves in a saucepan, pour in the water and bring to a boil. Reduce the heat to very low.

Melt 1 tablespoon [15 ml.] of the butter in a skillet, stir in the flour and cook for a few minutes. Dilute the mixture gradually with enough milk to give it a thick, creamy consistency; then add the remaining butter and the rice, and pour the mixture into the saucepan of tea. Bring to a boil, season to taste with salt and serve immediately.

ALEXANDER DIMITROV BELORECHKI AND
NIKOLAY ANGELOV DZHELEPOV
OBODRITELNITE PITIETA V NASHIYA DOM

Spiced Tea

To make 2 cups [½ liter]

2 cups	water	½ liter
4	whole cloves	4
½-inch	cinnamon stick	1-cm.
3	whole allspice	3
1 tbsp.	fresh lemon juice	15 ml.
½ tsp.	black tea leaves	2 ml.

Simmer the water and spices for 10 minutes and strain. Add the lemon juice to the water and bring to a boil. Place the tea leaves in a tea strainer set over a teapot and pour the spiced water slowly through the tea leaves. Serve hot in teacups.

ANNA G. EDMONDS (EDITOR)
AN AMERICAN COOK IN TURKEY

Tea Russian-Style

Le Thé à la Russe

A samovar is a metal urn with a vertical cylinder in the center and a spigot near the base. After the urn is filled with cold water, burning charcoal is dropped into the cylinder to heat the water to a boil for diluting a tea essence.

To make 2 cups [½ liter]

2 tbsp.	black tea leaves	30 ml.
2 cups	boiling water	½ liter
	sugar	
	lemon slices	
	jam	

Place the tea leaves in a small warmed teapot, fill it with the boiling water and let the tea infuse for 10 minutes. Set the pot on top of the cylinder of a samovar to keep this tea essence hot. For each serving, strain a little of the essence into a cup and add enough boiling water from the samovar to dilute the essence to taste. Serve the tea accompanied by sugar, lemon slices and jam.

ÉDOUARD DE POMIANE
LE CODE DE LA BONNE CHÈRE

Cardamom Tea

Ilaichi Chah

This mellow tea is flavored with green cardamom pods, which lend a tasty sweetness. This recipe describes the way Indians enjoy cardamom tea. You may omit the milk and sugar altogether, in which case reduce the tea to 3 teaspoons [15 ml.] or else the brewed tea will be too strong and bitter.

To make 1½ quarts [1½ liters]

12	green cardamoms	12
1½ quarts	cold water	1½ liters
3 tbsp.	black tea leaves	45 ml.
1	piece of lemon, lime or orange peel, 1 by ½ inch [2½ by 1 cm.]	1
	scalded milk and sugar	

Combine the cardamom pods and water in a deep saucepan and bring to a boil. Reduce the heat, cover, and simmer for five minutes. Then turn off the heat and let stand, covered, for 10 minutes. Meanwhile, rinse the teapot with boiling water. Add the tea leaves and the peel to the pot. Bring the cardamom water to a boil and pour it, pods and all, into the teapot. Let the tea infuse for two to three minutes before serving. Serve scalded milk and sugar separately.

JULIE SAHNI
CLASSIC INDIAN COOKING

Hot Orange Tea

To make about 2 ½ cups [625 ml.]

6 tbsp.	fresh orange juice	90 ml.
	boiling water	
2 tsp.	black tea leaves	10 ml.
	lemon slices	

Pour the orange juice into a jug, pour in 1 ¼ cups [300 ml.] of boiling water and stir. Pour the contents of the jug onto the tea leaves in a warmed 3-cup [¾-liter] teapot, and infuse for two minutes. Then fill the teapot with boiling water and infuse for another four minutes. Serve in heatproof glasses, with lemon slices on top.

RICHARD R. FULLER
TEA FOR THE CONNOISSEUR

Ginger Tea

If a stronger tea is desired, boil the water with the ginger or crush the ginger slices and add them to the pot with the tea.

To make about 1 ¼ cups [300 ml.]

1 tsp.	black tea leaves	5 ml.
4 or 5	thin slices fresh ginger	4 or 5
1 ¼ cups	boiling water	300 ml.
	sugar	

Heat a small teapot and add the tea leaves and two slices of the ginger. Pour in the boiling water. Infuse for three to five minutes. Strain the tea into a heated cup. Add the remaining ginger slices to the cup and serve the tea with sugar.

CHANDRA DISSANAYAKE
CEYLON COOKERY

Anise Tea

Shy mi Yansoon

To make 1 quart [1 liter]

1 tsp.	aniseed	5 ml.
2 cups	boiling water	½ liter
2 cups	hot black tea	½ liter
2 tbsp.	chopped walnuts	30 ml.

Place the aniseed in the boiling water. Let steep for 10 minutes. Strain and add the anise liquid to the hot black tea. Serve the anise tea at once, garnished with the walnuts.

HELEN COREY
THE ART OF SYRIAN COOKERY

Spicy Hot Tea

To make about 2 ½ quarts [2 ½ liters]

2 quarts	water	2 liters
4-inch	cinnamon stick	10-cm.
1 tsp.	whole cloves	5 ml.
3 tbsp.	black tea leaves	45 ml.
½ to ¾ cup	honey	125 to 175 ml.
2 ½ tbsp.	fresh lemon juice	37 ml.
1 cup	fresh orange juice	¼ liter

Bring the water, cinnamon and cloves to a boil. Remove the pan from the heat and add the tea leaves. Stir, cover and steep the tea for five minutes. Strain the tea and add honey to taste. Bring the lemon and orange juices to a boil and stir into the hot tea. Serve immediately.

HAZEL BERTO
COOKING WITH HONEY

Walnut Tea

He T'ao Jen Ch'a

To make about 1 ½ quarts [1 ½ liters]

½ cup	rice	125 ml.
6 cups	water	1 ½ liters
2 cups	walnuts, blanched and peeled	½ liter
2 cups	sugar	½ liter

Soak the rice in 3 cups [¾ liter] of the water for 15 minutes. Drain the rice in a sieve set over a bowl; reserve the water. Grind the rice and walnuts together in a mortar, adding the reserved rice water to the paste a little at a time. Line the sieve with a double thickness of cheesecloth or muslin and set it over a heavy saucepan. Pour in the paste and wring the cloth to extract the liquid. Discard the rice and walnuts.

Add the remaining water and the sugar to the walnut-flavored liquid. Stirring all the time, cook the mixture over medium heat for seven minutes. Serve hot.

DOLLY CHOW
CHOW!

Midnight Infusion

La Tisana di Mezzanotte

To make ¾ cup [175 ml.]

¾ cup	water	175 ml.
1 tsp.	dried camomile flowers	5 ml.
1	piece orange peel	1
1 tsp.	honey	5 ml.

Bring the water to a boil and pour it over the camomile, orange peel and honey. Stir, cover and leave in a warm place for 10 minutes. Strain into a cup and serve very hot.

PASQUALE MONTENERO, ANNA BASLINI ROSSELLI
AND MASSIMO ALBERINI
L'ARTE DI SAPER MANGIARE (SENZA RINUNCE)

Camomile Tea

Papatya

To make 1 cup [¼ liter]

2 tsp.	dried camomile flowers	10 ml.
1 cup	water	¼ liter
	sugar	

Put the camomile flowers in the water and boil for five minutes. Remove from the heat; add sugar to taste.

ANNA G. EDMONDS (EDITOR)
AN AMERICAN COOK IN TURKEY

Rose-hip Tisane

Otvara ot Shipki

To make about 1 cup [¼ liter]

1½ cups	water	375 ml.
¼ cup	dried rose-hip halves, filaments removed	50 ml.
2 tsp.	sugar	10 ml.

Bring the water to a boil in a saucepan with a tight-fitting lid. Add the rose-hip halves, cover the pan with the lid and simmer over very low heat for 20 to 30 minutes. Set the saucepan aside in a cool place for several hours, then strain the liquid, discarding the hips. Stir in the sugar and serve.

TASHO TASHEV, ZH. STOYANOVA AND YA. DZHAMBAZOVA
DIETICHNO HRANENE

Maté

The maté plant is sometimes known as Paraguay tea. Its leaves, which are rich in caffeine, are used in the preparation of an infusion that is both a stimulant and a tonic. Like tea, maté can be flavored with lemon juice, rum, kirsch, and so on. After straining, the leaves or grounds can be stirred once or twice into more hot water, producing a second and a third drink that are still quite pleasant.

To make 1 quart [1 liter]

¼ cup	maté leaves or powder	50 ml.
1 quart	boiling water	1 liter
	sugar (optional)	

Place the maté in a teapot and pour in the boiling water. Let infuse in a hot place for at least 10 minutes. Strain. Drink hot or cold, with or without sugar, according to taste.

PROSPER MONTAGNÉ
LAROUSSE GASTRONOMIQUE

Korean Ginger Tea

Sang-Cha

To make 1½ quarts [1½ liters]

⅓ cup	thinly sliced fresh ginger	75 ml.
5 cups	water	1¼ liters
¾ cup	sugar	175 ml.
½ tsp.	ground cinnamon	2 ml.
1 tbsp.	pine nuts	15 ml.
3	walnuts, shelled, blanched, peeled and chopped	3
2	dates, pitted and thinly sliced	2

Boil the ginger and water together for 20 minutes. Strain to remove the ginger. Add the sugar and cinnamon to the ginger water. While still hot, serve in cups, adding a small amount of pine nuts, walnuts and dates to each cup.

HARRIETT MORRIS
THE ART OF KOREAN COOKING

Garden Sage Tea

Adaçay

To make 1 cup [¼ liter]

1 cup	water	¼ liter
4	fresh or dried sage leaves	4
	sugar	

Bring the water to a boil and add the sage leaves as you would tea. Add sugar to taste.

ANNA G. EDMONDS (EDITOR)
AN AMERICAN COOK IN TURKEY

Violet Tea

To make 1 ¼ cups [300 ml.]

1¼ cups	boiling water	300 ml.
1 tsp.	dried violets	5 ml.
	honey	

Pour the water onto the violets and leave for five minutes. Strain the tea and sweeten it with honey to taste.

MRS. C. F. LEYEL AND MISS OLGA HARTLEY
THE GENTLE ART OF COOKERY

Iced Aniseed Tea

To make about 4 cups [1 liter]

2 tbsp.	aniseed	30 ml.
1 cup	water	¼ liter
2 cups	strong black tea	½ liter
about 1 cup	milk or cream	about ¼ liter
	sugar	
	crushed ice	

Boil the aniseed in the water until tender. Strain the liquid and pour it into the black tea. Add milk or cream and sugar to taste, and chill the mixture. To serve the tea, pour it into tall glasses filled with crushed ice.

PREMILA LAL
PREMILA LAL'S INDIAN RECIPES

Iced Tea Made with Cold Water

If you even just sort of follow these absurdly simple guidelines, you'll surely be captivated by the cool, clean brew that results. But you must start with tea leaves that are worth brewing in the first place. Tea should have a fascinating aroma. It does not last forever—either in your home canister or in the store. Take a good deep sniff before you infuse it; if it smells dusty or almost not-at-all, replace it.

To make 1 quart [1 liter]

3 tbsp.	black tea leaves	45 ml.
1 quart	cold water	1 liter
	superfine sugar	

Combine the tea and water in a 1-quart [1-liter] jar. Cap the jar and shake it, or stir the leaves with a spoon for a moment. Leave the jar in the refrigerator for at least 12 hours. (It may be left for days this way, if you like.)

When you want some, strain the tea and sweeten it to taste with superfine sugar. Add lemon, lime or orange slices or juice, or mint sprigs, as the tea flavor dictates.

HELEN WITTY AND ELIZABETH SCHNEIDER COLCHIE
BETTER THAN STORE-BOUGHT

Larned Tea Sherbet

A handful of strawberries, or bits of fresh orange peel, floating on the surface is a pretty touch that you may add to your sherbet. Or, you may mix your sherbet in a jug, and fill the mouth of it with sprays of fresh mint.

To make about 1 ½ quarts [1 ½ liters]

4 tsp.	Ceylon tea leaves	20 ml.
1 quart	boiling water	1 liter
	small block of ice or ice cubes	
1½ cups	sugar	375 ml.
⅓ cup	fresh lemon juice	75 ml.
2 cups	soda water, chilled	½ liter

Put the tea leaves in a jug and pour the boiling water upon them. Cover closely and let stand five minutes. Strain and leave to cool. Put the ice into a punch bowl and about it the sugar, and strain over this the lemon juice. Add the tea now and, just before the sherbet is served, the soda water.

MARION HARLAND AND CHRISTINE TERHUNE HERRICK
THE NATIONAL COOK BOOK

Coffees

Turkish Coffee

An ibrik is a small long-handled pot made of tinned copper or brass. A small saucepan may be used instead.

You might like to add a spice to the *ibrik* to boil with the water. Try a cardamom pod, a couple of cloves, a small stick of cinnamon or a pinch of freshly grated nutmeg.

To make ¾ cup [175 ml.]

¾ cup	water	175 ml.
1 tbsp.	sugar	15 ml.
1 tbsp.	pulverized coffee	15 ml.

In an *ibrik,* boil the water with the sugar. Add the coffee, stir well and return the pot to the heat. When the coffee froths up to the rim, remove the pot from the heat. Some people let a drop of cold water precipitate the grounds; others rap the pot smartly; still others let them settle by waiting for about two minutes. When the grounds have settled, repeat the heating and settling processes twice again.

Serve as soon as the grounds have settled for the last time, while the coffee is still hot. Pour or rather shake out a little froth for each small coffee cup. Some grounds will settle at the bottom of the cup. You are not supposed to eat them.

CLAUDIA RODEN
COFFEE

Serbian Coffee

Srpska Kafa

Džezva is the name by which the Turkish coffee pot is known in Serbia. It is a small long-handled pot with a lip but no lid.

To make ½ cup [125 ml.]

½ cup	cold water	125 ml.
1 tsp.	sugar	5 ml.
1½ tsp.	pulverized coffee	7 ml.

Put the water with sugar in the *džezva.* When the mixture boils, pour off about one third into a demitasse. Stir the coffee into the boiling syrup in the *džezva* and let it come to a boil once more. Remove from the heat, add the liquid from the cup and infuse for 30 seconds. Pour the coffee into demitasses and serve at once.

SPASENIJA-PATA MARKOVIC
YUGOSLAV COOKBOOK

Rumanian Coffee

Roumunsko Kafe

To make about 2 cups [½ liter]

3 tbsp.	pulverized coffee	45 ml.
4 tsp.	superfine sugar	20 ml.
2 tsp.	cocoa powder	10 ml.
2 cups	water	½ liter
	vanilla sugar	
	light cream	

Mix the coffee, superfine sugar and cocoa powder together in a Turkish coffee pot or a small saucepan and pour in the water. Over low heat, slowly bring the mixture to just below the boiling point, removing the pot from the heat before the froth starts to rise. Pour, without straining, into four demitasses. Serve vanilla sugar and light cream separately.

ALEXANDER DIMITROV BELORECHKI AND
NIKOLAY ANGELOV DZHELEPOV
OBODRITELNITE PITIETA V NASHIYA DOM

Cardamom Topper

To make about 5 cups [1¼ liters]

1 quart	hot strong coffee	1 liter
¼ tsp.	ground cardamom	1 ml.
⅛ tsp.	ground mace	½ ml.
¾ cup	heavy cream	175 ml.
1 tbsp.	sugar	15 ml.
1 tsp.	vanilla extract	5 ml.

Combine the coffee, half of the cardamom and all of the mace, and keep the mixture warm over low heat. Beat the cream, sugar and vanilla in a chilled bowl until peaks form. Pour the coffee into cups and top with the whipped cream mixture. Sprinkle the rest of the cardamom on top.

JAN BLEXRUD
A TOAST TO SOBER SPIRITS & JOYOUS JUICES

Ras el Hanout for Coffee

Maure Kaoua

Gum arabic, an aromatic flavoring often used in candymaking, is available at herbalists and pharmacies. Galingale, also known as laos, is a strong, ginger-like spice. It is sold dried, either ground or cut into small pieces, at herbalists and Indonesian or Asian food stores.

For those who love to play with spices, coffee with *ras el hanout* has got to be some kind of *ne plus ultra.* The mixture of peppery and sweet spices gives the coffee a flavor that is both sweet and warm, mysterious and indefinable.

	To make about ⅓ cup [75 ml.]	
2	whole nutmegs, grated, or 4 tsp. [20 ml.] grated nutmeg	2
2-inch	cinnamon stick, crushed, or 1 tsp. [5 ml.] ground cinnamon	5-cm.
6 to 8	dried rosebuds	6 to 8
12	whole cloves or ½ tsp. [2 ml.] ground cloves	12
⅛ tsp.	gum arabic	½ ml.
1 tbsp.	ground ginger	15 ml.
2	pieces galingale or about ½ tsp. [2 ml.] ground galingale	2
2	whole allspice or ⅛ tsp. [½ ml.] ground allspice	2
¾ tsp.	ground white pepper	4 ml.
3	blades mace or ½ tsp. [2 ml.] ground mace	3
15	white or green cardamoms	15
1 tsp.	fennel seeds	5 ml.
1 tsp.	aniseed	5 ml.
1 tbsp.	sesame seeds	15 ml.

Combine all of the ingredients in an electric spice grinder or blender. Grind them, then sieve and bottle them carefully to preserve the freshness.

When making coffee, add ¼ teaspoon [1 ml.] of *ras el hanout* to every ½ cup [125 ml.] of ground coffee, and then proceed to make coffee in your usual fashion.

PAULA WOLFERT
COUSCOUS AND OTHER GOOD FOOD FROM MOROCCO

Mexican Coffee

Café de Olla

To make about 1 cup [¼ liter]

1 cup	water	¼ liter
3 tbsp.	dark-roasted coffee, coarsely ground	45 ml.
1-inch	cinnamon stick	2½-cm.
	dark brown sugar	

In a heavy pot, bring the water to a boil. Add the coffee, the cinnamon and sugar to taste. Bring to a boil twice, then strain and serve.

DIANA KENNEDY
CUISINES OF MEXICO

Coffee with Chocolate

Caffè col Cioccolato

Chantilly cream is heavy cream whipped until it becomes soft and thick, sweetened to taste with sugar and, if you like, flavored with vanilla.

	To make about 1 quart [1 liter]	
2 cups	hot strong coffee	½ liter
2 cups	hot chocolate	½ liter
¾ cup	Chantilly cream or whipped heavy cream	175 ml.
1 tbsp.	orange peel, finely chopped	15 ml.

Pour equal quantities of coffee and chocolate into each cup. Cover this thick liquid with Chantilly cream or whipped cream, and sprinkle a few pieces of orange peel on top.

VINCENZO BUONASSISI
IL CAFFÈ

Café Nero

To make about 3½ cups [875 ml.]

6	sugar cubes	6
¾ cup	brandy	175 ml.
8	lemon peel julienne	8
8	orange peel julienne	8
12	apple peel julienne	12
12	whole cloves	12
2-inch	cinnamon stick, broken into bits	5-cm.
2½ cups	hot strong coffee	625 ml.

Into a chafing dish over low heat, place five of the sugar cubes with the brandy, lemon and orange peels, apple peel, cloves and cinnamon. When the mixture is hot, fill a ladle partway with the liquid, add the remaining sugar cube and dissolve it. Light the liquid in the ladle with a match and pour it into the chafing dish to set the mixture afire. Stirring constantly, let the liquid burn for one minute; then, while still burning, ladle the mixture into after-dinner coffee cups that have been filled two thirds full with the coffee.

MARTHA MEADE
RECIPES FROM THE OLD SOUTH

Orange-flavored Turkish Coffee

Portokalovo Kafe

The technique of making Turkish coffee appears on page 25.

To make 2½ cups [625 ml.]

2 cups	hot strong unsweetened Turkish coffee, strained	½ liter
	sugar	
½ cup	brandy	125 ml.
	finely grated orange peel	
	whipped cream	

Sweeten the coffee to taste and pour it into four warmed demitasses, filling them by about three quarters. Add the brandy. Sprinkle the surface with orange peel and add a dollop of whipped cream. Serve immediately.

ALEXANDER DIMITROV BELORECHKI AND
NIKOLAY ANGELOV DZHELEPOV
OBODRITELNITE PITIETA V NASHIYA DOM

Café Brûlot

A *brûlot* bowl is a large silver or copper bowl.

To make about 3 cups [¾ liter]

4-inch	cinnamon stick	10-cm.
12	whole cloves	12
2	oranges, peel thinly pared and cut into slivers	2
2	lemons, peel thinly pared and cut into slivers	2
6	sugar tablets	6
1 cup	brandy	¼ liter
¼ cup	Curaçao	50 ml.
2 cups	hot strong coffee	½ liter

In a *brûlot* bowl or chafing dish set over a lighted alcohol burner, mash the cinnamon, cloves, orange and lemon peels and the sugar tablets with a ladle. Add the brandy and Curaçao, and stir together until the sugar has dissolved. Carefully ignite the spirits. Gradually add the coffee and continue mixing until the flame flickers out. Serve hot in *brûlot* cups or in demitasses.

DEIRDRE STANFORTH (EDITOR)
BRENNAN'S NEW ORLEANS COOKBOOK

Spanish Coffee Punch

Mazagran

To make about 2 cups [½ liter]

1 cup	cold black coffee	¼ liter
⅔ cup	cold water	150 ml.
3 tbsp.	brandy or rum	45 ml.
¼ cup	sugar	50 ml.
1	lemon slice	1
1	ice cube	1

Mix all the ingredients together and stir until the sugar is dissolved. Strain and serve.

ROSARIO CIFNENTES
COCINA PRACTICA

Dublin Coffee James Joyce

This is excellent for after-dinner conversation.

To make about 1¼ cups [300 ml.]

1 tsp.	sugar	5 ml.
⅓ cup	Irish whiskey	75 ml.
⅔ cup	hot strong coffee	150 ml.
3 tbsp.	heavy cream	45 ml.

Put the sugar and Irish whiskey into a balloon wine glass. Pour in the black coffee and stir; as the contents revolve, add the cream in a circular motion. Let the cream float on top of the coffee. Do not stir again.

ALICE B. TOKLAS
THE ALICE B. TOKLAS COOK BOOK

Café Chiapas

To make about 1 cup [¼ liter]

1 cup	hot, freshly made coffee	¼ liter
1 tbsp.	Kahlúa	15 ml.
1 tbsp.	brandy	15 ml.
1	cinnamon stick	1
	heavy cream, whipped	

Pour the coffee into a cup or mug, add the Kahlúa and brandy, drop in the cinnamon stick and top the drink with a dab of whipped cream.

KAREN GOLDWACH STEVENS
DINING IN-CHICAGO

Viennese Coffee

Café Borgia

The author suggests that the coffee be spiced by brewing four whole cloves and a stick of cinnamon with the coffee.

To make about 1 ½ quarts [1 ½ liters]

4 oz.	sweet or semisweet chocolate	125 g.
	sugar or honey	
4 cups	hot coffee	1 liter
½ cup	heavy cream	125 ml.
	ground cinnamon, cocoa powder or grated orange peel	

In a heavy saucepan, melt the chocolate over low heat. Add sugar or honey to taste, and stir in ¼ cup [50 ml.] of the cream. Whisk in the hot coffee, a little at a time, and beat well until the mixture is frothy. Keep the mixture hot over low heat. Whip the remaining cream. Serve the coffee with the whipped cream, and sprinkle with a little cinnamon, cocoa powder or grated orange peel.

CLAUDIA RODEN
COFFEE

Cappuccino

There is a way of enjoying coffee that I learned when travelling near Sorrento. I asked for cold milk in my cappuccino to refresh me from the heat of the south, and the barman poured the milk first and then the coffee. Because of the differing temperatures, the two liquids did not mix and the coffee remained on top. I did not add sugar and did not stir, so the two liquids remained separate. When I sipped my cappuccino, the milk and the coffee reached my palate separately; one hot and one cold, one slightly sweet, the other bitter.

To make 3 ½ cups [875 ml.]

1¾ cups	cold milk	425 ml.
1¾ cups	very hot strong coffee	425 ml.
	sugar (optional)	
	cocoa powder, ground cinnamon or grated nutmeg (optional)	

Pour out the milk into individual cups and add the hot coffee. Add sugar to taste, if you like. Do not stir. Cocoa powder, ground cinnamon or grated nutmeg may be sprinkled on top.

VINCENZO BUONASSISI
IL CAFFÈ

Lady Granville's Iced Coffee

The technique of making iced coffee appears on pages 26-27.
   Marie, Lady Granville, was heiress to Talleyrand's close friend, the Duke of Dalberg. This is quite the best recipe for iced coffee that I know; even if you are obliged to reduce the quantity of cream slightly—alas, we are not all heiresses—it is still delicious. But do not economize on the coffee.

coffee
light cream
milk
sugar

Combine coffee, cream, milk in equal parts; sweeten to your taste, bearing in mind that adding ice diminishes sweetness.

JANE GRIGSON
FOOD WITH THE FAMOUS

Coffee Granita with Cream

Granita di Caffè con Panna

To make about 1 ½ quarts [1 ½ liters]

¾ cup	sugar	175 ml.
2 cups	water	½ liter
2 cups	hot strong coffee	½ liter
1 cup	heavy cream, whipped	¼ liter

Stir the sugar and water together over low heat until the sugar has dissolved. Add the coffee and let the mixture cool. Pour the mixture into a freezing tray. Stirring frequently, freeze to a mush—about three hours. Serve the granita in sherbet glasses, topping each glass with whipped cream.

ADA BONI
THE TALISMAN ITALIAN COOK BOOK

Spiced Coffee Frappé

To make about 3 cups [¾ liter]

2½ cups	hot, very strong coffee	625 ml.
2	cinnamon sticks	2
4	whole cloves	4
4	whole allspice	4
⅔ cup	heavy cream	150 ml.
5 or 6	ice cubes	5 or 6
	sugar (optional)	

Pour the coffee over the cinnamon, cloves and allspice, cover, cool to room temperature, then refrigerate for at least one hour. Strain the spiced coffee into a blender, add the cream, ice cubes and sugar to taste. Blend the coffee to a creamy froth and serve it immediately, as the froth soon subsides.

CLAUDIA RODEN
COFFEE

Juices

Russian Apple Water for Children

Yablochnaya Voda

This drink can be made in larger quantities and kept in the refrigerator for up to five days.

You can also make apple water from apple peelings and cores. Remove the seeds from the cores and chop the peel and cores very fine.

To make about 1 cup [1/4 liter]

1	medium-sized apple, unpeeled, sliced into wedges and the seeds removed	1
2 tsp.	fresh lemon juice	10 ml.
1/2 tsp.	finely chopped lemon peel	2 ml.
1 tbsp.	sugar	15 ml.
3/4 cup	water	175 ml.

Put the apple wedges, lemon juice and lemon peel in a small nonreactive saucepan. Add the sugar and water, and simmer over low heat for 15 to 20 minutes. Remove from the heat and let the mixture cool. Strain the apple water, and refrigerate it in a covered container until needed.

DETSKOE PITANIE

Apple-Apricot Frappé

To make about 3 1/2 cups [875 ml.]

1/2 cup	fresh apricot juice	125 ml.
3/4 cup	skim milk	175 ml.
1	medium-sized apple, peeled, cored and cut into chunks	1
	ground cinnamon	
4	ice cubes	4

Place the apricot juice, milk, apple chunks, a pinch of cinnamon and the ice cubes in the container of a blender or food processor, and blend until the mixture is thick and frothy—about three minutes. Hold down the top of the container until the ice cubes have been crushed a little. Before the ice has been completely crushed, it can be heard striking against the container; blend until it can no longer be heard.

Immediately, pour the frappé into tall, chilled glasses. Serve with long spoons.

CAROL CUTLER
THE WOMAN'S DAY LOW-CALORIE DESSERT COOKBOOK

Apple Tea

To make 1 cup [1/4 liter]

1	apple, cored and thinly sliced	1
1 tsp.	grated lemon peel	5 ml.
1 cup	boiling water	1/4 liter
	sugar	

Pour the boiling water over the apple slices and lemon peel, let the tea cool, then refrigerate it until cold. To serve, strain out the fruits and sweeten to taste.

HELEN WORTH
DAMNYANKEE IN A SOUTHERN KITCHEN

Apple Drink

Bibita alla Mela

Underripe eating apples or tart cooking apples will give this drink an assertive taste; fully ripened eating apples will give it a mild flavor. In either case, it is not necessary to peel or core the apples.

To make about 2 cups [1/2 liter]

3 to 4 tbsp.	fresh lemon juice	45 to 60 ml.
5	green apples, sliced	5
2 cups	boiling water	1/2 liter
2/3 cup	superfine sugar	150 ml.

Sprinkle the lemon juice over the apples and cover them with the water. Set the mixture aside until the apples are soft—this will take at least one hour. Strain the liquid, add the sugar and refrigerate it. Serve cold.

MILA CONTINI
FATTO IN CASA

Apricot Refreshment

Refresco de Albaricoque

Instead of jam, you can use 1 pound [1/2 kg.] of dried apricots soaked in warm water to cover for six hours, drained and sweetened with sugar to taste.

To make about 1 quart [1 liter]

2 cups	apricot jam	1/2 liter
2 cups	water	1/2 liter
1	lemon, the peel reserved, juice strained	1
	ice cubes	

Pass the apricot jam through a sieve into a heavy, nonreactive pan. Add the water and lemon peel, boil for two minutes, remove from the heat and pass the mixture through the sieve into a bowl or jug. Stir in the lemon juice and let the mixture cool. To serve, pour into small glasses and add an ice cube to each drink.

MANUAL DE COCINA

Cranberry Juice

Reserve the fruit pulp, if you like, to make cranberry sauce.

To make 5 cups [1 ¼ liters]

1 lb.	cranberries	½ kg.
5 cups	water	1 ¼ liters
	salt	
2 or 3	orange slices (optional)	2 or 3
about ½ cup	sugar	about 125 ml.

Wash the cranberries and put them into a nonreactive saucepan with the water, a pinch of salt and, if you wish, the orange slices. Cook over medium heat until all the berries burst—about 10 minutes.

Pour the fruit and liquid into a cheesecloth-lined sieve. Strain the juice without pressing down on the fruit.

Return the juice to the saucepan, add the sugar and boil for two or three minutes. Taste and add more sugar if it is needed. Cool and chill the juice before serving.

HELEN WITTY AND ELIZABETH SCHNEIDER COLCHIE
BETTER THAN STORE-BOUGHT

Fizzy Drink

Perldrink

Strawberries, raspberries or gooseberries may be substituted for the currants.

To make about 1 quart [1 liter]

2 lb.	red currants	1 kg.
about ½ cup	sugar	about 125 ml.
about 3 cups	soda water	about ¾ liter
	ice cubes	

Rub the berries through a sieve. Sweeten the resulting juice to taste. Pour the juice into a jar, cover and leave for a day. To serve, pour into glasses, top with soda water and add an ice cube to each glass.

URSULA GRÜNIGER
COOKING WITH FRUIT

Jim-Jams

The technique of making currant and raspberry juices is shown on page 37. You will need 3 pounds [1 ½ kg.] or 8 cups [2 liters] of each fruit to produce 1 quart [1 liter] of juice.

To make about 2 ½ quarts [2 ½ liters]

1 quart	currant juice	1 liter
1 quart	raspberry juice	1 liter
1 cup	fresh orange juice	¼ liter
1 lb.	raisins	½ kg.
1 ½ cups	sugar	375 ml.

Mix all of the ingredients in a nonreactive saucepan, and heat them until the sugar is dissolved. Strain out the raisins; reserve them. Cool the liquid, then replace the raisins and bottle the drink.

DAUGHTERS OF THE AMERICAN REVOLUTION,
TIMOTHY BIGELOW CHAPTER
A BOOK OF BEVERAGES

Grapefruit Carrot Cocktail

To make about 5 cups [1 ¼ liters]

3	medium-sized carrots, coarsely chopped and cooked in a small amount of salted water until tender, drained and ¼ cup [50 ml.] of the cooking liquid reserved	3
4 cups	fresh grapefruit juice	1 liter
1 ½ tbsp.	grenadine	22 ml.
	ground ginger	
1 ½ cups	crushed ice	375 ml.

In a blender, purée the carrots with the reserved liquid for a few seconds. Add the grapefruit juice, grenadine, a pinch of ground ginger and the crushed ice and blend until frothy. Serve immediately.

BETTY ROLLIN
THE NON-DRINKER'S DRINK BOOK

Grapefruit and Tangerine Squash

Spremuta di Pompelmo e Mandarino

To make about 1 ½ cups [375 ml.]

½ cup	fresh grapefruit juice	125 ml.
½ cup	fresh tangerine juice	125 ml.
1 tsp.	honey	5 ml.
about ½ cup	water	about 125 ml.
1	ice cube (optional)	1

Pour the grapefruit and tangerine juices into a tall 14-ounce [425-ml.] glass, add the honey and stir until it dissolves. Top up the glass with water and, if you wish, add an ice cube.

PASQUALE MONTENERO, ANNA BASLINI ROSSELLI
AND MASSIMO ALBERINI
L'ARTE DI SAPER MANGIARE

Guava Juice

To make about 2 quarts [2 liters]

5 lb.	half-ripe or firm, ripe guavas, unpeeled, the flesh cut from the seeds and the seeds discarded	2½ kg.
about 2 quarts	water	about 2 liters

Put the guavas in a large, nonreactive pan with just enough water to cover the fruit. Boil for 15 to 20 minutes, until the fruit is very soft. Pour the mixture into a jelly bag and hang the bag over a bowl to drip. Do not squeeze the bag, lest the juice become cloudy.

FAVORITE ISLAND COOKERY: BOOK II

Lemonade à la Soyer

To make about 1 quart [1 liter]

1 quart	water	1 liter
2	dried figs, halved	2
1	lemon, peeled, halved and one half thinly sliced	1
1 tsp.	honey	5 ml.

Put the water and figs into a saucepan and boil for 15 minutes. Add the lemon peel and lemon slices and boil for two minutes. Pour the lemonade into a jug, cover tightly and leave until cold. Strain the lemonade and add the honey.

WILLIAM BERNHARD
THE BOOK OF ONE HUNDRED BEVERAGES

Lemon-Honey Kvass

To make about 3 quarts [3 liters]

2	lemons, the peel thinly pared and the juice strained	2
½ cup	honey	125 ml.
2 to 3 tbsp.	sugar	30 to 45 ml.
3 quarts	hot water (140° to 160° F. [65° to 70° C.])	3 liters

Add the lemon peel and juice, the honey and sugar to the water and mix well. Let stand for 24 hours. Strain the mixture through a sieve lined with muslin or cheesecloth. Bottle and cork it. The kvass will be ready to serve in one to one and a half weeks.

N. I. GEORGIEVSKY, M. E. MELMAN, E. A. SHADURA
AND A. S. SHEMJAKINSKY
UKRAINIAN CUISINE

Spiced Lemonade

To make 1 ½ quarts [1 ½ liters]

4-inch	cinnamon stick	10-cm.
4	whole cloves	4
1 tsp.	ground allspice	5 ml.
2 cups	water	½ liter
1 quart	chilled lemonade, made with ¾ cup [175 ml.] fresh lemon juice, 1 quart [1 liter] water and sugar to taste	1 liter
	ice cubes	
	lemon slices, studded with whole cloves	
	freshly grated nutmeg	

Combine the cinnamon, cloves and allspice with the water in a saucepan. Bring to a boil, reduce the heat and simmer uncovered for about eight minutes. Strain and chill the liquid. Add the spiced liquid to the chilled lemonade. To serve, pour the spiced lemonade into tall glasses partly filled with ice cubes. Garnish each drink with a lemon slice and a sprinkling of nutmeg.

BETTY ROLLIN
THE NON-DRINKER'S DRINK BOOK

Frosty Pink Lemonade

To make about 5 cups [1 ¼ liters]

1 cup	fresh lemon juice	¼ liter
1 cup	sugar	¼ liter
12 to 16	ice cubes	12 to 16
2 ½ cups	cold water	625 ml.
1	lemon, cut into thin slices	1
	red food coloring	

In a large pitcher, combine the lemon juice and sugar; stir with a long-handled spoon until the sugar dissolves. Add the ice cubes, cold water and lemon slices; stir briskly until the pitcher is frosty. Stir in a few drops of food coloring to make the lemonade pink.

JOE CARCIONE
THE GREENGROCER COOKBOOK

Lemonade

To make about 13 cups [3 ¼ liters]

6	lemons, the peel finely chopped, the juice strained	6
2 ½ quarts	water	2 ½ liters
about 2 cups	sugar syrup (recipe, page 164)	about ½ liter

Stir the lemon peel into the water and pour in the lemon juice; add syrup to taste. Mix the ingredients well and let them stand at room temperature for three or four hours. Strain the liquid through a colander lined with muslin or cheesecloth, and refrigerate it until thoroughly chilled—about three hours.

G. A. JARRIN
THE ITALIAN CONFECTIONER

Rose-flavored Lemon Drink

To make about 1 quart [1 liter]

1 ½ tbsp.	sugar	22 ml.
½ cup	fresh lemon juice	125 ml.
1 quart	ice water	1 liter
1 tbsp.	rose water	15 ml.
	crushed ice	

Mix the sugar and the lemon juice, stirring until the sugar is completely dissolved. Add the ice water and rose water. To serve, pour the mixture into tall glasses partly filled with crushed ice.

PREMILA LAL
PREMILA LAL'S INDIAN RECIPES

Papaya Drink

As a variation, prepare the drink with a banana or mango.

To make about 2 ½ cups [625 ml.]

1	very ripe papaya, peeled, halved, seeded and mashed	1
1 tbsp.	sugar	15 ml.
1 ¼ cups	water, coconut milk (recipe, page 165) or milk	300 ml.
1 tbsp.	fresh lemon juice	15 ml.

Mix the papaya with the sugar and the water, coconut milk or milk. Add the lemon juice and serve cold.

JANNY VAN DER MEER AND BEATRICE R. MANSUR (EDITORS)
TANZANIAN FOOD WITH TRADITIONAL AND NEW RECIPES

Milk and Papaya Refresher

Refresco de Lechosa

The technique of making coconut milk is demonstrated on pages 38-39.

To make about 3 cups [¾ liter]

1	ripe papaya, peeled, halved, seeded and coarsely chopped	1
⅓ cup	milk or coconut milk	75 ml.
3 tbsp.	fresh lime juice	45 ml.
½ tsp.	grated lime peel	2 ml.
¼ cup	vanilla sugar, or ¼ cup [50 ml.] superfine sugar and 1 tsp. [5 ml.] vanilla extract	50 ml.
½ cup	finely crushed ice	125 ml.
3 or 4	lime slices	3 or 4

Combine the papaya, milk or coconut milk, lime juice and peel, vanilla sugar (or superfine sugar and vanilla extract) and the ice in an electric blender or food processor, and blend at high speed until the mixture is smooth and thick. Serve in chilled glasses, garnished with the lime slices.

ELISABETH LAMBERT ORTIZ
CARIBBEAN COOKING

Apéritif from Lake Chapala

Aperitivo Chapala

Serve this as a chaser to tequila or as an apéritif before luncheon or dinner.

To make about 1 ¼ cups [300 ml.]

1 cup	fresh orange juice	¼ liter
3 tbsp.	grenadine	45 ml.
1 tsp.	cayenne pepper	5 ml.
	salt	

Mix the ingredients thoroughly and chill before serving.

ELISABETH LAMBERT ORTIZ
THE COMPLETE BOOK OF MEXICAN COOKING

Orange Gingerade

To make about 2 quarts [2 liters]

½ lb.	candied ginger, finely chopped (about 1 cup [¼ liter])	¼ kg.
2 cups	water	½ liter
1½ cups	sugar	375 ml.
1 cup	fresh grapefruit juice	¼ liter
3 cups	fresh orange juice	¾ liter
	ice, crushed	

Cook the chopped ginger for 10 minutes with the water and sugar. Add the grapefruit and orange juices. Cool the mixture. Strain and blend with the crushed ice.

DELINEATOR HOME INSTITUTE
BEVERAGES FOR PARTIES

Fresh Nectarine Nectar

To make about 2½ cups [625 ml.]

3 or 4	nectarines, peeled, halved, pitted and sliced	3 or 4
½ cup	fresh orange juice	125 ml.
1 tbsp.	fresh lemon juice	15 ml.
1 tbsp.	sugar	15 ml.
1 cup	crushed ice	250 ml.

Place all of the ingredients in an electric blender. Cover and blend until the mixture is smooth—about one minute. Serve the nectar at once.

JEAN H. SHEPARD
THE FRESH FRUITS AND VEGETABLES COOKBOOK

Fresh Orangeade

Orangeade

The authors suggest that instead of rubbing sugar tablets on the lemons to flavor the syrup, you can increase the sugar by about 3 tablespoons [45 ml.] and infuse thin parings of lemon peel in the syrup as demonstrated on page 34.

To make about 3 quarts [3 liters]

⅔ cup	sugar, plus 10 sugar tablets	150 ml.
3	lemons	3
2 cups	water	½ liter
12	oranges	12
2 quarts	soda water, chilled, or ice water	2 liters
	ice cubes or crushed ice	

Rub the sugar tablets on the peel of the lemons, then warm 2 cups [½ liter] of water and in it dissolve the tablets and the remaining sugar. When this syrup has cooled, squeeze the lemons and 10 of the oranges. Combine the fruit juice with the syrup. Refrigerate the orangeade until very cold.

Peel the two remaining oranges and cut them into thin slices. Dilute the orangeade with the soda water or ice water. Serve immediately with a slice of the peeled orange and a little ice in each glass.

F. M. STOLL AND W. H. DE GROOT
HET HAAGSE KOOKBOEK

Mango-Orange Drink

As a variation, use papaya instead of mango.

To make about 2 quarts [2 liters]

3 cups	water	¾ liter
½ cup	sugar	125 ml.
1 tbsp.	grated orange peel	15 ml.
2 cups	mashed mango flesh	½ liter
1 cup	fresh orange juice	¼ liter
½ cup	fresh lemon juice	125 ml.

Heat the water with the sugar and the orange peel over low heat until the sugar is dissolved. Cool down to room temperature. Add the mango flesh and the orange and lemon juices, and mix well. Serve cold.

JANNY VAN DER MEER AND BEATRICE R. MANSUR (EDITORS)
TANZANIAN FOOD WITH TRADITIONAL AND NEW RECIPES

Summer Drink

Payasam

The technique of extracting coconut milk is demonstrated on page 38.

To make about 2 quarts [2 liters]		
6	ripe mangoes	6
1	coconut, milk extracted	1
½ cup	sugar	125 ml.
½ tsp.	ground cardamom	2 ml.
	powdered saffron	
	cashews, chopped	
	ghee	
	ice cubes	

Peel the mangoes, squeeze out the pulp into a bowl and re-serve it. Place the mango pits in another bowl, pour in a little hot water and strip the pits clean of all pulp; discard the pits and add the water to the bowl of pulp.

Grate the coconut and use 1 cup [¼ liter] of hot water to extract the milk. Grind the coconut in a food grinder or processor and use another cup of water to extract thinner milk. Add the coconut milk, sugar, cardamom and a pinch of saffron to the mango pulp and mix well.

Fry a few cashews in a little *ghee*. Add them to the mango mixture and stir well. Chill the drink thoroughly and serve, poured over ice cubes, in tall glasses.

PREMILA LAL
PREMILA LAL'S INDIAN RECIPES

Fresh Limeade

To make about 1 quart [1 liter]		
1 cup	fresh lime juice	¼ liter
1 cup	sugar syrup *(recipe, page 164)*	¼ liter
	ice cubes	
2 cups	soda water, chilled, or ice water	½ liter
	lime slices, studded with whole cloves	

Combine the lime juice with the sugar syrup and mix well. Cool the mixture. To serve, pour ⅓ cup [75 ml.] of the lime syrup into a tall glass and add ice cubes. Fill the glass to the top with soda water or water. Stir the limeade and garnish each glass with a clove-studded lime slice.

JOE CARCIONE
THE GREENGROCER COOKBOOK

Pineapple Peel Drink

To make 1 quart [1 liter]		
1	large pineapple, peel only	1
1 quart	water	1 liter
4	whole cloves	4
about ¼ cup	sugar	about 50 ml.

Place the pineapple peel in an enameled or other nonreactive pan, add the water and bring to a boil over medium heat. Boil gently for about 10 minutes. Remove the pan from the heat, add the cloves and sugar to taste, stir the mixture and let it stand until cold. Strain, then refrigerate the drink to chill it thoroughly. Serve chilled.

ELLEN GIBSON WILSON
A WEST AFRICAN COOK BOOK

Pineapple Drink

Garapiña

To make 2½ cups [625 ml.]		
1	pineapple, peel only	1
2½ cups	water	625 ml.
	sugar	

Place the pineapple peelings in a pitcher or a widemouthed jar. Add the water, cover and let stand for 24 hours in a warm place until it ferments, and bubbles form. Strain the liquid, add sugar to taste and serve very cold.

BERTA CABANILLAS AND CARMEN GINORIO
PUERTO-RICAN DISHES

Pineapple Water

The pineapple can be puréed in a food processor.

To make about 6 cups [1½ liters]		
1	large pineapple, peeled, quartered, cored and pounded to a purée	1
2 cups	boiling sugar syrup *(recipe, page 164)*	½ liter
3 tbsp.	fresh lemon juice	45 ml.
1 quart	water	1 liter

Put the pineapple purée in a large earthenware bowl, pour in the syrup and lemon juice, stir and cover. Let the mixture sit for two hours, then strain the liquid through a fine sieve and add the water.

LAURA S. FITCHETT (EDITOR)
BEVERAGES AND SAUCES OF COLONIAL VIRGINIA

Pineapple Squash

This is a good way to use up leftover pineapple skins and cores. Keep the squash refrigerated.

Wash the pineapples before peeling them. To use the squash, pour ¼ cup [50 ml.] of pineapple squash into a glass, and top up with cold water.

To make about 2 quarts [2 liters]

	peel and core of 1 pineapple, cut into small pieces	
about 1 quart	water	about 1 liter
about 4 cups	sugar	about 1 liter
½ cup	fresh lemon juice	125 ml.

Put the pineapple peel and core in a nonreactive saucepan and add enough water to cover them. Bring to a boil, then simmer for 30 minutes. Strain the liquid through a cloth and press the juice out of the peel and core. Measure the mixture, and for each cup [¼ liter] use 1 cup of sugar. Heat the juice with the sugar over low heat until the sugar is dissolved. Cool the mixture. Add the lemon juice. Pour into clean bottles, cork and store.

JANNY VAN DER MEER AND BEATRICE R. MANSUR (EDITORS)
TANZANIAN FOOD WITH TRADITIONAL AND NEW RECIPES

Pineapple Sherbet

The technique of making a granita is shown on pages 26-27.
Adding sugar to the egg whites gives body to the sherbet.

To make 2½ quarts [2½ liters]

1	pineapple, peeled, quartered, cored and chopped	1
2 quarts	water	2 liters
2 cups	sugar	½ liter
¾ cup	fresh lemon juice	175 ml.
5	egg whites, stiffly beaten	5

Steep the pineapple in the water for two hours. Strain. Add all except 3 tablespoons [45 ml.] of the sugar to the pineapple liquid. Stir in the lemon juice. Fold the reserved sugar into the beaten egg whites, then stir all gently together. Freeze at once.

THE BUCKEYE COOKBOOK: TRADITIONAL AMERICAN RECIPES

Pineapple Snow

To make ½ cup [125 ml.]

3 tbsp.	chopped pineapple	45 ml.
1 tbsp.	fresh lime juice	15 ml.
1½ tsp.	sugar	7 ml.
½ cup	crushed ice	125 ml.
1	slice fresh lime (optional)	1

Combine the pineapple, lime juice and sugar in the container of an electric blender, and blend them rapidly for a few seconds. Put the ice in a chilled 6-ounce [180-ml.] glass and pour the pineapple mixture over it. Garnish with a lime slice, if you like.

JAN BLEXRUD
A TOAST TO SOBER SPIRITS & JOYOUS JUICES

Strawberry Granita

Granita di Fragole

The technique of making a granita is shown on pages 26-27.
On account of the sugar, the freezing will take about an hour more than the usual time taken for making ice.

To make about 1 quart [1 liter]

2 lb.	strawberries, hulled (5 cups [1¼ liters])	1 kg.
1 tbsp.	fresh lemon juice	15 ml.
3 to 4 tbsp.	fresh orange juice	45 to 60 ml.
1 cup	sugar	¼ liter
⅔ cup	water	150 ml.

Boil the sugar and water together for five minutes. Cool this syrup to room temperature. Put the strawberries through a sieve. Add the lemon and orange juices to the strawberry pulp. Stir in the syrup. Freeze in an ice tray for about three hours, stirring frequently.

ELIZABETH DAVID
ITALIAN FOOD

Strawberry Sherbet

To make about 7 cups [1¾ liters]

2¾ lb.	strawberries, hulled, ½ cup [125 ml.] reserved whole, the rest crushed	1¼ kg.
2 cups	sugar	½ liter
1 quart	cold water	1 liter
3 tbsp.	fresh lemon juice	45 ml.
1 tbsp.	maraschino liqueur	15 ml.

Press the crushed strawberries through a sieve lined with muslin or cheesecloth and place over a bowl containing the sugar. Set the bowl in a cold place, stirring the contents now and then until the sugar dissolves. Then add the water, lemon juice and maraschino. Cover tightly and refrigerate the mixture for at least an hour. Before you serve the sherbet, throw in the reserved whole strawberries, so that one or two float on the surface in each glass.

MARION HARLAND AND CHRISTINE TERHUNE HERRICK
THE NATIONAL COOK BOOK

Raspberry and Lime Swizzle

To make 2½ quarts [2½ liters]

1½ cups	sugar	375 ml.
8 cups	water	2 liters
1⅔ cups	fresh lime juice	400 ml.
1⅔ cups	raspberry purée	400 ml.
	lime slices	

Combine the sugar, 2 cups [½ liter] of the water and ⅓ cup [75 ml.] of the lime juice in a nonreactive saucepan. Stir the mixture until the sugar dissolves. Bring to a boil and boil for five minutes, then remove the syrup from the heat. Pour the syrup into a large bowl or heatproof jar and cool it slightly. Stir in the raspberry purée and the remaining water and lime juice. Chill the drink thoroughly. Serve garnished with lime slices.

JEAN H. SHEPARD
THE FRESH FRUITS AND VEGETABLES COOKBOOK

Raspberry Granita

Granita di Lampone

The technique of making granita is shown on pages 26-27. If desired, lemon or orange juice may be added.

To make about 2 cups [½ liter]

¾ cup	raspberries, puréed through a sieve	175 ml.
1 cup	water	¼ liter
⅓ cup	sugar	75 ml.

Stir the raspberry purée, water and sugar together. Pour the mixture into an ice tray and place in the freezer. Stir the mixture at regular intervals while it freezes.

ELENA SPAGNOL
I GELATI FATTI IN CASA CON O SENZA MACCHINA

Rhubarb Drink

Napójz Rabarbaru

To make about 5 cups [1¼ liters]

2 cups	water	½ liter
1 lb.	rhubarb, rinsed and chopped	½ kg.
	sugar	
1 tsp.	grated lemon peel (optional)	5 ml.

Bring the water to a boil in a heavy, nonreactive pan, add the rhubarb, cover the pan and boil the rhubarb for 10 minutes. Strain the juice, add sugar to taste, and pour the drink into a bowl or jug to cool. Stir in the lemon peel, if you are using it.

ZOFIA CZERNY AND MARIA STRASBURGER
ZYWIENIE RODZINY

Avocado Apéritif

To make about 1 quart [1 liter]

1	medium-sized avocado, halved, pitted, peeled and chopped	1
1	large cucumber, peeled, halved, seeded and chopped	1
½ cup	chopped parsley	125 ml.
3 tbsp.	fresh lemon juice	45 ml.
1 tbsp.	olive oil	15 ml.
2 cups	crushed ice	½ liter
	lemon slices or cucumber-rind strips	

In a blender combine the avocado, cucumber, parsley, lemon juice and oil. Blend until smooth. Add the ice and blend again. Strain the mixture into chilled glasses. Garnish each drink with a lemon slice or a strip of cucumber rind.

GAIL SCHIOLER
THE NON-DRINKER'S DRINK BOOK

Carrot and Orange Juice

Succo di Carota e Arancia

To make about 2 cups [½ liter]

1 lb.	carrots, chopped (about 2 cups [½ liter])	½ kg.
1	orange, peeled and halved	1
	ice cubes	
	salt	

Place the carrots in the juicing attachment of a food processor with the orange and a few ice cubes, and process until the juices have been extracted. Add a pinch of salt.

MILA CONTINI
FATTO IN CASA

Sauerkraut Cocktail

The technique of making tomato juice is shown on page 37.

To make 2 cups [½ liter]		
½ cup	sauerkraut juice	125 ml.
1½ cups	tomato juice	375 ml.
	fresh lemon juice	
	Worcestershire sauce	
	salt and coarsely ground black pepper	

Mix the sauerkraut and tomato juices with a dash each of lemon juice and Worcestershire sauce. Add salt and a few grindings of pepper. Chill and serve in cocktail glasses.

BETTY ROLLIN
THE NON-DRINKER'S DRINK BOOK

Tomato Juice

Succo di Pomodoro

The tomatoes may be puréed through the fine disk of a food mill as shown on page 37. Chervil may replace the parsley.

To serve the juice as an apéritif, pour the juice into a cocktail shaker, add a few drops of Worcestershire sauce and some ice cubes, and shake vigorously. Garnish the drink with a sprig of parsley.

To make about 3 cups [¾ liter]		
1½ lb.	ripe tomatoes, chopped	¾ kg.
	salt and pepper	
3 tbsp.	fresh lemon juice	45 ml.
2 tbsp.	chopped fresh parsley	30 ml.

Purée the tomatoes through a sieve and pour the juice into a carafe. Add a pinch of salt, some pepper, the lemon juice and chopped parsley, and stir. Refrigerate until chilled.

MILA CONTINI
FATTO IN CASA

Tomato Apéritif

Sangrita

The volatile oils in chilies may irritate your skin. Wear rubber gloves when you are handling them or wash your hands immediately afterwards.

Customarily, a *sangrita* is drunk by sipping it alternately with a glass of tequila. It is served with halved limes and salt on the side. Many people add a little lime juice to either the *sangrita* or the tequila, or take a little suck of lime between sips. The serrano chilies may be replaced by cayenne pepper. A proper *sangrita* is quite fiery.

To make about 1 quart [1 liter]		
6	medium-sized tomatoes, peeled and seeded	6
1½ cups	fresh orange juice	375 ml.
⅓ cup	fresh lime juice	75 ml.
1	small white onion, chopped	1
1 tsp.	sugar	5 ml.
	salt	
4 to 6	fresh green serrano chilies, stemmed, seeded and chopped	4 to 6

Place all the ingredients in an electric blender and blend until smooth. If the ingredients exceed the capacity of the container, process a small quantity at a time. Chill the mixture well. Pour into small glasses to serve.

ELISABETH LAMBERT ORTIZ
THE COMPLETE BOOK OF MEXICAN COOKING

Vegetable Cocktail

To make 3 to 4 cups [¾ to 1 liter]		
3	medium-sized ripe tomatoes, peeled, seeded and chopped	3
½	medium-sized cucumber, peeled, halved, seeded and chopped	½
⅔ cup	chopped celery	150 ml.
1 tbsp.	soy sauce	15 ml.
1 tsp.	mint leaves	5 ml.
	salt and black pepper	
1 to 2 cups	water	¼ to ½ liter
	fresh cress or coriander leaves	

Combine the vegetables and the seasonings in a blender and blend until smooth. Gradually blend in cold water until the cocktail has the consistency you want. Serve chilled with a few cress or coriander leaves on top.

MALA YOUNG
DRINKS & SNACKS

Sesame-Seed Drink

Horchata de Ajonjolí

To make about 1 1/2 quarts [1 1/2 liters]

2 cups	sesame seeds	1/2 liter
1 quart	hot water	1 liter
2 cups	cold water	1/2 liter
1 cup	superfine sugar	1/4 liter
	mint leaves or lemon slices	

Wash the seeds and soak them in water for two hours. Drain them. Grind them in a mortar. Add the hot water to the ground seeds, then strain the mixture through a colander lined with muslin or cheesecloth; squeeze the cloth to extract all of the sesame-seed liquid. Add the sugar and cold water to the strained liquid. Serve very cold and garnish with mint leaves or lemon slices.

BERTA CABANILLAS AND CARMEN GINORIO
PUERTO-RICAN DISHES

Cumin Seed Appetizer

Jeera Pani

Jaggery is coarse brown Indian sugar made from palm sap. Asafetida is a pungent musky-flavored spice. Jaggery and ground dried asafetida are available from Indian grocers.

To make about 3 cups [3/4 liter]

1 1/2 tbsp.	brown sugar or jaggery	22 ml.
1	walnut-sized piece dried tamarind pulp	1
3 cups	water	3/4 liter
	asafetida powder	
1/4 tsp.	pepper	1 ml.
2 tsp.	cumin seeds, toasted in a skillet over low heat for 1 minute, then ground	10 ml.
10 to 15	fresh mint leaves	10 to 15
2 tsp.	salt	10 ml.

If you are using jaggery, put it in 1/3 cup [75 ml.] of the water to soak. Leave for one hour. Soak the tamarind in 1 cup [1/4 liter] of the water for 20 minutes. Strain the tamarind liquid through a cloth, squeezing well to extract all of the juice from the pulp. Add the sugar or jaggery, a pinch of asafetida powder, the pepper, cumin seeds, mint leaves and salt. Then stir in the rest of the water.

KALA PRIMLANI
INDIAN COOKING

Melon Seed Drink

Horchata

Horchata is Spanish for orgeat, originally a refreshing barley water, which the French changed by making it with almonds. But Spaniards and Mexicans, who have more melons than almonds, substitute cantaloupe, watermelon, cucumber and pumpkin seeds. So today in Mexico you will get a fine cooler made of any of these seeds or all of them put together.

To make about 1 quart [1 liter]

2 cups	fresh melon seeds	1/2 liter
1 quart	water	1 liter
1/2 cup	sugar	125 ml.
2 tsp.	ground cinnamon	10 ml.
	ice	

Wash the seeds thoroughly and grind them fine, shells and all. Stir the seeds into the water with the sugar and cinnamon. Let stand in the refrigerator, stirring occasionally. When all the succulent seed flavor has gone into the water, after about three hours, strain through a very fine sieve. Add ice and serve.

CORA, ROSE AND BOB BROWN
THE SOUTH AMERICAN COOK BOOK

Peanut Milk

To make about 1 quart [1 liter]

1/2 cup	peanut butter	125 ml.
1 quart	water	1 liter
1/2 tsp.	salt	2 ml.
	sugar (optional)	

Put the peanut butter into a pan and add the water very gradually, stirring steadily, until the ingredients are thoroughly blended. Bring the mixture to a boil and cook over medium heat for 10 minutes, stirring occasionally. Add salt (and sugar, if desired). Beat with a whisk or rotary beater just before serving.

ELLEN GIBSON WILSON
A WEST AFRICAN COOK BOOK

Coconut Refresher

Refresco de Coco

To make about 1 quart [1 liter]

¼ cup	sugar	50 ml.
⅔ cup	water	150 ml.
2½ cups	coconut milk *(recipe, page 165)*	625 ml.
	grenadine or fresh pomegranate juice (optional)	

Dissolve the sugar in the water over low heat, cool it, and whisk in the coconut milk. You can color the drink pleasantly with a few drops of grenadine or fresh pomegranate juice.

CORA, ROSE AND BOB BROWN
THE SOUTH AMERICAN COOK BOOK

Rice Water

To make about 1½ cups [375 ml.]

1 tbsp.	rice	15 ml.
2 cups	water or milk	½ liter
1 tsp.	sugar	5 ml.
	ground cinnamon or grated nutmeg, or grated orange or lemon peel (optional)	

Put the rice into a pan with the water or milk and set over medium heat. Bring to a boil, then reduce the heat and simmer the mixture for 30 minutes. Strain, add the sugar and a pinch of spice or peel as desired. Chill and serve.

ELLEN GIBSON WILSON
A WEST AFRICAN COOK BOOK

Indian Meal Gruel

Sugar and a sprinkling of grated nutmeg can be added in place of the salt and cream.

To make about 3 cups [¾ liter]

2 tsp.	cornmeal, mixed with 2 tbsp. [30 ml.] cold water to form a smooth paste	10 ml.
2½ cups	water	625 ml.
	salt	
2 tbsp.	cream	30 ml.

In a pan, stir the cornmeal paste into the water. Stirring constantly, bring to the boiling point, then simmer for half an hour. Strain, add a pinch of salt and the cream, stir, and serve immediately.

BERTHA E. L. STOCKBRIDGE
WHAT TO DRINK

Oatmeal and Ginger Drink

The oatmeal called for in this recipe is a form of ground oat kernel—not the familiar rolled oats. Oatmeal is available from health-food stores.

To make about 5 cups [1¼ liters]

2 tbsp.	fine oatmeal	30 ml.
½ tsp.	ground ginger	2 ml.
1 tbsp.	brown sugar	15 ml.
1	lemon, the peel grated and the juice strained	1
5 cups	boiling water	1¼ liters

Mix the oatmeal, ginger, sugar and lemon peel together in a heavy saucepan. Pour in the boiling water, stirring all the time. Set the pan over low heat and continue stirring until the mixture comes to a boil. Stir in the lemon juice. Simmer the mixture for 10 to 15 minutes longer, then strain it into a warmed jug.

FLORENCE B. JACK
ONE HUNDRED DRINKS & CUPS

Chocolate-flavored Atole

Champurrado

Masa harina is dried corn treated with lime and ground to a flourlike texture. It can be purchased in stores where Mexican foods are sold.

Though there are many variations, basically *atole* is a gruel thickened with *masa harina*, sweetened with sugar and flavored with crushed fruits—such as pineapple and strawberries—or seasoned with chili.

To make about 2½ cups [625 ml.]

2½ cups	water	625 ml.
½ cup	*masa harina*	125 ml.
1½ oz.	semisweet chocolate, grated	45 g.
1-inch	cinnamon stick	2½-cm.
	brown sugar	

Bring 1½ cups [375 ml.] of the water to a boil. Mix the *masa harina* with the remaining water and strain it into the boiling water, stirring the mixture well so that it is completely smooth. Add the chocolate, cinnamon and brown sugar to taste. Keep stirring the mixture until it thickens and is well flavored—about five minutes.

DIANA KENNEDY
CUISINES OF MEXICO

Another Recipe for Barley Water

	To make 5 cups [1 ¼ liters]	
3 tbsp.	pearl barley	45 ml.
	water	
¼ cup	fresh lemon juice	50 ml.
	sugar	

Wash the pearl barley in a bowl of cold water, changing the water several times. Then put the barley in a saucepan with 5 cups [1 ¼ liters] of fresh water. Bring the mixture to a boil and allow it to simmer for 10 minutes. Strain the barley water, then add the lemon juice and sugar to taste.

MRS. C. F. LEYEL AND MISS OLGA HARTLEY
THE GENTLE ART OF COOKERY

Wheat Drink with Syrup

Zhitna Sliz sus Sirop

Whole-wheat kernels are available at health-food stores. The technique of making a fruit syrup is shown on pages 40-41.

	To make 1 ¼ cups [300 ml.]	
½ cup	whole-wheat kernels, rinsed in cold water	125 ml.
4 cups	water	1 liter
2 tbsp.	cherry, raspberry or strawberry syrup, made by the recipe for basic fruit syrup (recipe, page 164)	30 ml.

Put the wheat and the water in a heavy saucepan and simmer over low heat for three to four hours. Pass through a sieve and discard the residue. Return the wheat liquid to the saucepan and simmer for two to three minutes. Serve hot, sweetened with the syrup.

TASHO TASHEV, ZH. STOYANOVA AND YA. DZHAMBAZOVA
DIETICHNO HRANENE

Honey Drink

Napój z Miodu

You can use juice squeezed from red or black currants, cranberries or grated rhubarb.

	To make 2 quarts [2 liters]	
⅓ cup	honey	75 ml.
1 ½ quarts	warm water	1 ½ liters
2 cups	uncooked fruit juice	½ liter

Dissolve the honey in the warm water. Stir in the fruit juice.

ZOFIA CZERNY AND MARIA STRASBURGER
ZYWIENIE RODZINY

Syrups

Apricot Syrup

For the apricot purée you will need 4 pounds [2 kg.] of apricots. Blanch, peel, halve and pit fresh apricots, then press them through a sieve or food mill. Soak dried apricots in water to cover for eight hours before puréeing them. Citric acid is sold at pharmacies. To make a smaller quantity, reduce the ingredients proportionately. The syrup can be safely refrigerated for about a month, but must be used within two weeks after a bottle is opened.

When serving this syrup, add a little cream or ice cream to each drink.

	To make about 10 quarts [10 liters]	
8 quarts	boiling sugar syrup (recipe, page 164)	8 liters
8 cups	apricot purée	2 liters
2 tsp.	citric acid, dissolved in ¼ cup [50 ml.] water	10 ml.

Add the sugar syrup to the purée. Mix well and add the citric-acid solution; stir occasionally until the mixture cools.

ALBERT A. HOPKINS
HOME MADE BEVERAGES

Orange Syrup

The original version of this recipe calls for 36 pounds [18 kg.] of fruit and yields about 3 gallons [12 liters] of syrup. The quantities here are reduced proportionately. The syrup can be safely refrigerated for about a month, but must be used within two weeks after the bottle is opened.

	To make about 1 quart [1 liter]	
2 cups	fresh orange juice	½ liter
¾ cup	fresh lemon juice	175 ml.
¾ cup	fresh tangerine juice	175 ml.
4 tsp.	grated lemon peel	20 ml.
4 tsp.	grated tangerine peel	20 ml.
about 5 cups	sugar	about 1 ¼ liters

In a nonreactive pan, combine the fruit juices and peels with sugar to taste. Allow the mixture to stand overnight in a cool place. Warm the mixture just enough to dissolve the sugar. Bottle and cork it. To serve, mix the syrup with ice water to taste.

ANNA G. EDMONDS (EDITOR)
AN AMERICAN COOK IN TURKEY

Currant Syrup

The syrup can be safely refrigerated for about a month, but must be used within two weeks after a bottle is opened.

To make about 7 cups [1¾ liters]

3 lb.	currants, white or red	1½ kg.
1 lb.	raspberries	½ kg.
1 lb.	sour cherries, pitted	½ kg.
	sugar	

Mash the fruits together, and let them stand in a warm place for a day. Strain the juice into a nonreactive pan, and add 4 cups [1 liter] of sugar to each 2½ cups [625 ml.] of liquid; place over low heat or inside a pan partly filled with simmering water, and stir to dissolve the sugar. Cool the syrup, then skim it, pour it into bottles and cork them tightly.

WILLIAM BERNHARD
THE BOOK OF ONE HUNDRED BEVERAGES

Catalan Grape Syrup

Arrop

The technique for extracting the juice from grapes is demonstrated on page 34. The syrup can be safely refrigerated for about a month, but must be used within two weeks after a jar is opened.

To make about 2 cups [½ liter]

4 lb.	well-ripened grapes, juice extracted	2 kg.

In a large, nonreactive saucepan, cook the grape juice over low heat until it is reduced to one quarter of its original volume. Strain it and return it to the heat until it thickens. Pour the syrup into glass jars and seal them tightly.

CATALUNYA LLAMINERA

Quince Syrup

Sciroppo di Mele Cotogne

The syrup can be safely refrigerated for about a month, but must be used within two weeks after a bottle is opened.

To make about 2 quarts [2 liters]

3 lb.	quinces, sliced	1½ kg.
2 quarts	water	2 liters
	sugar	

Put the quinces in a heavy, nonreactive pan. Add the water and bring to a boil. Stirring frequently with a wooden spoon, cook over low heat for 45 minutes, or until the quinces are soft. Strain, then let the juice ferment in a cool place for two and one half days. Remove the scum from the surface, mea-sure the juice into the pan and add 6 cups [1½ liters] of sugar for each quart [1 liter] of juice. Boil the syrup for a few minutes, remove the pan from the heat, cool the syrup and pour it into bottles.

MILA CONTINI
FATTO IN CASA

Lemon Syrup

Siroppo di Limone

To make a smaller quantity, reduce the ingredients proportionately. The syrup can be safely refrigerated for approximately a month, but must be used within two weeks after a bottle is opened.

To make about 4 quarts [4 liters]

12	lemons, the peel thinly pared and the juice strained	12
4½ quarts	water	4½ liters
14 cups	sugar, dissolved in water	3½ liters

Put the lemon peel and water into a large, nonreactive pan, bring to a boil, then simmer uncovered for 20 minutes. Strain the liquid into another pan, stir in the dissolved sugar and cook uncovered over medium heat for 10 minutes. Remove the syrup from the heat and stir in the lemon juice. Let the syrup cool, then bottle it.

IL CUOCO MILANESE E LA CUCINIERA PIEMONTESE

Pomegranate Syrup

Jarabe de Granada (Granadina)

The syrup can be safely refrigerated for about a month, but must be used within two weeks after a bottle is opened.

To make about 2 quarts [2 liters]

12 lb.	pomegranates	6 kg.
12 cups	sugar	3 liters
⅓ cup	fresh lemon juice	75 ml.
	red food coloring	

Remove the seed clusters from the pomegranates and pull the seeds away from the bitter white membranes that connect them. Wrap the seeds in cloth and crush them by striking the parcel two or three times with a wooden mallet. Wring the parcel vigorously to extract all of the juice.

Measure the juice—there should be approximately 2 quarts [2 liters]. Pour it into a nonreactive saucepan, add the sugar and stir until the sugar dissolves. Add the lemon juice, put the pan over medium heat and bring the liquid to a boil. Continue boiling for 10 minutes. Off the heat, add a few drops of red food coloring. Strain the syrup through filter paper or a cloth, then pour it into bottles.

MARÍA MESTAYER DE ECHAGÜE
CONFITERÍA Y REPOSTERÍA

Lemon Ginger Syrup

The syrup can be safely refrigerated for about a month, but must be used within two weeks after a bottle is opened.

To make about 5 cups [1¼ liters]

¼ cup	chopped fresh ginger	50 ml.
5 cups	water	1¼ liters
2	lemons, the peel of 1 thinly pared	2
	sugar	

Combine the ginger, water and lemon peel in a saucepan. Bring to a boil and simmer gently for 45 minutes, making good any water boiled away. Strain the mixture and measure the liquid. Add 2 cups [½ liter] of sugar and the strained juice of one lemon to every 2½ cups [625 ml.] of liquid; stir until the sugar dissolves. Cool and bottle the syrup.

F. W. BEECH (EDITOR)
HOME-MADE WINES, SYRUPS AND CORDIALS

Raspberry Vinegar Syrup

Sirop de Vinaigre Framboisé

The syrup can be safely refrigerated for about a month, but must be used within two weeks after a bottle is opened.

To make about 1½ quarts [1½ liters]

½ lb.	raspberries (about 2 cups [½ liter])	¼ kg.
1 quart	wine vinegar	1 liter
	sugar	

Steep the raspberries in the wine vinegar for eight to 10 days. Strain the liquid through a cloth, pressing the berries to extract all of their juice. Measure the liquid into a non-reactive pan and add 3 cups [¾ liter] of sugar for every 4 cups [1 liter] of liquid. Heat the mixture in a water bath—stirring occasionally and skimming off the scum—until the sugar dissolves. Cool the mixture and bottle it.

SIMIN PALAY
LA CUISINE DU PAYS

Red Currant Syrup

Sirop de Groseilles

The syrup can be safely refrigerated for about a month, but must be used within two weeks after a bottle is opened.

To make about 1 quart [1 liter]

4 lb.	red currants, slightly underripe	2 kg.
2 lb.	morello cherries, pitted	1 kg.
	sugar	

Crush the red currants and cherries together and put them into an earthenware pot. Let the crushed fruits ferment for 24 hours, then press them through a muslin- or cheesecloth-lined sieve. Wring the cloth to ensure that all the liquid is extracted. Measure the liquid and add 3½ cups [875 ml.] of sugar to each 2 cups [½ liter] of liquid. Pour the mixture into a heavy, nonreactive pan and cook over low heat, stirring from time to time, until the sugar dissolves. Then increase the heat and let the syrup come to a boil, take it off the heat and skim it. Let the syrup cool a little, then bottle it. The next day, cork the bottles and store them in a cool place.

ÉMILE DUMONT
LA BONNE CUISINE FRANÇAISE

Raspberry Shrub

The syrup can be safely refrigerated for about a month, but must be used within two weeks after a bottle is opened.

Raspberry shrub mixed with cold water is a pure, delicious drink for summer.

To make about 1½ quarts [1½ liters]

2 lb.	raspberries (about 4 pints [2 liters])	1 kg.
about 2 cups	vinegar	about ½ liter
	sugar	

Put the raspberries in a nonreactive pan and scarcely cover them with vinegar. Add 2 cups [½ liter] of sugar for each 2 cups of raspberries. Bring the mixture to a boil, skim it and let it cool. Strain and bottle the liquid.

MRS. CHILD
THE AMERICAN FRUGAL HOUSEWIFE

Clover Honey Syrup

This syrup can be safely refrigerated for about a month, but must be used within two weeks after a bottle is opened.

This syrup is a pleasant addition to soda water, lemonade or dry white wine.

To make about 5 cups [1¼ liters]

1 quart	fresh clover heads	1 liter
¼ cup	fresh mint leaves	50 ml.
1 quart	boiling water	1 liter
2 cups	clover honey	½ liter

Put the clover heads and mint leaves in a saucepan, pour in the water, cover the pan with a tight-fitting lid, and simmer gently for five minutes. Remove the pan from the heat and let the mixture steep—still covered—for 20 minutes. Strain the infusion through muslin or cheesecloth and add the clover honey. Then return the liquid to the saucepan and boil it for three minutes. Bottle the syrup and cork it.

BLANCHE POWNALL GARRETT
CANADIAN COUNTRY PRESERVES & WINES

Mint Syrup

This syrup can be safely refrigerated for about a month, but must be used within two weeks after the bottle is opened.
Use the mint syrup as a flavoring in drinks, punches or even homemade ice cream.

To make about 1 ½ cups [375 ml.]

20 to 30	fresh mint leaves	20 to 30
1 cup	sugar	¼ liter
1 cup	boiling water	¼ liter

Using a pestle, crush the mint leaves and the sugar to a coarse paste in a mortar or heavy bowl. Transfer the mixture to a pan, add the boiling water and stir over low heat until the sugar dissolves. Simmer for three to five minutes to thicken the syrup. Remove the syrup from the heat, allow it to cool, then strain out the mint leaves. Bottle.

JOEL, DAVID AND KARL SCHAPIRA
THE BOOK OF COFFEE & TEA

Elder Flower Syrup

The author specifies that the elder flowers be picked on a dry day. The syrup can be safely refrigerated for about a month, but must be used within two weeks after a bottle is opened.

To make about 1 ½ quarts [1 ½ liters]

4 cups	fresh elder flowers	1 liter
about 4 cups	water	about 1 liter
	sugar	

Put the elder flowers into a heavy pan. Pour in enough water to just cover the flowers, bring to a boil and simmer over low heat for 30 minutes, making good any water cooked away. Line a sieve with a double layer of dampened muslin or cheesecloth, place the sieve over a large bowl and strain the mixture through it; squeeze the cloth thoroughly to extract all the liquid. Measure the liquid and return it to the pan. Add 1 ½ cups [375 ml.] of sugar for every 2 ¼ cups [550 ml.] of liquid, bring to a boil, stirring constantly, and simmer undisturbed for 10 minutes, skimming if necessary. Let the syrup cool, then bottle it.

F. W. BEECH (EDITOR)
HOME-MADE WINES, SYRUPS AND CORDIALS

Almond Orgeat

Jarabe de Horchata de Almendras

An alternative way to concentrate the flavor of the almond liquid is to let the crushed almonds steep in the water for up to 12 hours; you need then strain it only once. This technique is demonstrated on pages 42-43. The syrup can be safely refrigerated for about a month, but must be used within two weeks after a bottle is opened.

To make about 1 quart [1 liter]

1 cup	almonds, blanched and peeled	¼ liter
1 quart	water	1 liter
3 cups	sugar	¾ liter
1	lemon peel	1

Soak the almonds for two to three hours. Drain them, crush them in a mortar, transfer them to a large bowl and mix them with the water. Place a double layer of dampened muslin or cheesecloth in a sieve, set the sieve over another large bowl and strain the almond-and-water mixture through it, squeezing the cloth well. Spoon the pulp back into the almond water and strain the mixture through the cloth again; repeat this process once or twice to extract as much flavor as possible. Pour the almond liquid into a saucepan, add the sugar and lemon peel and cook the mixture over medium heat, stirring constantly, until it is just about to boil. Cool the orgeat, remove the lemon peel and bottle the orgeat.

VICTORIA SERRA SUÑOL
SABORES: COCINA DEL HOGAR

Violet Syrup

Sirop de Violettes

The syrup can be safely refrigerated for about a month, but must be used within two weeks after a bottle is opened.

To make about 3 quarts [3 liters]

1 ½ cups	freshly picked violets, stems and leaves removed	375 ml.
2 quarts	boiling water	2 liters
4 lb.	sugar cubes	2 kg.

Crush the violets in a mortar and transfer them to a large bowl. Dilute with the boiling water. Leave the mixture to infuse for 10 hours. Strain the infusion through a colander that has been lined with dampened muslin or cheesecloth and placed over a heatproof bowl. Set the bowl in a large pan partly filled with almost-boiling water. Add the sugar to the strained liquid and simmer over low heat, stirring until the sugar dissolves. Remove the syrup from the heat and filter it. Bottle the syrup while it is still warm.

C. DURANDEAU
GUIDE DE LA BONNE CUISINIÈRE

Milk Drinks

Cocoa

To make 1 quart [1 liter]

¼ cup	cocoa powder	125 ml.
1 cup	boiling water	¼ liter
⅛ tsp.	salt	½ ml.
2 to 4 tbsp.	sugar	30 to 60 ml.
½ tsp.	ground cinnamon	2 ml.
	ground cloves or nutmeg	
3 cups	milk, scalded	¾ liter
1 tsp.	vanilla extract	5 ml.

Combine the cocoa powder, water, salt and sugar in the top of a double boiler, stir, and boil for two minutes over direct but low heat. Add the cinnamon and a pinch of cloves or nutmeg. Place the top of the double boiler over boiling water and add the scalded milk. Stir and heat the cocoa. Cover and keep it over hot water for 10 more minutes. Add the vanilla and beat the cocoa with a wire whisk before serving.

IRMA ROMBAUER AND MARION ROMBAUER BECKER
THE JOY OF COOKING

Hot Cocoa

To make 1 quart [1 liter]

1 quart	milk	1 liter
¼ cup	cocoa powder	50 ml.
¼ cup	sugar	50 ml.
	salt	
1	cinnamon stick	1
	freshly grated nutmeg	

Place the milk in the top of a double boiler, set above cold water. Cover and place the pan on a burner to heat the milk. While the milk is heating, mix together the cocoa powder, sugar and a pinch of salt in a small bowl. When the milk is quite hot pour about a cup of it into the bowl containing the cocoa mixture. Mix well and then pour this cocoa mixture into the milk in the double boiler. Stir until well mixed. Add the cinnamon stick and a good grating of nutmeg. Cook the cocoa for 15 minutes. Turn off the heat and let the cocoa rest over the hot water until you are ready to serve it.

EDNA LEWIS
THE TASTE OF COUNTRY COOKING

French Chocolate

To make about 1 ½ quarts [1 ½ liters]

2 oz.	unsweetened baking chocolate	60 g.
½ cup	cold water	125 ml.
¾ cup	sugar	175 ml.
	salt	
½ cup	heavy cream, whipped	125 ml.
1 quart	milk	1 liter

Put the chocolate and cold water in a saucepan and stir over low heat until the chocolate melts. Add the sugar and a pinch of salt, and cook until the mixture is thick—about 10 minutes. Let the mixture cool and then fold in the whipped cream. Heat the milk in a double boiler, pour it into six cups and top each serving with the chocolate cream.

FANNIE MERRITT FARMER
THE FANNIE FARMER COOKBOOK

French Hot Chocolate

You might like to try replacing half the milk with strong, hot black coffee, for a cup of hot mocha chocolate.

To make 1 ½ cups [375 ml.]

1 cup	milk	¼ liter
2 oz.	semisweet baking chocolate	60 g.
1	egg yolk	1

Heat the milk, but do not let it boil. Pour three quarters of it into a mug and then add the chocolate to the remaining milk. Melt the chocolate over low heat and blend it thoroughly with the milk. Return the rest of the milk to the saucepan, remove the pan from the heat, and stir.

Take a teaspoonful of the chocolate-and-milk mixture and stir it into the egg yolk. Add a few more spoonfuls and then pour the yolk mixture into the saucepan. Whisk the drink to a froth and pour into the serving mug.

NORMAN KOLPAS
THE CHOCOLATE LOVERS' COMPANION

Brazilian Chocolate

To make about 3 ½ cups [875 ml.]

1 oz.	sweet baking chocolate	30 g.
¼ cup	sugar	50 ml.
⅛ tsp.	salt	½ ml.
1 cup	boiling water	¼ liter
½ cup	milk, heated	125 ml.
½ cup	cream, heated	125 ml.
1 ½ cups	hot, freshly made strong black coffee	375 ml.
1 tsp.	vanilla extract	5 ml.
	ground cinnamon (optional)	

Melt the chocolate with the sugar and salt in the top of a double boiler set over hot water. Stir in the boiling water, and cook for three to five minutes. Then add the hot milk, cream and coffee. Beat the mixture well and add the vanilla and, if you wish, a pinch of cinnamon.

IRMA ROMBAUER AND MARION ROMBAUER BECKER
THE JOY OF COOKING

German or Sweetened Vanilla Chocolate

To make about 3 cups [¾ liter]

2 cups	hot milk	½ liter
2 oz.	sweet chocolate	60 g.
2 to 3 tbsp.	hot water	30 to 45 ml.
½ cup	heavy cream	125 ml.
2 tbsp.	superfine sugar	30 ml.
¼ tsp.	vanilla extract	1 ml.

Over low heat, melt the chocolate in the hot water. Stir to a smooth paste; add the milk gradually and stir the mixture for five minutes.

Flavor the cream with the sugar and the vanilla, then whip it. Serve the hot chocolate in cups three quarters full, with 2 or 3 tablespoons [30 or 45 ml.] of whipped cream on top of each cup.

MRS. MARY J. LINCOLN
MRS. LINCOLN'S BOSTON COOK BOOK

Mexican Chocolate Drink

Mexican chocolate is a granular sweet chocolate, flavored with almonds and cinnamon. It is obtainable in bar form where Latin American foods are sold. A molinillo is a special tool for beating chocolate: a deeply indented wooden ball at-tached to a long, rounded wooden handle. The molinillo is placed upright in the pan and rotated by spinning the handle back and forth between the palms of both hands.

To make about 1 ¼ cups [300 ml.]

1 cup	water	¼ liter
1 ½ oz.	Mexican chocolate	45 g.

Heat the water in a saucepan. As it comes to a boil, break the chocolate into it and stir until the chocolate has melted. Let the mixture boil gently for about five minutes so that all the flavor comes out, then beat it with a *molinillo* or whisk or in a blender until it is frothy.

DIANA KENNEDY
CUISINES OF MEXICO

Spanish Chocolate
Chocolate Español

To make about 2 ½ cups [625 ml.]

2 cups	milk	½ liter
2 oz.	sweet chocolate, broken or grated	60 g.
½ tsp.	ground cinnamon	2 ml.
2	eggs, beaten	2

Stir the milk with the chocolate and the cinnamon over low heat until the chocolate dissolves. Add the eggs and beat the mixture until it becomes thick, taking care not to let it boil.

SYBILLE SCHALL
COCINA RAPIDA

Chocolate Delight
La Delice au Chocolat

To make 2 quarts [2 liters]

¾ cup	cocoa powder	175 ml.
⅔ cup	sugar	150 ml.
1 quart	milk	1 liter
1 ½ cups	strong black coffee	375 ml.
1 cup	kirsch or brandy	¼ liter
1 cup	heavy cream, whipped with 2 tbsp. [30 ml.] sugar	¼ liter

Blend the cocoa with the sugar in a heavy saucepan. Gradually stir in the milk. Heat to the boiling point. Remove from the heat and add the coffee and the kirsch or brandy. Chill the mixture. For each serving, fill a 10- to 12-ounce [300- to 360-ml.] glass two thirds full with the cocoa mixture. Add about ¼ cup [50 ml.] of the whipped cream and blend well. Serve the drink at once.

NIKA STANDEN HAZELTON
THE SWISS COOKBOOK

Brown Russian

To make about 1 ¼ cups [300 ml.]

1 cup	milk	¼ liter
2 oz.	semisweet chocolate	60 g.
2 tbsp.	vodka	30 ml.

Heat the milk gently. Pour three quarters of it into a mug. Add the chocolate to the remaining milk and melt over low heat until thoroughly blended. Return the rest of the milk to the pan, remove from the heat and stir. Pour the drink back into the mug. Stir in the vodka and serve.

NORMAN KOLPAS
THE CHOCOLATE LOVERS' COMPANION

Coffee Milk Shake with Alcohol

Mokka-Shake met Alcohol

Instead of beating the ingredients by hand, you can use an electric blender. The technique of making milk shakes in a blender is demonstrated on page 53.

To make about 3¾ cups [925 ml.]

2 cups	milk	½ liter
¼ cup	coffee liqueur	50 ml.
1 cup	coffee ice cream (recipe, page 166)	¼ liter
2	egg yolks	2
4 tbsp.	sweetened whipped cream	60 ml.
2 tbsp.	almonds, cut into slivers	30 ml.

Beat the milk, coffee liqueur, coffee ice cream and egg yolks vigorously together until everything is well mixed and frothy. Serve the still-frothy coffee milk shake in tall glasses. Decorate each glass with a spoonful of whipped cream, sprinkled with almond slivers.

HET VOLKOMEN ZUIVELBOEK

Egg Flip

To make about ¾ cup [175 ml.]

1	egg	1
1 tsp.	superfine sugar	5 ml.
⅔ cup	milk	150 ml.
	nutmeg (optional)	

Break the egg into a tumbler, add the sugar and beat well with a fork. Heat the milk in a saucepan without letting it boil, and pour it over the egg, beating all the time. Then pour the drink backward and forward from the tumbler to the saucepan until frothy. Serve hot. A little nutmeg may be grated over the top.

FLORENCE B. JACK
ONE HUNDRED DRINKS AND CUPS

Meringue Milk

Leche Merengada

The technique of making meringue milk is shown on pages 48-49. The milk can be served when thoroughly chilled or frozen until firm.

To make about 1½ quarts [1½ liters]

1 quart	milk	1 liter
1½ cups	sugar	375 ml.
1	piece lemon peel	1
1 tsp.	fresh lemon juice	5 ml.
3-inch	cinnamon stick	8-cm.
4	egg whites	4
	ground cinnamon	

Place the milk in a saucepan with 1 cup [¼ liter] of the sugar, the lemon peel and cinnamon stick. Simmer for five minutes, then let the milk cool.

When the milk has completely cooled, strain it into a bowl and place it in the freezer. Beat the egg whites with the remaining sugar and a few drops of lemon juice until stiff peaks are formed. When the milk starts to set, beat in the egg whites little by little. Return the bowl to the freezer and let the meringue milk freeze until firm.

To serve, fill glasses with the meringue milk, mounding it up, and dust it with ground cinnamon.

REPOSTERIA COCINA TIPICA

Zabaglione Shake

Frappé di Zabaione

To make about 1½ cups [375 ml.]

½ cup	light cream	125 ml.
4	egg yolks	4
4 tsp.	sugar	20 ml.
4 tsp.	Marsala	20 ml.
4 tbsp.	crushed ice	60 ml.

Put all the ingredients together into a blender and blend them at high speed for one to two minutes.

VERA
SI FA COSÌ

Coffee Cocktail

Mokkacocktail

To make about 2 cups [1/2 liter]

1/4 cup	double-strength coffee	50 ml.
1/3 cup	brandy	75 ml.
1 cup	milk	1/4 liter
2	egg yolks	2
1 tbsp.	cocoa powder	15 ml.
2 tbsp.	superfine sugar	30 ml.
	ice cubes	

Thoroughly mix all the ingredients, except the ice cubes, in a blender or by hand. Pour into glasses. Finally, add ice cubes.

HET VOLKOMEN ZUIVELBOEK

Havana Almond Drink

Amande

The original version of this recipe calls for 20 sweet and two bitter almonds. Bitter almonds contain traces of poisonous prussic acid, and are unavailable in the United States. Almond extract makes a suitable substitute.

To make about 1 quart [1 liter]

20	almonds, blanched and peeled	20
1/4 tsp.	almond extract	1 ml.
1 quart	milk	1 liter
1-inch	piece vanilla bean, slit to expose the seeds	2 1/2-cm.
1 cup	sugar	1/4 liter
	ice cubes	

Using a mortar and pestle, pound the almonds and almond extract to a pulp. Pour the milk into a pan, stir in the almond pulp and bring the mixture almost to a boil over medium heat. Remove the pan from the heat, and add the vanilla bean and the sugar to the almond-and-milk mixture; the vanilla seeds will spice the drink. Stir, heat again, then strain the drink and cool it. Serve with plenty of ice.

CORA, ROSE AND BOB BROWN
THE SOUTH AMERICAN COOK BOOK

Milk of Almonds

To make 4 quarts [4 liters]

1 1/2 cups	almonds, blanched and peeled	375 ml.
1 2/3 cups	superfine sugar	400 ml.
1 quart	water	1 liter
3 quarts	milk	3 liters
1/3 cup	orange-flower water	75 ml.

Mix the almonds with half of the sugar and put through a food grinder four times. Then pound this paste in a mortar, little by little and as fine as possible. Combine the paste with the water and let it infuse overnight.

Add the remainder of the sugar to the milk. Flavor the almond-paste mixture with the orange-flower water, strain it through a fine-meshed sieve and mix it with the sweetened milk. Serve the drink very cold.

LATIFA BENNANI-SMIRES
MOROCCAN COOKING

Cobra Cooler

Harira

Nagapanchmi in July or August is a day set aside for the cobra. It is meritorious on this day to feed cobras, which are sacred to the Hindus, with an offering of milk. Usually there is a bit of milk left over in the pantry after feeding the snakes. Always the day is hot, so almonds and spices will be mixed with the leftover milk and made into a cooling liquid.

To make about 3 cups [3/4 liter]

15	black peppercorns	15
about 3 tbsp.	sugar	about 45 ml.
3	whole cardamoms, pods removed and seeds separated	3
1/2 cup	large seedless raisins	125 ml.
1/3 cup	almonds, blanched and peeled	75 ml.
1 cup	water	1/4 liter
2 cups	milk	1/2 liter

Drop the peppercorns into a blender and pulverize them. Then add the sugar, cardamom seeds, raisins, almonds and water. Process to a very fine purée. Add the milk and blend at high speed for one minute. Taste for sweetness and add up to 1 tablespoon [15 ml.] more sugar if desired. Strain through fine muslin or several thicknesses of dampened cheesecloth, and chill before drinking.

SHIVAJI RAO AND SHALINI DEVI HOLKAR
COOKING OF THE MAHARAJAS

Coconut Milk Drink

To make about 2 cups [1/2 liter]

1 cup	milk	1/4 liter
1 cup	coconut milk *(recipe, page 165)*	1/4 liter
1 tbsp.	heavy cream	15 ml.
2 tbsp.	freshly grated coconut	30 ml.
1/2 tbsp.	ground pistachios	7 ml.

Mix the milk with the coconut milk and beat until frothy. Top the drink with the cream and grated coconut and a sprinkling of ground pistachios.

JACK SANTA MARIA
INDIAN SWEET COOKERY

Holstein Tea

Holsteiner Thee

To make about 5 cups [1 1/4 liters]

1 quart	milk	1 liter
4 tsp.	black tea leaves	20 ml.
3	egg yolks	3
3 to 4 tbsp.	sugar	45 to 60 ml.

Bring the milk to a boil. Add the tea leaves, cover the pan and infuse over low heat for five minutes. Then strain the milk. Whisk the egg yolks lightly with the sugar and add the hot milk, stirring constantly. Heat, still stirring, but do not let the mixture boil.

HET VOLKOMEN ZUIVELBOEK

Cambric Tea

This tea, being white, takes its name from the fine white linen fabric called cambric after the French city of Cambrai, where it was originally made.

To those whose nerves forbid the use of tea or coffee, this mild, nutritious beverage is cordially commended. There is no milk-and-water insipidity about it, if the cream be genuine and the water on a fresh, violent boil.

To make 3/4 cup [175 ml.]

1	sugar cube	1
1/4 cup	heavy cream	50 ml.
1/2 cup	boiling water	125 ml.

Put the sugar in a cup; add the cream; let stand a minute to melt the sugar, and fill up the cup with the boiling water.

MARION HARLAND AND CHRISTINE TERHUNE HERRICK
THE NATIONAL COOK BOOK

Hot Semolina Drink

Salep

Although Turkey is extremely hot in the summer, it can be bitterly cold in winter, especially in the eastern districts near the Caucasus Mountains. This drink is sold in the streets during the winter and is a warming comfort when the winds are blowing down from Central Asia.

To make 2 1/2 cups [625 ml.]

2 1/2 cups	milk	625 ml.
1 tbsp.	semolina	15 ml.
	sugar	
	ground cinnamon	

Place the milk, semolina and sugar to taste in a pan and cook gently over low heat for 10 minutes, stirring frequently. To serve, pour into heatproof glasses and sprinkle ground cinnamon on top.

VENICE LAMB
THE HOME BOOK OF TURKISH COOKERY

Slemp

This is the drink the children have on the evening of the St. Nicolas Festival (December 5).

To make 3 cups [3/4 liter]

8	whole cloves	8
1	cinnamon stick	1
1	blade mace	1
	saffron threads	
1 quart	milk	1 liter
1/2 cup	sugar	125 ml.
2 tbsp.	cornstarch, dissolved in 1/4 cup [50 ml.] water	30 ml.
	water	

Wrap the cloves, cinnamon, mace and a few saffron threads in a piece of cheesecloth and put them in a heavy saucepan. Add the milk. Heat the milk until small bubbles appear around the edges of the pan, then reduce the heat to low and simmer, covered, for 30 minutes. Stir in the sugar and dissolved cornstarch. Simmer for five minutes more. Press the bag of spices between two spoons to extract the last bit of flavor, then discard it. Serve the drink hot in mugs.

C. COUNTESS VAN LIMBURG STIRUM
THE ART OF DUTCH COOKING

Saffron Milk

Saffraanmelk

To make about 1 quart [1 liter]

1 quart	milk, brought to a boil	1 liter
6	threads saffron or a pinch of powdered saffron	6
3 to 4 tbsp.	sugar	45 to 60 ml.
1½ tbsp.	cornstarch, mixed with ¼ cup [50 ml.] cold water or cold milk	22 ml.

Pour the milk into a pan and add the saffron. Cover the pan with its lid and bring the milk to a simmer over low heat. If using saffron threads, let the mixture infuse for 15 minutes, stirring from time to time to avoid sticking. Remove and discard the threads. If using powdered saffron, there is no need to let the milk infuse. Stir the sugar into the hot milk. Stir in the cornstarch mixture to thicken the milk. Stirring constantly, simmer the saffron milk for two minutes.

HET VOLKOMEN ZUIVELBOEK

Anise Milk

Anijs Melk

To make about 1 quart [1 liter]

1 quart	milk	1 liter
1 tbsp.	aniseed, crushed to a powder	15 ml.
½ cup	sugar	125 ml.
2 tbsp.	cornstarch, dissolved in ¼ cup [50 ml.] water	30 ml.

Scald the milk with the aniseed, add the sugar and simmer for five minutes. Add the dissolved cornstarch. Stirring constantly, cook over low heat until the mixture has thickened slightly—about five minutes.

C. COUNTESS VAN LIMBURG STIRUM
THE ART OF DUTCH COOKING

Buttermilk Lemonade

To make about 1 quart [1 liter]

2 tbsp.	sugar	30 ml.
¼ cup	fresh lemon juice	50 ml.
1 quart	buttermilk	1 liter

In a large bowl, mix the sugar with the lemon juice and stir until dissolved; add the buttermilk, stirring constantly.

BERTHA E. L. STOCKBRIDGE
WHAT TO DRINK

Buttermilk and Beets

Buttermilch und Rote Beete

To make about 1½ cups [375 ml.]

2 cups	peeled and coarsely chopped beets	½ liter
1 cup	buttermilk	¼ liter
about 1 tbsp.	fresh lemon juice	about 15 ml.
	sugar or honey	

Pass the beets through the fine disk of a food grinder, put the purée in a square of muslin or a double layer of cheesecloth, and twist the cloth tightly to extract the juice. Mix the juice with the buttermilk. Add some lemon juice and a little sugar or honey to taste.

GERDA RICHTER
WUNDERQUELLE MILCH

Tangy Cultured Milk

Kefir

This delicious Middle Eastern beverage can be briefly described as one of the family of cultured milk products that includes yogurt, buttermilk and sour cream. To get started, purchase *kefir* (usually to be found at a health-food store). Whole milk makes a smoother product than skimmed milk. The culture acts quite rapidly to create a junket-like milk product. To preserve the *kefir* as a liquid, shake it each time you serve it to break up the curds; it then becomes a thoroughly creamy, not curdy, drink. You may add fresh or frozen fruit, puréed and sweetened, to make flavored *kefir*.

Use a starter from a previous batch to make the next one. Flavored as well as plain *kefir* can be used as a starter.

To make 1 quart [1 liter]

1 quart	whole or skimmed milk	1 liter
¼ cup	prepared *kefir*	50 ml.

Heat the milk to lukewarm (110° F. [44° C.]). Mix in the *kefir* starter and pour into a jar. Cover and leave at room temperature for eight to 24 hours (depending upon air temperature), until thick and custard-like. Shake the *kefir*, then chill it thoroughly. Shake again before serving.

HELEN WITTY AND ELIZABETH SCHNEIDER COLCHIE
BETTER THAN STORE-BOUGHT

Banana Shake

This also works like a dream with peaches, apricots, or stewed and peeled prunes. Other fruits, however, may require adding spices. For example, if you want to use apples, add a dash of cinnamon.

To make about 2 cups [½ liter]

1 cup	yogurt (recipe, page 165)	¼ liter
1	large ripe banana, sliced	1
¼ tsp.	sugar	1 ml.
	ice cubes (optional)	

Put the yogurt, banana, sugar and ice cubes, if you like, in an electric blender and blend for a minute or so. Serve in a chilled glass.

CAROL ANN RINZLER
THE SIGNET BOOK OF YOGURT

Fruit Lassi

The techniques of making yogurt and fruit lassi are demonstrated on pages 50-51. The drink can be garnished with pieces of fruit instead of with flower petals.

To make about 2½ cups [625 ml.]

1 cup	plain yogurt (recipe, page 165)	¼ liter
2 tsp.	honey	10 ml.
3 tbsp.	fresh lemon juice	45 ml.
½ cup	finely chopped soft fruit: mango, papaya, banana	125 ml.
1 cup	water	¼ liter
	flower petals	

Beat the yogurt and mix in all the ingredients thoroughly. Serve decorated with flower petals.

JACK SANTA MARIA
INDIAN SWEET COOKERY

Minty Yogurt Refresher

Mattha

Literally translated, *mattha* means "buttermilk." Its taste and consistency, however, bear no resemblance to commercial buttermilk. Indian buttermilk is much thinner, more like skimmed milk, and has a buttery-yogurt flavor. *Mattha* is so flavorful that it is frequently served just by itself, though it is quite common to add a little salt, crushed cumin and a few fragrant herbs. It is a perfect drink for summer. For the best flavor, the yogurt should be a little tangy.

Mattha may be made a day ahead and refrigerated. Just before serving, blend again to froth the drink. Do not add more ice cubes, or it will taste weak and flavorless.

To make about 2 cups [½ liter]

1 cup	plain yogurt (recipe, page 165)	¼ liter
¾ cup	cold water	175 ml.
12	mint leaves	12
½ tsp.	cumin seeds, toasted in a skillet over low heat for 1 minute, then ground	2 ml.
½ tsp.	coarse salt	2 ml.
8 or 9	ice cubes	8 or 9

Put the yogurt, water and eight mint leaves in the container of an electric blender, and blend for half a minute or until the mint is finely chopped. Add the cumin, salt and ice cubes, and continue blending for an additional half minute, or until the drink is frothy (the ice cubes will not disintegrate fully).

Pour the drink with the ice into tall glasses. Squeeze the four remaining mint leaves lightly in your fingers to release the fragrance, and place them on top. Serve immediately.

JULIE SAHNI
CLASSIC INDIAN COOKING

Suzy Sunflower

The technique of making pineapple juice is demonstrated on pages 36-37.

To make about 1 cup [¼ liter]

½ cup	yogurt (recipe, page 165)	125 ml.
½ cup	fresh orange or pineapple juice	125 ml.
¼ cup	raw unsalted sunflower seeds, hulled	50 ml.

Combine all of the ingredients in a blender or food processor. Blend until smooth. Pour into a tall glass.

GAIL SCHIOLER
THE NON-DRINKER'S DRINK BOOK

Tiger's Milk

To make about 2 cups [1/2 liter]

3/4 cup	yogurt *(recipe, page 165)*	175 ml.
3/4 cup	fresh orange juice	175 ml.
1	banana, sliced	1
3 tbsp.	brewer's yeast	45 ml.
1	egg	1
1 to 2 tbsp.	honey	15 to 30 ml.

Combine all of the ingredients in a blender or food processor and blend until smooth. Serve at once.

GAIL SCHIOLER
THE NON-DRINKER'S DRINK BOOK

Yogurt Drink

Ayran

The original version of this recipe calls for Bulgarian yogurt—an especially thick type not available in America. Drained yogurt makes a suitable substitute.

To make about 2 1/2 quarts [2 1/2 liters]

8 cups	yogurt *(recipe, page 165)*, placed in a cheesecloth-lined colander set over a bowl, refrigerated and drained for 24 hours	2 liters
5 cups	cold water, soda water or sparkling mineral water	1 1/4 liters
	crushed ice (optional)	

Put the drained yogurt in a large bowl and beat it with a wooden spoon or wire whisk until creamy. Add the water gradually, beating all the time. Pour the drink into a large serving pitcher and add crushed ice, if you like.

K. KATRANDZHIEV
BULGARSKOTO KISELO MLYAKO

Rose-flavored Yogurt Drink

Lassi

For a classic *lassi*, the quality of the yogurt is of prime importance. It should be slightly sour so that when it is diluted it still retains a strong yogurt flavor. Also, it is essential that

the yogurt be rich and creamy, or else the *lassi* will taste watery. Since commercial yogurt lacks the right creaminess, you will need to add a little cream to enrich it.

To make about 2 cups [1/2 liter]

1 1/2 cups	plain yogurt *(recipe, page 165)*	375 ml.
1 tbsp.	rose water	15 ml.
3 tbsp.	heavy cream	45 ml.
6 tbsp.	sugar	90 ml.
9 or 10	ice cubes	9 or 10

Put the yogurt, rose water, cream and sugar in the container of an electric blender, and blend for half a minute, or until the sugar is fully dissolved. Add the ice cubes, and continue blending for another half minute, or until the yogurt drink is frothy (the ice cubes will not disintegrate fully). Pour the drink into tall glasses and serve.

JULIE SAHNI
CLASSIC INDIAN COOKING

Soda Fountain Drinks

Chocolate Ice Cream Shake

The technique of making milk shakes is demonstrated on page 53. The shake can be varied by using any fruit syrup instead of chocolate syrup, or substituting another flavor of ice cream. For a malted milk shake, add a spoonful of malted-milk powder.

To make about 1 cup [1/4 liter]

2 tbsp.	chocolate syrup	30 ml.
3/4 cup	half-and-half cream, chilled	175 ml.
about 1 tsp.	superfine sugar	about 5 ml.
1/4 cup	vanilla ice cream *(recipe, page 165)*	50 ml.
	heavy cream, whipped	

Place the chocolate syrup, milk, sugar to taste, and the vanilla ice cream in a blender. Blend the ingredients until the mixture is smooth. Pour the milk shake into a chilled tall glass and serve at once, the top covered with a generous dollop of whipped heavy cream.

LOUIS P. DE GOUY
THE GOLD COOK BOOK

Chocolate Syrup

To make 2 cups [½ liter]

2 to 3 oz.	unsweetened chocolate, cut into small pieces	60 to 90 g.
1 cup	sugar	¼ liter
¼ tsp.	salt	1 ml.
1¼ cups	boiling water	300 ml.

In the top of a double boiler, combine the chocolate with the sugar and salt; gradually add the boiling water and cook this syrup over direct low heat for five minutes, stirring constantly. Place over hot water and let the syrup simmer gently for 10 minutes. Now beat the syrup hard with a rotary beater until it is thick; pour the syrup into a sterilized jar with a tight-fitting cover. Chill and store the syrup in the refrigerator; it will keep for months.

LOUIS P. DE GOUY
THE GOLD COOK BOOK

Frosted Chocolate Shake

The technique of making milk shakes in an electric blender is demonstrated on page 53.

To make about 1½ cups [375 ml.]

¾ cup	milk, chilled	175 ml.
2 to 3 tbsp.	chocolate syrup	30 to 45 ml.
1 tsp.	sugar	5 ml.
½ tsp.	vanilla extract	2 ml.
2 scoops	vanilla ice cream (recipe, page 165)	2 scoops

Combine the chocolate syrup, milk, sugar and vanilla extract in a shaker or glass jar; shake vigorously. Add the ice cream and shake again. Serve immediately, pouring the mixture into a tall glass.

JOSH GASPERO (EDITOR)
HERSHEY'S 1934 COOKBOOK

Chocolate Ice Cream Soda

To make 1¼ cups [300 ml.]

3 tbsp.	chocolate syrup	45 ml.
1 tbsp.	heavy cream	15 ml.
1 scoop	chocolate, mint or vanilla ice cream	1 scoop
	soda water	

Put the syrup and cream in a tall glass. Mix well. Add the ice cream and fill up with soda water. Stir thoroughly.

FANNIE MERRITT FARMER
THE FANNIE FARMER COOKBOOK

Banana Milk Shake

Bananenmilkshake

To make about 3 cups [¾ liter]

2 cups	milk	½ liter
2	bananas, sliced	2
¼ cup	heavy cream	50 ml.
2 tbsp.	sugar	30 ml.
1 tsp.	fresh lemon juice	5 ml.
1	egg yolk	1
	ice cubes	

Place the milk, bananas, cream, sugar, lemon juice and egg yolk in a blender, and blend until they become a smooth, homogeneous mixture. Place ice cubes in glasses and pour the banana milk shake over them.

FEEST: TIPS EN RECEPTEN VOOR PARTIJTJES THUIS EN BUITEN

Chilled Fresh Lemon Frosted

To make about 1 quart [1 liter]

¾ cup	sugar	175 ml.
4	lemons, peeled, the juice strained	4
3 cups	water	¾ liter
6 scoops	lemon sherbet	6 scoops
12	fresh or candied mint leaves	12

Combine the sugar, lemon juice and ¾ cup [175 ml.] of the water in a nonreactive saucepan. Boil the mixture for two minutes, then remove it from the heat and add the lemon peel. Let stand for five minutes. Discard the lemon peel, add the remaining water and chill. For each serving, put one scoop of lemon sherbet into a 5- to 6-ounce [150- to 180-ml.] glass. Fill the glass with the chilled lemonade. Garnish the drinks with the mint leaves.

IDA BAILEY ALLEN
BEST LOVED RECIPES OF THE AMERICAN PEOPLE

Orange Shake

Oranjeshake

To make about 3 cups [¾ liter]

2 cups	milk	½ liter
2 tbsp.	heavy cream	30 ml.
1 cup	fresh orange juice	¼ liter
1 tbsp.	fresh lemon juice	15 ml.
3 tbsp.	sugar	45 ml.
	ice cubes	

Put all the ingredients, except the ice cubes, into a blender and blend for two minutes. Put one or two ice cubes into each glass, pour the drink over them and serve immediately.

FEEST: TIPS EN RECEPTEN VOOR PARTIJTJES THUIS EN BUITEN

Peach Honey Float

To make about 2 ½ quarts [2 ½ liters]

3	medium-sized ripe peaches, peeled, halved, pitted and coarsely crushed	3
½ cup	honey	125 ml.
1 quart	milk	1 liter
½ tsp.	almond extract	2 ml.
1 quart	vanilla ice cream (recipe, page 165)	1 liter

Combine the peaches and honey. Add half of the milk; beat or blend, then add the rest of the milk, the almond extract and half of the ice cream. Beat until smooth. Pour into tall glasses and top with the remaining ice cream.

HAZEL BERTO
COOKING WITH HONEY

Coffee-Maple Punch

To make about 5 cups [1 ¼ liters]

1	egg	1
2 tbsp.	crushed ice	30 ml.
¼ cup	maple syrup	50 ml.
3 cups	light cream	¾ liter
1 cup	cold strong coffee	¼ liter
4 scoops	vanilla ice cream (recipe, page 165)	4 scoops

Put the egg, the crushed ice, the maple syrup, 1 cup [¼ liter] of the cream, and the coffee into a shaker. Shake thoroughly,

strain into a pitcher, add the rest of the cream and stir well. Pour into four tall glasses and top with the ice cream before serving. Serve with a straw and a long-handled spoon.

BERTHA E. L. STOCKBRIDGE
WHAT TO DRINK — THE BLUE BOOK OF BEVERAGES

Old-fashioned Root Beer

To make a smaller quantity of root beer, reduce the ingredients proportionately.

To make about 10 quarts [10 liters]

2 oz.	bottle root-beer concentrate	60 ml.
8 cups	sugar	2 liters
10 quarts	water, plus 1 cup [¼ liter]	10 liters
¼ oz.	package active dry yeast or ⅗ oz. [18 g.] cake fresh yeast, mixed with 1 cup [¼ liter] tepid water and left to stand for 10 minutes	7 g.

Add the root-beer concentrate to the sugar, mix well and dissolve in 10 quarts [10 liters] of tepid water. Add the yeast mixture, stir well and bottle the root beer immediately, fastening the caps securely. Set in a warm, draft-free place for three to four days until the root beer becomes effervescent. Serve chilled.

DELINEATOR HOME INSTITUTE
BEVERAGES FOR PARTIES

Ginger Rickey

To make 1 cup [¼ liter]

	crushed ice	
2 tbsp.	ginger syrup	30 ml.
2 tbsp.	cherry syrup, made by the recipe for basic fruit syrup (recipe, page 164)	30 ml.
1 tsp.	fresh lime juice	5 ml.
⅔ cup	soda water, chilled	150 ml.
	lemon slices	
	maraschino cherries	

Fill a chilled, tall 12-ounce [375-ml.] glass one quarter full with crushed ice. Add the ginger syrup, cherry syrup and lime juice, and fill with soda water. Stir well and decorate with lemon slices and cherries.

C. H. BOEGLIN
SUNDAES

Ginger Syrup for Home-Style Ginger Ale

Use this concentrated ginger syrup for mixing with soda water to produce an amazingly bright-tasting, vividly gingery drink by blending about 1 tablespoon [15 ml.] of syrup with ¾ cup [175 ml.] of chilled soda water. Incidentally, although this syrup is intended as a beverage base, a spoonful over vanilla ice cream is luscious.

To make 2 cups [½ liter]		
6 oz.	fresh ginger, peeled and finely chopped (about 1 cup [¼ liter])	175 g.
2 cups	water	½ liter
1 ¼ cups	sugar	300 ml.

Bring the ginger to a boil with the water in an enameled or stainless-steel saucepan. Simmer for five minutes, then let stand for 12 to 24 hours, covered with a cloth.

Strain through a sieve lined with two layers of cheesecloth; squeeze the pulp in the cloth to extract all possible juice. Return the juice to the saucepan, add the sugar and bring to a boil over medium heat, stirring. Boil gently for five minutes, skimming off any froth. Cool the mixture, strain it into a bottle and refrigerate.

HELEN WITTY AND ELIZABETH SCHNEIDER COLCHIE
BETTER THAN STORE-BOUGHT

Ginger Beer

This is the traditional homemade soft drink in much of West Africa. There are many variations in the proportion of ginger to water and in the kind of fruit added (sometimes pineapple is used instead of citrus). Some versions add yeast. This recipe was developed from directions of friends in Sierra Leone. It makes a strong "beer" that can be diluted with water or soda water to produce a lighter drink, although some people prefer to serve it full-strength over ice cubes.

To make about 1 ½ quarts [1 ½ liters]		
¾ to 1 cup	grated fresh ginger	175 to 250 ml.
3 cups	boiling water, plus 3 cups [¾ liter] cold water	¾ liter
½ cup	fresh lime or lemon juice	125 ml.
6	whole cloves or one 1-inch [2½-cm.] cinnamon stick (optional)	6
1 ½ cups	sugar	375 ml.

Place the ginger in a large, heavy earthenware or wooden bowl. Set the bowl on a pad or folded towel and pound the ginger with a wooden masher. (Use a mortar and pestle if you have one, of course.) The root fibers must be well broken down, as near to a pulp as you can get them. When the ginger is well pounded, pour the boiling water over the pulp. Let the ginger stand for two hours. Strain through several thicknesses of cheesecloth, pressing and squeezing the pulp to extract all of the liquid. Return the liquid to the bowl. Add the cold water, lime or lemon juice, and the cloves or cinnamon, if you are using it. Stir the mixture and set it aside for an hour or so to settle. Decant the liquid carefully, keeping back the sediment. Add the sugar and stir the ginger beer until the sugar dissolves. Serve chilled.

ELLEN GIBSON WILSON
A WEST AFRICAN COOK BOOK

Ginger Ale

Boiling the ginger twice gives the drink a richer flavor. This ginger ale will keep for a week at room temperature; in a refrigerator, it will keep for four to five weeks.

To make about 3 quarts [3 liters]		
2 tbsp.	finely chopped fresh ginger	30 ml.
1 tsp.	peppercorns	5 ml.
2 ½ quarts	water	2 ½ liters
2 ½ cups	sugar	625 ml.
12 to 16	lemons, the juice strained	12 to 16

In a mortar, grind the ginger to a paste. Mix the ginger paste and peppercorns with 1 quart [1 liter] of water. Bring to a boil and simmer for two to three minutes. Cool; then strain the liquid through a colander lined with muslin or cheesecloth. Reserve the strained liquid. Return the ginger and pepper remaining in the cloth to the pan; add another quart of water and bring to a boil. Simmer for a few minutes, strain and mix with the reserved ginger liquid.

Over low heat, dissolve the sugar in the remaining water without letting this syrup boil. Cool, and strain the syrup into the ginger liquid. Add lemon juice to taste.

KALA PRIMLANI
INDIAN COOKING

Broths

Seven-Vegetable Broth

The technique of making vegetable broth is demonstrated on pages 56-57, where the water is added to the vegetables and then brought slowly to a boil in order to draw out the maximum scum from the ingredients. Turnips can be used instead of the parsnips, and the celeriac can be omitted.

To make 1 quart [1 liter]

2 to 3 quarts	cold water	2 to 3 liters
4	large carrots, finely chopped	4
4	medium-sized onions, finely chopped	4
2	leeks, white part only, finely chopped	2
1 cup	tomatoes, skinned and seeded	¼ liter
2	celery ribs, finely chopped	2
2	parsnips, finely chopped	2
1	celeriac	1
4	sprigs parsley	4
2	garlic cloves	2
1	bay leaf	1
1½ tsp.	salt	7 ml.
10	black peppercorns	10
½ tsp.	sugar	2 ml.
2 tsp.	fresh lemon juice	10 ml.
	freshly ground pepper	
2 tbsp.	finely cut fresh chives, or 2 scallions, white and green parts, thinly sliced	30 ml.

Bring 2 quarts [2 liters] of cold water to a boil. Add all of the vegetables—except the celeriac—and the parsley, garlic, bay leaf, salt and peppercorns. Peel and chop the celeriac and add it immediately to the rest of the vegetables—it darkens quickly when left exposed to air.

Reduce the heat and simmer the broth gently, partially covered, for two hours. As the water evaporates, add fresh cold water; you must keep the level constant throughout the two hours. Strain the broth and discard the solids. Return the broth to the saucepan and, over medium heat, reduce the broth until only 1 quart [1 liter] remains. Add the sugar and lemon juice. Taste for seasoning and adjust if needed. Sprinkle the chives or scallions over the broth before serving.

MICHÈLE URVATER AND DAVID LIEDERMAN
COOKING THE NOUVELLE CUISINE IN AMERICA

Vegetable Bouillon

Il Brodo Vegetale

To make about 2 quarts [2 liters]

2	large carrots, chopped	2
2	large potatoes, diced	2
2	small onions	2
1	leek, white and green parts, chopped	1
2	celery ribs with leaves, chopped	2
2	zucchini, chopped	2
3	large ripe tomatoes, peeled, seeded and chopped	3
1 cup	chopped cabbage leaves	¼ liter
1 cup	chopped green beans	¼ liter
⅓ cup	parsley sprigs	75 ml.
2 tbsp.	fresh basil leaves or 1 tsp. [5 ml.] dried basil	30 ml.
½ tsp	dried thyme	2 ml.
1 tbsp.	salt	15 ml.
1 tsp.	pepper	5 ml.
3 quarts	water	3 liters

Combine all the ingredients in a large, deep kettle. Bring to the boiling point. Reduce the heat to very low and simmer, covered, for about three hours, skimming when necessary. Stir occasionally. Strain the bouillon through a triple layer of cheesecloth, moistened and wrung dry.

NIKA HAZELTON
THE REGIONAL ITALIAN KITCHEN

Chicken Broth

To make about 1 quart [1 liter]

one 4 to 5 lb.	stewing chicken	one 2 to 2½ kg.
	cold water	
¼ cup	coarsely ground white rice	50 ml.
¼ cup	pearl barley	50 ml.
3 tbsp.	honey	45 ml.
	salt	

Cover the chicken with cold water in a large saucepan; put in the ground rice and barley and, when the water boils, add the honey. Let all simmer slowly for three hours, skimming often; when you find the liquid is reduced by a third of its original quantity, strain off the broth and season it with salt.

MRS. RUNDELL
MODERN DOMESTIC COOKERY

Plain Chicken Broth

Once the broth has been made, the chicken pieces can be eaten. If you use a stewing chicken to make this broth, you may have to cook it for two and one half hours.

To make about 1 quart [1 liter]

3 to 4 lb.	chicken, quartered	1½ to 2 kg.
5 cups	water	1¼ liters
	salt	
1	lettuce heart, chopped	1
	fresh chervil leaves	

Put the chicken pieces into a stewpan with the water and a very little salt; set it to boil, skim it well and then add the lettuce heart and a handful of chervil. Simmer the broth for about one hour, then strain it through a cloth into a bowl.

CHARLES ELMÉ FRANCATELLI
THE MODERN COOK

Vegetable Broth
Akhni

Ghee is Indian cooking fat, either clarified butter or made from vegetable fats. It can be bought from Indian grocers.

To make about 1½ quarts [1½ liters]

3 tbsp.	ghee or light vegetable oil	45 ml.
2	small unpeeled onions, quartered	2
1	carrot, cut into 1-inch [2½-cm.] slices	1
1	large unpeeled garlic clove, crushed	1
¼-inch	slice fresh ginger	6-mm.
1 tsp.	cumin seeds	5 ml.
2 tsp.	coriander seeds	10 ml.
3-inch	cinnamon stick	7½-cm.
3	black cardamoms or 6 green cardamoms	3
8	whole cloves	8
1 tsp.	black peppercorns	5 ml.
1 tsp.	coarse salt	5 ml.
2 quarts	cold water	2 liters

Heat the *ghee* or vegetable oil in a 3-quart [3-liter] stockpot or deep saucepan, and add all the other ingredients except the water. Fry the vegetables and spices over medium heat for 10 minutes, or until the onions are wilted and begin to brown. Add the water and bring it to a boil. Reduce the heat, cover the pot partially with a lid and let the mixture simmer for at least one hour, preferably two hours. When cool, strain the broth through a double layer of cheesecloth into a con-

tainer and refrigerate for two hours. Spoon off the fat from the surface, then refrigerate the broth until needed. It may be stored indefinitely in the refrigerator if boiled for five minutes every four days, or may be frozen.

JULIE SAHNI
CLASSIC INDIAN COOKING

Garlic Soup
Aïgo-Bouido

The technique of making garlic soup is shown on pages 58-59.

Aïgo-bouido is Provençal for "boiled water." It is believed to be a cure-all. The rustic accompaniment is always dried bread crusts. The simplest version—reserved for those who are seriously ill—is nothing but a couple of cloves of garlic boiled in water with a branch of thyme and a sage leaf, strained over some crusts of dried bread soaked in olive oil. A rich *aïgo-bouido* (more garlic and egg yolks) is an obligatory course in every Provençal Christmas Eve menu.

To make about 1 quart [1 liter]

1 quart	water	1 liter
10 to 15	garlic cloves, unpeeled and lightly crushed	10 to 15
1	bay leaf	1
2 or 3	sage leaves	2 or 3
½ tsp.	thyme	2 ml.
	salt	
	dried bread crusts, crumbled	
Binding pommade		
1	egg	1
2	egg yolks	2
⅓ cup	freshly grated Parmesan cheese, or mixed Parmesan and Gruyère	75 ml.
	freshly ground pepper	
¼ cup	olive oil	50 ml.

Bring the water to a boil and add the herbs, garlic and salt to taste. Cover and simmer for 40 minutes, strain through a sieve, discard the herbs and press the garlic through into the liquid. Taste for salt.

Combine the egg, egg yolks, grated cheese and pepper in a bowl, stir and then beat with a small whisk until creamy. Slowly pour in the oil, beating all the time; then whisk in a ladleful of the bouillon. Stir the contents of the bowl into the bouillon, transfer it to a saucepan and whisk it over low-to-medium heat until it thickens slightly—just enough not to be watery. Pour it over a handful of dried crusts of bread in a preheated tureen, and serve immediately.

RICHARD OLNEY
THE FRENCH MENU COOKBOOK

Mutton Broth

If mutton is unavailable, lamb neck can be substituted. Other vegetables, such as an onion, a carrot and a garlic clove, may be added if desired; a bouquet garni may be substituted for the parsley and thyme.

To make about 7 cups [1 ¾ liters]

3 lb.	mutton neck, cut into pieces	1½ kg.
2 quarts	cold water	2 liters
2	turnips, sliced	2
3 or 4	sprigs parsley	3 or 4
1	sprig thyme	1
	salt	

Put the mutton into a stewpan with the water; place the stewpan on the heat to boil, skim it well, and then add the turnips, parsley, thyme and a little salt. When it has boiled gently by the side of the heat for one and one half hours, skim off the fat from the surface, and then let the broth be strained through a sieve lined with muslin into a bowl.

CHARLES ELMÉ FRANCATELLI
THE MODERN COOK

Savory Beef Tea

Be careful not to have too much of any one vegetable, but rather an agreeable blending of flavors. One small teacupful of the vegetables cut up and mixed will be quite sufficient. Any flavoring that is objected to may be omitted.

To make about 2½ cups [625 ml.]

½ lb.	lean juicy beef, finely chopped	¼ kg.
about 2 cups	cold water	about ½ liter
½ tsp.	salt	2 ml.
1	small piece each carrot, turnip, onion and celery, diced	1
1	small bouquet garni	1
3 or 4	peppercorns	3 or 4
1	small mace blade	1

Place all the ingredients in a heatproof jar. Stir well, cover, and place the jar in a saucepan with cold water to reach three quarters of the way up the sides. Bring to a boil and simmer for two to three hours, replenishing the water in the saucepan as necessary. Remove the jar from the saucepan, stir the contents with a fork, and strain the tea through a sieve, pressing well.

FLORENCE B. JACK
COOKERY FOR EVERY HOUSEHOLD

Beers and Wines

Cherry Ale

To make a smaller quantity of ale, reduce the ingredients proportionately.

Some makers add a few cloves to make the ale spicy. When all is drunk, the cherries are used like those of cherry brandy, as preserves in tarts and pies.

To make 4½ quarts [4½ liters]

3 to 4 lb.	morello cherries	1½ to 2 kg.
4 to 6 cups	sugar	1 to 1½ liters
3½ quarts	ale or strong beer	3½ liters

Prick the cherries with a needle and put them in an earthenware jar or wooden tub. Sprinkle over them the sugar according to the sweetness liked, but never in greater proportion than 6 cups [1½ liters] of sugar to 4 pounds [2 kg.] of cherries, as the fermentation will not absorb it. Then fill the jar or tub with the beer or ale, cover and leave to ferment in a warm place. Cork down when fermentation has ceased and store for at least six months—a year is better.

MARY AYLETT
COUNTRY WINES

Dandelion Beer

To make about 4 quarts [4 liters]

1 quart	young dandelion plants, washed, the hairs removed from the taproots	1 liter
1-inch	piece fresh ginger, bruised	2½-cm.
1	lemon, the peel thinly pared, the juice strained	1
4 quarts	water	4 liters
2¼ cups	brown sugar	550 ml.
¼ cup	cream of tartar	50 ml.
¼ oz.	package beer yeast	7 g.

Boil the dandelion plants, ginger and lemon peel in the water for 10 minutes. Place the sugar and cream of tartar in an earthenware jar and strain the boiling mixture over them. Stir until they are dissolved. When the mixture is lukewarm, add the lemon juice and yeast, cover the jar, and leave in a warm place for three days. Siphon off into screw-top bottles and leave for a week before drinking.

WILMA PATERSON
A COUNTRY CUP

Black Currant and Lemon Beer

Shypuchka

To make about 8 quarts [8 liters]

2 lb.	black currant leaves	1 kg.
8 quarts	boiling water	8 liters
2	lemons, thinly sliced, the seeds removed	2
2 cups	sugar	½ liter
¼ oz.	package beer yeast, mixed with a little tepid water and left to stand for 10 minutes	7 g.
	raisins	

Place the black currant leaves in a large pot and pour the boiling water over them. Add the lemon slices and the sugar. Cover the pot with a cloth and let the mixture cool until it is lukewarm. Add the dissolved yeast. Put the pot in a warm place and let it stand for 24 hours, or until bubbles form on the surface of the mixture.

Strain the mixture through cheesecloth or muslin, then bottle it—adding one raisin to each bottle. Cap the bottles. Two hours before serving, place a bottle on ice or in the refrigerator to chill it.

N. I. GEORGIEVSKY, M. E. MELMAN, E. A. SHADURA
AND A. S. SHEMJAKINSKY
UKRAINIAN CUISINE

Kvass from Black Rye Bread

Kvas od Suvog Hleba

Kvass is the national drink in Eastern European countries. It is slightly effervescent.

To make about 15 quarts [15 liters]

6 lb.	very dry black rye bread, sliced	3 kg.
about 18 quarts	boiling water	about 18 liters
four ¼ oz.	packages active dry yeast mashed to a paste with a little tepid water, or four ⅗ oz. [18 g.] cakes fresh yeast	four 7 g.
2 cups	sugar	½ liter
1	lemon, sliced, the seeds removed	1
	seedless white raisins	

Put the bread in a large pot or bucket and pour the boiling water over it. Cover with a cloth and leave for eight hours. Then strain the liquid into another large container, discarding the bread. Add the yeast paste, sugar and lemon slices. Mix well, cover the container and let the mixture stand for another eight hours. Then strain the liquid through a sieve lined with cheesecloth or muslin and pour it into bottles. Drop two raisins into each bottle, cork tightly and store the bottles in a cool place. In a couple of days the kvass will be ready to drink.

SPASENIJA-PATA MARKOVIĆ (EDITOR)
VELIKI NARODNI KUVAR

Small Beer

Diod Fain

To make a smaller quantity of beer, reduce the ingredients proportionately.

To make about 23 quarts [23 liters]

3 cups	dandelion leaves	¾ liter
2 cups	nettle leaves	½ liter
23 quarts	water	23 liters
two 4-inch	pieces fresh ginger, bruised	two 10-cm.
2 tsp.	grated lemon peel	10 ml.
2 tbsp.	grated orange peel	30 ml.
8 cups	granulated sugar	2 liters
2½ cups	brown sugar	625 ml.
five ¼ oz.	packages beer yeast	five 7 g.
	sugar syrup (recipe, page 164)	

Wash the dandelion and nettle leaves, put them in a large pan, cover them with 14 quarts [14 liters] of the water and add the ginger and the lemon and orange peels. Bring the mixture to a boil and simmer for about 30 minutes. Put the sugar in another large pan and strain the boiling liquid into it, stirring well until the sugar has dissolved. Then add the remaining 9 quarts [9 liters] of cold water to this mixture. Let the liquid cool until it is lukewarm, then stir in the yeast. Cover the pan with a clean cloth and leave in a warm place until fermentation has ceased. Skim the surface and bottle the beer, adding 1 tablespoon [15 ml.] of sugar syrup to each bottle. Cap securely. The beer will be ready for drinking in seven days.

S. MINWEL TIBBOTT
WELSH FARE

Quickly Made Ginger Beer

The technique of making ginger beer is shown on pages 66-67.

To make about 4 quarts [4 liters]

3-inch	piece fresh ginger, peeled and chopped (about 1 ½ oz. [45 g.])	8-cm.
1 ½ cups	sugar	375 ml.
1	lemon, the peel thinly pared, the juice strained	1
4 quarts	boiling water	4 liters
¼ oz.	package beer yeast, mixed with a little tepid water and left to stand for 10 minutes	7 g.

Crush the ginger in a mortar. Put the ginger in a large bowl with the sugar and lemon peel, and pour in the boiling water. Leave the mixture until it is lukewarm, then add the lemon juice and yeast mixture. Cover the bowl and let the mixture ferment for 12 hours or overnight. Strain the ginger beer through several layers of dampened cheesecloth or muslin; bottle it in strong 12-ounce [375-ml.] bottles.

MRS. LESLIE
THE AMERICAN FAMILY COOK BOOK

Cider

The technique of making cider is shown on pages 72-73.

To prevent bacteria from spoiling the cider, it is essential to sterilize the apples. The apples can be chopped and puréed—a small batch at a time—in a food processor; there will then be no need to add the sugar syrup or to crush them daily while they ferment. Because of the low alcohol content of cider it may sour unless it is racked through filter paper.

To make about 4 quarts [4 liters]

7 quarts	water	7 liters
1	Campden tablet, crushed	1
10 lb.	apples	5 kg.
	sugar syrup made with ½ cup [125 ml.] sugar and 1 quart [1 liter] water, cooled	
2 tbsp.	fresh lemon juice	30 ml.
⅙ oz.	package all-purpose wine yeast, mixed with a little tepid water and left to stand for 10 minutes	5 g.

To sterilize the apples, put 7 quarts [7 liters] of water into a bucket and dissolve the Campden tablet in it. Add the apples and stir. Cover the bucket and leave it for two minutes; then drain the apples and rinse them under cold running water. Rinse the bucket.

Slice the apples, cutting out any bruised parts lest they impair the color and the flavor of the cider. Put the sugar syrup and lemon juice into the bucket and add the sliced apples. Add the yeast to the apples and stir well.

Crush the apples with a pestle. Cover the bucket and leave the mixture to ferment in a warm place for a week, crushing the apples daily.

Put the apple pulp or purée through a wine press and collect the juice in a 4-quart [4-liter] fermentation jug. Fit in a fermentation lock and leave the cider in a cool place for about two weeks to allow the sediment to settle. Rack the cider through filter paper into a clean jar and bottle it immediately. Store the bottles upright in a cool place until the cider has completely cleared.

PETITS PROPOS CULINAIRES

Maple Cider Wine

The technique of making cider is demonstrated on pages 72-73. Use genuine maple syrup—not maple-flavored pancake syrup—for the wine.

To make about 3 ½ quarts [3 ½ liters]

2 cups	maple syrup	½ liter
3 quarts	freshly made apple cider	3 liters
⅙ oz.	package all-purpose wine yeast	5 g.

Put the maple syrup in a pan and heat it until it is lukewarm. Pour the cider into a crock and stir the warm syrup into it. Sprinkle the yeast into the mixture and cover the crock with a heavy towel. Keep it in a warm place for two weeks, stirring daily. Strain the wine into a fermentation jar, cover it with a fermentation lock and set the wine away in a cool place to work quietly for three to four months. Bottle when it is perfectly clear and still.

BLANCHE POWNALL GARRETT
CANADIAN COUNTRY PRESERVES & WINES

Mulberry Wine, Port-Style

The technique of making wine is shown on pages 74-75.

To make 4 quarts [4 liters]

5 lb.	mulberries, stems attached	2 ½ kg.
4 quarts	water, plus 2 cups [½ liter] cooled boiled water	4 liters
2	Campden tablets, crushed separately	2
6 cups	sugar	1 ½ liters
2 ½ tbsp.	citric acid	37 ml.
¼ tsp.	grape tannin	1 ml.
⅙ oz.	package port wine yeast or all-purpose wine yeast	5 g.
	yeast nutrient	

Place the mulberries in a nonreactive pan with 4 quarts [4 liters] of water and bring to a boil. Add the sugar and simmer for a few minutes, stirring until the sugar has dissolved. Cool the mixture. Add the citric acid, grape tannin and one crushed Campden tablet. Pour the mixture into a wide-necked fermentation jar, cover the jar securely with plastic wrap and let it stand overnight. Add the yeast and nutrient, replace the cover and leave the mixture in a warm—70° F. [20° C.]—place for about a week, stirring daily.

Strain the mulberry mixture through a cheesecloth-lined sieve and pour the liquid into a 4-quart fermentation jug. Top up with the cooled boiled water if necessary, and fit with a fermentation lock. Rack into a clean jug after all fermentation has ceased—in about three weeks—and add the other Campden tablet. Let the wine clear, and rack again before bottling. The wine will be ready in about 18 months.

S. M. TRITTON
GUIDE TO BETTER WINE AND BEER MAKING FOR BEGINNERS

Blueberry Wine

The technique of making wine is shown on pages 74-75.

	To make 4 quarts [4 liters]	
3 quarts	hot water, plus about 2 cups [½ liter] cooled boiled water	3 liters
3 lb.	blueberries	1½ kg.
5 cups	sugar	1¼ liters
1 tsp.	acid blend	5 ml.
	yeast nutrient	
½ tsp.	pectic enzyme powder	2 ml.
¼ tsp.	grape tannin	1 ml.
⅙ oz.	package all-purpose wine yeast	5 g.
1	Campden tablet, crushed	1
	sugar syrup (recipe, page 164) (optional)	

Pour the hot water over the blueberries. Add the sugar and stir until it dissolves. Let the mixture cool to 70° F. [20° C.]. Add the acid blend, yeast nutrient, pectic enzyme powder, grape tannin and yeast. Stir the mixture and let it stand for five days, stirring once each day. Strain the mixture and pour the juice into a 4-quart [4-liter] fermentation jug. Top up the jug with cooled boiled water, attach a fermentation lock to the jug, and set the wine aside in a warm place to ferment for about four weeks. When the wine is completely still, add the Campden tablet to it and rack the wine. Adjust the sweetness, if desired, by adding sugar syrup. Return the wine to the fermentation jug and attach the lock, in case the wine ferments further. Rack the wine a second time when clear. Bottle immediately.

DONALD L. ACE AND JAMES H. EAKIN JR.
WINEMAKING AS A HOBBY

Red Currant Wine

The technique of making wine is shown on pages 72-73.

	To make 4 quarts [4 liters]	
2½ lb.	red currants (about 5 cups [1¼ liters])	1¼ kg.
1 lb.	seedless white raisins, chopped	½ kg.
14 cups	water, plus about 2 cups [½ liter] cooled boiled water	3½ liters
1	Campden tablet, crushed and dissolved in ⅓ cup [75 ml.] tepid water	1
5 cups	sugar	1¼ liters
⅙ oz.	package all-purpose wine yeast, mixed with ¼ cup [50 ml.] tepid water and left to stand for 10 minutes	5 g.
	yeast nutrient	
3	ripe bananas	3

Put the currants in a large, wide-necked fermenting vessel, such as a bucket, and crush them well with a pestle. Add the raisins and mix in 2 quarts [2 liters] of the water. Add the Campden solution.

Put half of the sugar and 1 quart [1 liter] of the water in a pan, bring to a boil, and boil for two minutes. Cool this syrup, then mix it into the currant pulp. Add the yeast mixture and the nutrient. Cover the fermenting vessel with a tight lid or a sheet of plastic wrap tied down with string. Let the mixture ferment for eight days, stirring daily. After four days, peel the bananas, mash them to a pulp and add them to the fermenting mixture.

After eight days, strain the wine through a sieve lined with a double layer of dampened cheesecloth or muslin. Gather up the edges of the cloth and squeeze tightly to extract all of the liquid from the pulp. Clean the fermenting vessel and return the strained wine to it. Boil the rest of the sugar in the remaining 2 cups [½ liter] of water for two minutes, let the syrup cool and add it to the wine. Cover the fermenting vessel as before and let the wine ferment for three to four days. Carefully pour the wine into a 4-quart [4-liter] fermentation jug, leaving behind as much sediment as you can. Then fill up the jug to where the neck begins with cooled boiled water; fit a fermentation lock in the neck of the jug and leave the wine until all fermentation has ceased—about four weeks. Bottle and store the wine.

H. E. BRAVERY
THE COMPLETE BOOK OF HOME WINEMAKING

Date Wine

Isinglass is a clarifying agent. If it is not available, substitute ½ teaspoon [2 ml.] of pectic enzyme powder. The technique of making wine is demonstrated on pages 74-75.

	To make about 4 quarts [4 liters]	
4 quarts	water, plus 2½ quarts [2½ liters] boiling water	4 liters
3 to 4 lb.	dried dates, halved, pitted and chopped, about 10 pits reserved	1½ to 2 kg.
2	lemons, the peel thinly pared, the juice strained	2
½ oz.	isinglass	15 g.
⅙ oz.	package all-purpose wine yeast, mixed with a little tepid water and left to stand for 10 minutes	5 g.

Pour 4 quarts [4 liters] of water into a large pan and add the dates and the reserved date pits. Bring the mixture to a boil and simmer for two hours. When the cooking is almost done, add the lemon peel; finish simmering, remove the pan from the heat and add the lemon juice.

Leave the mixture in the pan until it is tepid, then strain it into a cask or another large container. Reserve the date pulp. Ladle about ½ cup [125 ml.] of the warm, strained liquid into a glass. Melt the isinglass in it, then stir the mixture well into the liquid in the cask. Add the yeast. Leave the cask, covered, in a warm place for five days for the wine to ferment. Put the date pulp in a basin, pour 2½ quarts [2½ liters] of boiling water over it and store it in a cool place.

Rack off the wine into a 4-quart [4-liter] fermentation jug. Strain the liquid from the date pulp and use it to top up the wine in the jug so that it comes to just above the neck. Cover the jug with a fermentation lock. The wine can be drunk in a few months, but it will be much improved if it is racked into a clean cask after about six months and kept for a year before it is bottled.

MARY AYLETT
COUNTRY WINES

Plum Port

The technique of making wine is shown on pages 74-75.

	To make about 4 quarts [4 liters]	
8 lb.	ripe, firm blue plums, pitted, 6 pits reserved	4 kg.
½ cup	lemon juice	125 ml.
4 quarts	boiling water	4 liters
⅙ oz.	package all-purpose wine yeast, mixed with a little tepid water and left to stand for 10 minutes	5 g.
6 cups	sugar	1½ liters

Put the plums and reserved plum pits in a large crock and crush them with a wooden mallet, until the juice runs freely. Add the lemon juice and boiling water. Leave this mixture until it is lukewarm, then add the yeast mixture and 2 cups [½ liter] of the sugar.

Cover the crock and let it stand in a warm place for two weeks, stirring the mixture several times each day.

Put the remaining sugar in a large vessel and strain the plum mixture over the sugar, through a sieve lined with cheesecloth or muslin. Stir until the sugar is dissolved.

Transfer the mixture to a 4-quart [4-liter] fermentation jug, fit a fermentation lock in the jug and keep it in the same warm place for six weeks. Rack the liquid into a clean jug and set it away in a cool place for a couple of months until it is still and clear. Bottle, and store in a cool, dark corner for at least a year.

BLANCHE POWNALL GARRETT
CANADIAN COUNTRY PRESERVES & WINES

Elderberry Wine

The technique of making wine is shown on pages 74-75.

	To make 4 quarts [4 liters]	
3 lb.	elderberries (about 6 cups [1½ liters])	1½ kg.
½ lb.	seedless white raisins, chopped	¼ kg.
4 cups	sugar	1 liter
1 tsp.	acid blend	5 ml.
½ tsp.	pectic enzyme powder	2 ml.
1 tsp.	malt extract	5 ml.
14 cups	water, plus about 2 cups [½ liter] cooled boiled water	3½ liters
1 lb.	bananas, ripened until black	½ kg.
1	Campden tablet	1

Place the elderberries in a nylon or cheesecloth bag along with the raisins; tie the bag and drop it into a plastic bucket.

Add the sugar, acid blend, pectic enzyme powder and malt extract. Add 3 quarts [3 liters] of hot water and stir to dissolve the sugar.

Peel the bananas, cut them into pieces and simmer for 30 minutes in 2 cups [½ liter] of water. Strain the bananas without pressing the pulp and add the liquid to the bucket. Cover the container. When cooled to 75° F. [22° C.], add the yeast, and ferment for seven days, turning the bag of fruit each day. Lift the bag from the liquid and suspend it to drain; do not press. Place the liquid in a 4-quart [4-liter] jug, top up with cooled boiled water, attach a fermentation lock and ferment. Rack when fermentation is completed and add the Campden tablet. Rack again in two months and bottle. Age at least two years.

DONALD L. ACE AND JAMES H. EAKIN JR.
WINEMAKING AS A HOBBY

Carrot Wine

The technique of making wine is shown on pages 74-75.

To make 4 quarts [4 liters]

4 lb.	carrots, tops and hair roots removed, chopped	2 kg.
4 quarts	water, plus 2 cups [½ liter] cooled boiled water	4 liters
4 cups	sugar	1 liter
1 lb.	seedless white raisins, finely chopped	½ kg.
½ tsp.	grape tannin	2 ml.
1	Campden tablet, crushed	1
⅙ oz.	package all-purpose wine yeast	5 g.
½ tsp.	yeast energizer	2 ml.

Bring the carrots to a boil in 4 quarts [4 liters] of water and simmer them for about 15 minutes, or until they are tender. Place the sugar in a wide-necked fermentation jar. Strain the boiled carrot mixture through a cheesecloth-lined sieve, discard the carrots and pour the hot liquid over the sugar, stirring until the sugar has dissolved. Mix in the raisins, grape tannin and the crushed Campden tablet. Cover the jar securely with plastic wrap and let it stand overnight. Add the yeast and energizer, replace the cover and allow the mixture to ferment in a warm place—70° F. [20° C.]—for three to five days. Strain out the pulp and pour the liquid into a 4-quart fermentation jug. Top up with the cooled boiled water if necessary, and fit with a fermentation lock. When fermentation is complete—in about three weeks—rack the wine into a clean jug. Allow the wine to clear for about two months. Rack again before bottling.

S. M. TRITTON
GUIDE TO BETTER WINE AND BEER MAKING FOR BEGINNERS

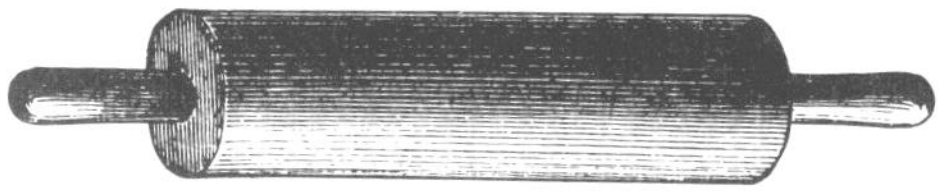

Rhubarb and Apple Wine

Instead of being crushed with a rolling pin, the rhubarb may be pulped in a blender or food processor. The technique of making wine is demonstrated on pages 74-75.

To make 4 quarts [4 liters]

1½ lb.	rhubarb, the leaves removed, the stalks wiped clean with a damp cloth and cut into small chunks	¾ kg.
1 lb.	sweet apples, washed, cored and peeled	½ kg.
1 lb.	raisins, chopped	½ kg.
3½ quarts	water, plus about 2 cups [½ liter] cooled boiled water	3½ liters
1	Campden tablet, crushed and dissolved in ⅓ cup [75 ml.] tepid water	1
3 cups	sugar	¾ liter
2 cups	freshly made strong black tea	½ liter
⅙ oz.	package all-purpose wine yeast, mixed with a little tepid water and left to stand for 10 minutes	5 g.
½ tsp.	yeast energizer	2 ml.

On a tray, crush the rhubarb chunks with a rolling pin, being careful not to lose any juice. Put the pulp and juices in a fermenting vessel. Chop the apples fine without losing the juice and add them to the rhubarb along with the raisins. Mix in 2 quarts [2 liters] of water and add the Campden solution. Cover and allow the mixture to stand overnight.

Bring half of the sugar and 1 quart [1 liter] of water to a boil and boil for two minutes. Let this syrup cool, then add it to the mixture in the fermenting vessel. Add the tea, yeast mixture and energizer. Cover the fermenting vessel with a tight lid or a sheet of plastic wrap tied down with string. Leave to ferment for 10 days, stirring daily.

Strain the mixture through a sieve lined with a double layer of dampened cheesecloth or muslin. Gather up the edges of the cloth and squeeze tightly to extract all of the liquid from the pulp. Clean the fermenting vessel and return the strained wine to it. Boil the rest of the sugar in 2 cups [½ liter] of water for two minutes and, when cooled, add it to the wine. Cover as before and leave for two to three days.

After this, pour the wine carefully into an 4-quart [4-liter] fermentation jug, leaving behind as much sediment as you can. Then fill up the jug to where the neck begins with cooled boiled water; fit a fermentation lock into the jug and leave the wine until all fermentation has ceased. Bottle and store the wine.

H. E. BRAVERY
THE COMPLETE BOOK OF HOME WINEMAKING

Pineapple and Grapefruit Wine

The technique of making wine is shown on pages 74-75.

To make 4 quarts [4 liters]		
4	fresh pineapples	4
4	grapefruits, juice strained	4
1 lb.	seedless white raisins, chopped	½ kg.
4 quarts	water	4 liters
2	Campden tablets, each crushed separately	2
½ tsp.	pectic enzyme powder	2 ml.
6 cups	sugar	1½ liters
	yeast nutrient	
⅙ oz.	package all-purpose wine yeast	5 g.

Top and tail the pineapples, but do not peel them. Cut them into small chunks and place them in a bucket. Add the grapefruit juice and raisins, and pour in 4 quarts [4 liters] of cold water. Add one crushed Campden tablet and the pectic enzyme. Cover the bucket and leave for 24 hours in a warm place. Stir in 2 cups [½ liter] of the sugar, the wine yeast and nutrient. Ferment for four to six days, then strain off the solids. Stir in the rest of the sugar and continue the fermentation in a 4-quart jug fitted with a fermentation lock. When fermentation is finished, rack the wine into a clean storage jar and add another crushed Campden tablet. When the wine is clear, rack it again and store it for six to nine months. Then bottle the wine and leave it for a further six months before serving it.

BEN TURNER
WINEMAKING & BREWING

Beet Wine

The technique of making wine is shown on pages 74-75. Carrots or turnips may be substituted for the beets.

To make 4 quarts [4 liters]		
3 lb.	beets, with the tops and taproots removed, coarsely chopped	1½ kg.
3 quarts	water, plus about 2 cups [½ liter] cooled boiled water	3 liters
6	oranges, the peel thinly pared, the juice strained	6
4-inch	piece fresh ginger, coarsely chopped	10-cm.
5½ cups	sugar	1⅜ liters
⅙ oz.	package all-purpose wine yeast	5 g.
	yeast nutrient	

Place the beets and 3 quarts [3 liters] of water in a stainless-steel pot and boil them until the beets are tender — about 30 minutes. Drop the orange peel into the beet mixture. Add the ginger and orange juice. Simmer the mixture for 15 minutes. Strain the mixture, add the sugar and stir until it is dissolved, then let the liquid cool to 70° F. [20° C.]. Add the yeast, pour the mixture into a 4-quart [4-liter] fermentation jug, top up with cooled boiled water, and ferment under a fermentation lock. Rack the wine when it is done fermenting; adjust the sweetness. Rack the wine again in a couple of months and bottle it.

DONALD L. ACE AND JAMES H. EAKIN JR.
WINEMAKING AS A HOBBY

Barley Wine

The technique of making wine is shown on pages 74-75.

To make about 4 quarts [4 liters]		
1 lb.	old potatoes, scrubbed and chopped	½ kg.
6 cups	sugar	1½ liters
1 lb.	pearl barley, crushed (about 2 cups [½ liter])	½ kg.
1 lb.	raisins, coarsely chopped	½ kg.
4 quarts	boiling water	4 liters
⅙ oz.	package all-purpose wine yeast	5 g.

Put the potatoes, sugar, crushed barley and raisins into a large bowl. Add the boiling water, stir until the sugar is dissolved and, when cool, add the yeast. Pour the mixture into a widemouthed 4-quart [4-liter] jar. There will then be approximately 1 quart [1 liter] of liquid surplus that should be kept in a bottle and allowed to ferment alongside the contents of the jar. This can be used for topping up during fermentation or at the time of storage.

Keep the filled jar and bottle on a tray in a warm room. Soon froth will form and the jar should be kept full so that the froth is forced out. When froth ceases to form, strain the contents of the jar and the bottle through muslin. Pour the liquid into a 4-quart fermentation jug, insert a fermentation lock and allow the liquid to ferment again. When gas bubbles cease to form, siphon the wine, without disturbing the yeast deposit, into a clean jug which should be full when corked. Keep the wine in a cool place for several months, or until completely clear. Siphon off the clear liquid, bottle, cork and leave the bottles on their sides to store.

F. W. BEECH (EDITOR)
HOME-MADE WINES, SYRUPS AND CORDIALS

Honeysuckle Wine

The technique of making wine is shown on pages 74-75.

	To make about 4 quarts [4 liters]	
4 cups	fully opened honeysuckle blossoms	1 liter
2 quarts	boiling water, plus 2 quarts [2 liters] cold water	2 liters
5 cups	sugar	1¼ liters
1	Campden tablet, crushed	1
1	orange, the peel thinly pared, the juice strained	1
1	lemon, the peel thinly pared, the juice strained	1
⅙ oz.	package all-purpose wine yeast, mixed with a little tepid water and left to stand for 10 minutes	5 g.
	yeast nutrient	

Place the blossoms, sugar and Campden tablet in a crock, and cover with the boiling water. Add the cold water. When lukewarm, add the fruit juices and peels, the yeast and nutrient. Strain into a fermentation jug, fit with a fermentation lock and leave in a warm place to ferment. Rack when clear, then rack a second time and bottle when fermentation has ceased.

WILMA PATERSON
A COUNTRY CUP

Tomato Wine

The technique of making wine is shown on pages 74-75.

	To make 4 quarts [4 liters]	
5 lb.	tomatoes	2½ kg.
3½ quarts	water, plus 2 cups [½ liter] cooled boiled water	3½ liters
½ tsp.	pectic enzyme powder	2 ml.
1½ tbsp.	citric acid	22 ml.
5 cups	sugar	1¼ liters
1	Campden tablet, crushed	1
⅙ oz.	package all-purpose wine yeast	5 g.
	yeast nutrient	

Place the tomatoes and 1½ quarts [1½ liters] of water in a nonreactive pan. Bring the water to a boil and boil the tomatoes for about five minutes, until they are very soft. Transfer the mixture to a wide-necked jar, mash the tomatoes with a pestle and add 2 quarts [2 liters] of water, the pectic enzyme powder, citric acid, sugar and the crushed Campden tablet. Stir the mixture well. Cover the mixture and let it stand overnight.

Add the yeast and nutrient, cover the jar securely and leave it in a warm—70° F. [20° C.]—place for about a week. Strain the mixture through a cheesecloth-lined sieve and pour the liquid into a 4-quart [4-liter] fermentation jug. Top up with the cooled boiled water if necessary, and fit with a fermentation lock. Allow the wine to ferment. When all fermentation has ceased, rack the wine again into a clean jug. Bottle and cork the wine.

S. M. TRITTON
GUIDE TO BETTER WINE AND BEER MAKING FOR BEGINNERS

Dandelion Wine

The technique of making wine is shown on pages 74-75.
Pick the dandelions on a hot, dry day, when the petals are fully open and fairly bug-free.

	To make 4 quarts [4 liters]	
9 cups	dandelion petals, washed, the stems and pods removed	2¼ liters
1	lemon, thinly sliced	1
1	orange, thinly sliced	1
4 quarts	boiling water	4 liters
6 cups	sugar	1½ liters
1 lb.	seedless white raisins	½ kg.
⅙ oz.	package all-purpose wine yeast, dissolved in a little tepid water	5 g.

Place the dandelion petals in a crock, adding the lemon and orange slices. Pour the boiling water over them and stir well. Cover with a tea towel and let the mixture stand for 10 days. Strain off the liquid through a cheesecloth bag into a large bowl, then discard the petals and fruit slices. Return the liquid to a clean crock. Stir in the sugar and raisins, then the yeast. Cover the crock and leave undisturbed for three days. Strain into a 4-quart [4-liter] jug, and top with a fermentation lock or loose cork. Rack after three months. Bottle when fermentation has ceased and the wine is clear. Age for six months to one year before serving.

NORMA JEAN AND CAROLE DARDEN
SPOONBREAD AND STRAWBERRY WINE

Mead

The technique of making mead is shown on pages 76-77.

To make about 4 quarts [4 liters]		
1 quart	water, plus 3 quarts [3 liters] cooled boiled water	1 liter
4 cups	clover honey	1 liter
1	lemon, the peel grated and the juice strained	1
2½ tbsp.	tea leaves	37 ml.
⅙ oz.	package all-purpose wine yeast, mixed with a little tepid water and left to stand for 10 minutes	5 g.
½ tsp.	yeast energizer	2 ml.

Pour 1 quart [1 liter] of fresh water into a large saucepan. Add the honey, lemon peel and juice and the tea leaves. Place the pan over medium heat and stir the mixture until the honey has dissolved. Then bring the mixture to a boil and simmer for 10 minutes. Let the mixture cool until it is tepid.

Pour 1 quart of the cooled boiled water into a 4-quart [4-liter] fermentation jug. Set a funnel in the jug and place a cheesecloth- or muslin-lined sieve over the funnel. Strain the honey mixture through the sieve into the jug. Pour another quart of the cooled boiled water into the honey mixture and add the yeast mixture and energizer. Fit a fermentation lock into the neck of the jug. Shake the jug well and let the liquid ferment in a warm place for three to four weeks. Top up the jug with cooled boiled water, refit the fermentation lock, and return the jug to the warm place until fermentation has ceased—that is, when bubbles stop rising in the liquid and no air moves through the lock.

Rack the mead into a clean jug and top up to the neck with more cooled boiled water. Replace the fermentation lock: The racking may have released some carbon dioxide. Put the jug in a cool place to allow the mead to clear. Sediment will slowly settle to the bottom of the jug and the mead will clear in about four weeks. Rack the cleared mead into bottles. Cork the bottles and store the mead for at least two years, preferably five. Serve it chilled.

PETITS PROPOS CULINAIRES

Liqueurs

Apricots in Eau de Vie
Abricots à l'Eau de Vie

The author recommends using a colorless eau de vie; flavorless vodka can be substituted.

To make about 1½ quarts [1½ liters]		
2 lb.	firm, ripe apricots	1 kg.
1 quart	eau de vie	1 liter
1½ cups	heavy sugar syrup (recipe page 164)	375 ml.

Wipe the apricots with a cloth and prick them with a skewer. Blanch the apricots by plunging them into a pan of boiling water, lifting them out after a few seconds, and putting them immediately into a bowl of cold water. Drain the blanched apricots and put them into preserving jars. Mix the *eau de vie* with the sugar syrup, strain the mixture and pour it over the apricots. Seal the preserving jars and leave the flavored *eau de vie* for at least two months.

SIMIN PALAY
LA CUISINE DU PAYS

Blackberry Cordial

To make the blackberry juice, combine 7 pounds [3½ kg.]—about 5½ quarts [5½ liters]—of blackberries and ½ cup [125 ml.] of water in a heavy, nonreactive pan. Cook the berries over low heat for 15 to 20 minutes, or until very juicy. Strain the juice through a double layer of dampened cheesecloth, wringing the cloth to extract all of the liquid.

To make about 2½ quarts [2½ liters]		
2 quarts	blackberry juice	2 liters
2 cups	sugar	½ liter
3 tbsp.	freshly grated nutmeg	45 ml.
1 tbsp.	ground cloves	15 ml.
1 tbsp.	ground allspice	15 ml.
1½ tbsp.	ground cinnamon	22 ml.
2 cups	brandy	½ liter

Simmer the blackberry juice, sugar and spices together for 30 minutes in a closely covered stewpan. Leave to cool and strain through a cloth when cold. Add the brandy.

HELEN BULLOCK
THE WILLIAMSBURG ART OF COOKERY

Wild-cherry Bounce

To make about 2 quarts [2 liters]

2 quarts	wild cherries	2 liters
about 1½ quarts	brandy or Scotch	about 1½ liters
⅔ cup	sugar	150 ml.

Pack the cherries into two 1-quart [1-liter] jars, strewing sugar over each layer and pounding the cherries hard with a small stick to bruise them and allow the juice to escape.

When the cherries and sugar are well mixed and fill the jars, pour in as much of the brandy or Scotch as can find room for itself between fruit and sugar. It will be gradually soaked up. Return to each jar until the contents of both are saturated and the liquor stands on top. Screw on covers and do not trouble yourself to think of the bounce again for four months. Then turn out the contents into a bowl, pound and crush the cherries with a potato masher, and strain and squeeze 1 cup [¼ liter] at a time through a cloth. The liquor will improve with age and keep for years.

MARION HARLAND AND CHRISTINE TERHUNE HERRICK
THE NATIONAL COOK BOOK

Cranberry Cordial

If you start this in early fall, when the berries first appear in the market, the cordial will be ready for holiday guests.

To make about 3 cups [¾ liter]

1 lb.	cranberries, coarsely chopped	½ kg.
3 cups	sugar	¾ liter
2 cups	light rum	½ liter

Place the chopped cranberries in a 2-quart [2-liter] jar that has a tight-fitting lid. Add the sugar and rum. Adjust the lid securely and place the jar in a cool, dark place. Invert the jar and shake it every day for six weeks. Strain the cordial into bottles and seal with corks.

MARGARET WOOLFOLK
COOKING WITH BERRIES

Currant Rum

To make about 3 quarts [3 liters]

1 quart	black currants (about 2 lb. [1 kg.])	1 liter
3 cups	heavy sugar syrup (recipe, page 164)	¾ liter
2 quarts	rum	2 liters

Boil the black currants with the sugar syrup and strain the liquid through cheesecloth or muslin, pressing the fruit well. When the liquid is nearly cold, add the rum and bottle it.

DOROTHY HARTLEY
FOOD IN ENGLAND

Fig Ratafia

Ratafia de Figues Sèches

The name ratafia comes from the Middle Ages custom of having the parties to a legal agreement celebrate its ratification by sharing a drink. The author recommends using a colorless eau de vie; flavorless vodka can be substituted.

To make about 1 quart [1 liter]

1½ lb.	dried figs	¾ kg.
¾ cup	sugar	175 ml.
1 quart	eau de vie	1 liter

Wash and dry the figs and put them in a 1½-quart [1½-liter] jar. Add the sugar and pour in the *eau de vie*. Cover the jar tightly. The ratafia will be ready in a month.

CHRISTIANE SCHAPIRA
LA CUISINE CORSE

Zesty Winter Cordial

Zest is the colored, flavorful layer of citrus peel.

To make 5 cups [1¼ liters]

3 cups	vodka or gin	¾ liter
2 cups	orange, lemon, grapefruit or lime zest	½ liter
2 cups	sugar syrup (recipe, page 164)	½ liter

Mix all the ingredients in a container, cover and let stand in a cool place or in the refrigerator for three months. Strain the cordial before serving it.

JULIE DANNENBAUM
FAST & FRESH

Plum Brandy

Slivyanka

To make about 3 quarts [3 liters]

2 quarts	very strong vodka	2 liters
2 lb.	ripe plums	1 kg.
4 cups	sugar, or 1½ quarts [1½ liters] light sugar syrup (recipe, page 164), cooled	1 liter

Put the plums in a crock. Add the vodka, seal the crock and set it in a dark place for four to six weeks. Drain off the vodka and reserve it. Add the sugar or cooled syrup to the crock and mix it with the plums. Let this mixture stand for two weeks: The sugar will draw the alcohol out of the plums.

Drain the syrup from the plums and add it to the reserved vodka. Discard the plums. Strain the brandy and pour it into bottles. Seal them and store for six months before serving.

N. I. GEORGIEVSKY, M. E. MELMAN, E. A. SHADURA
AND A. S. SHEMJAKINSKY
UKRAINIAN CUISINE

Peach Ratafia

Ratafia de Pêches

To make a smaller quantity of ratafia, reduce the ingredients proportionately. The authors recommend using a colorless eau de vie; flavorless vodka can be substituted. The technique of using a fruit press is shown on pages 72-73.

	To make about 13 quarts [13 liters]	
12 lb.	ripe, unblemished peaches, halved and pitted	6 kg.
9 quarts	*eau de vie*	9 liters
8 cups	sugar	2 liters

Put the peach halves, a few at a time, into a cloth bag, place them in a wine press and squeeze out the juice into a 16-quart [16-liter] stoneware jar. The peaches will yield a total of about 4 quarts [4 liters] of juice. Add the *eau de vie* to the juice, cover the jar tightly with a large plate that will just fit into the top and leave the mixture for five to six weeks.

Place a sieve lined with a double layer of dampened cheesecloth or muslin over the top of another 16-quart stoneware jar and carefully decant the mixture from the first jar through the sieve into the second jar. Stir in the sugar and leave the jar tightly covered for a day or two, stirring daily, to let the sugar dissolve. Strain the liqueur as before and bottle it.

VIARD AND FOURET
LE CUISINIER ROYAL

Curaçao

To make a smaller quantity, reduce the ingredients proportionately. The author recommends using a colorless eau de vie; flavorless vodka can be substituted.

	To make 11 quarts [11 liters]	
5 cups	bitter-orange peel, dried in a 250° F. [120° C.] oven for 30 minutes	1¼ liters
10 quarts	*eau de vie*	10 liters
¼ cup	ground cinnamon	50 ml.
¼ cup	ground cloves	50 ml.
1 quart	light sugar syrup (*recipe, page 164*)	1 liter

Put the orange peel into a large jar and add the *eau de vie*, cinnamon and cloves. Cork the jar tightly and let the mixture infuse for 12 to 15 days; place the jar in a sunny place or on a warm stove and shake it well each day. When the cordial is ready, strain the infusion and add the sugar syrup.

C. DURANDEAU
GUIDE DE LA BONNE CUISINIÈRE

Black Currant Liqueur

Cassis

The author suggests using a colorless eau de vie; flavorless vodka can be substituted.

	To make about 1 quart [1 liter]	
2 lb.	black currants (5 cups [1¼ liters]), the stems removed	1 kg.
4	whole cloves	4
1-inch	cinnamon stick	2½-cm.
about 3 cups	*eau de vie*	about ¾ liter
about 1 cup	sugar	about ¼ liter

Fill a large glass jar with the black currants; add the cloves and cinnamon and cover them with the *eau de vie*. Let the mixture infuse for at least two months, shaking it from time to time. Then strain the liquid and sweeten it, using 1 cup [¼ liter] of sugar for every quart [1 liter] of liquid. Strain the liqueur and bottle it.

SIMIN PALAY
LA CUISINE DU PAYS

Pomegranate Ratafia

Le Ratafia de Grenades

To make a smaller quantity, reduce the ingredients proportionately. The author recommends using a colorless eau de vie; flavorless vodka can be substituted. To make pomegranate juice, you will need 10 to 12 pomegranates. Wrap the seeds of a few pomegranates at a time in a piece of cheesecloth or muslin. Squeeze the wrapped seeds vigorously to extract all the juice.

	To make about 4 quarts [4 liters]	
2 cups	sugar	½ liter
1 quart	pomegranate juice	1 liter
3 quarts	*eau de vie*	3 liters
1	cinnamon stick	1

Dissolve the sugar in the pomegranate juice and stir in the *eau de vie*. Pour the liquid into a large glass jar and add the cinnamon stick. Cork or cover the jar tightly and leave it in a warm place for 30 to 40 days to infuse. Strain and bottle the ratafia.

AUSTIN DE CROZE
LES PLATS RÉGIONAUX DE FRANCE

Fresh Peach Cordial

To make 5 cups [1 ¼ liters]

3 cups	vodka or gin	¾ liter
6	peaches, pricked, blanched and cooled	6
2 cups	heavy sugar syrup (recipe, page 164)	½ liter
¼ cup	almonds	50 ml.

Mix all the ingredients in a container and cover. Let the cordial mellow in a cool place or in the refrigerator for three months. Strain the cordial before serving.

JULIE DANNENBAUM
FAST & FRESH

— · —

Raspberry Liqueur

Liqueur de Framboises

The author recommends using a colorless eau de vie; flavorless vodka can be substituted. One cup [¼ liter] of bilberries or red currants, or ½ cup [125 ml.] of orange peel, may be used instead of the raspberries; a ⅛-inch [3-mm.] fragment of cinnamon stick may be added to the mixture. The technique of corking bottles is demonstrated on page 9.

To make about 2 quarts [2 liters]

1 quart	eau de vie	1 liter
1 pint	raspberries	½ liter
3 cups	sugar	¾ liter
2 cups	water	½ liter

Place the *eau de vie* and the raspberries in a bottle. Cork the bottle lightly and put it in a sunny place for about two months. Shake the bottle often.

Mix the sugar and water in a saucepan and bring them to a boil. Skim off the scum, remove the saucepan from the heat and let the syrup cool. Strain the flavored *eau de vie* into a bowl through a sieve lined with a double layer of dampened cheesecloth or muslin, and add the sugar syrup. Bottle the liqueur, cork the bottles and store them.

FRANÇOIS VOEGELING
LA GASTRONOMIE ALSACIENNE

— · —

Grenoble Liqueur

Ratafia de Grenoble

To make a smaller quantity, reduce the ingredients proportionately. To obtain the raspberry juice, rub 8 pounds [4 kg.] of raspberries through a sieve. To obtain the cherry juice, pit 3 pounds [1 ½ kg.] of ripe red or black cherries and crush them in a mortar or press them through a food mill, then squeeze the pulp in a square of cheesecloth or muslin. The author recommends using a colorless eau de vie; flavorless vodka can be substituted.

To make about 7 quarts [7 liters]

4 quarts	eau de vie	4 liters
2 quarts	raspberry juice	2 liters
2 cups	cherry juice	½ liter
4 to 5 cups	sugar	1 to 1 ¼ liters

Combine all of the ingredients in a large glazed crock and allow the mixture to stand until the sugar has completely dissolved. Strain through cheesecloth or muslin and pour into bottles; cork very firmly.

ROSALIE BLANQUET
LE PÂTISSIER DE MÉNAGES

— · —

Fruit Vodka

Varenukha

To make the flour-and-water paste, mix flour with just enough water to make it cohere. Adding a few drops of oil will keep the paste from becoming brittle when it dries.

To make about 1 quart [1 liter]

½ cup	dried apples	125 ml.
¼ cup	cherries, pitted	50 ml.
½	small pear, thickly sliced	½
2 or 3	plums, halved and pitted	2 or 3
1 quart	vodka	1 liter
⅔ cup	honey	150 ml.
⅛ tsp. each	ground ginger, cinnamon, cloves and black pepper	½ ml. each
1	bay leaf	1
	flour-and-water paste	

Place each of the four fruits in a separate bowl. Cover the fruits with the vodka. Let them stand for five to six hours.

Pour the vodka and the fruits into a crock. Stir in the honey, spices and bay leaf. Cover the crock with its lid and seal the edges with flour-and-water paste. Bake in a 200° F. [100° C.] oven for 10 to 12 hours. Strain the mixture through a sieve lined with a double layer of cheesecloth or muslin. Serve either hot or cold.

N. I. GEORGIEVSKY, M. E. MELMAN, E. A. SHADURA
AND A. S. SHEMJAKINSKY
UKRAINIAN CUISINE

Orange and Coffee-bean Cordial

During storage, the liquid will probably turn dark from the coffee beans, but the orange flavor will still be there and the cordial will look deliciously unusual.

	To make about 5 cups [1 ¼ liters]	
3	oranges	3
27	coffee beans, plus ¼ cup [50 ml.] coffee beans	27
2 cups	sugar syrup (recipe, page 164)	½ liter
3 cups	tequila	¾ liter

Cut three slits down the sides of each orange. Insert three coffee beans into each slit. Put the oranges into a jar and add the rest of the coffee beans. Add the sugar syrup and tequila, and seal. Store in the refrigerator for three months. To serve, strain the liquid into frosted cordial glasses.

JULIE DANNENBAUM
FAST & FRESH

Coffee Liqueur

Liqueur de Café

The author recommends using a colorless eau de vie; flavorless vodka can be substituted.

	To make about 5 cups [1 ¼ liters]	
½ cup	freshly roasted coffee beans	125 ml.
1 quart	*eau de vie*	1 liter
1 cup	heavy sugar syrup (recipe, page 164)	¼ liter

Put the coffee beans into the *eau de vie* and let them macerate for 24 hours. Add the sugar syrup and mix all the ingredients together. Strain out the coffee beans; bottle the liqueur.

MANUEL PRATIQUE DE CUISINE PROVENÇALE

Spiced Eau de Vie

Rossolis

The author of this 17th Century recipe suggests tying small quantities of musk and ambergris in a cloth and placing them

in the bag through which the sweetened eau de vie is strained. Modern cooks do not add perfume to food or drink.

The author recommends using a colorless eau de vie; flavorless vodka can be substituted. The technique of corking bottles is demonstrated on page 9.

	To make about 5 cups [1 ¼ liters]	
1 quart	*eau de vie*	1 liter
3	fresh hot chilies	3
12	whole cloves, coarsely crushed	12
1	sprig fresh anise	1
½ tsp.	ground coriander	2 ml.
1 ½ cups	sugar	375 ml.
½ cup	water	125 ml.
12	almonds, coarsely crushed	12

Combine the *eau de vie* with the chilies and spices; let them infuse for about two hours. Strain the liquid into a bowl.

In a saucepan dissolve the sugar in the water, then cook the syrup over medium heat until it reaches the soft-ball stage—234° to 240° F. [112° to 116° C.] on a candy thermometer. Remove the syrup from the heat. Pour in the spiced *eau de vie* and stir well. Place the crushed almonds in a cheesecloth-lined sieve set over a bowl, and strain the sweetened *eau de vie*. Bottle the drink and cork it.

L'ESCOLE PARFAITE DES OFFICIERS DE BOUCHE

Angelica Cordial

Crème d'Angélique

The author recommends using a colorless eau de vie; flavorless vodka can be substituted.

	To make about 5 quarts [5 liters]	
½ lb.	candied green angelica	¼ kg.
1-inch	cinnamon stick	2½-cm.
4	whole cloves	4
3 quarts	*eau de vie*	3 liters
7 cups	sugar	1¾ liters
1 quart	water	1 liter

Put the angelica, cinnamon, cloves and *eau de vie* in a glass jar. Cover the jar and let the mixture infuse for one and a half months. Then strain it through a sieve into a large bowl. Mix the sugar and water in a saucepan and stir over low heat until the sugar dissolves. Increase the heat and let the mixture boil for about one minute, without stirring. Skim this syrup, then add it to the flavored *eau de vie*. Cool the cordial and bottle it.

TANTE MARIE
LA VÉRITABLE CUISINE DE FAMILLE

Avignon Milk Liqueur

Liqueur de Lait d'Avignon

Flavorless vodka can be substituted for the eau de vie.

To make 1 quart [1 liter]

2 cups	eau de vie	½ liter
2 cups	milk	½ liter
2 cups	sugar	½ liter
1	vanilla bean	1
1	lemon, quartered	1

Put the *eau de vie*, milk, sugar, vanilla bean and lemon quarters into a glass jar and mix them well together. Let the mixture macerate for 12 days, stirring it from time to time. Then strain the liqueur through a sieve lined with a double layer of dampened cheesecloth or muslin and decant it.

LUCETTE REY-BILLETON
LES BONNES RECETTES DU SOLEIL

Seven Seeds' Liqueur

Ratafia de Sept Graines

To make a smaller quantity, reduce the ingredients proportionately. The author recommends using a colorless eau de vie; flavorless vodka can be substituted.

To make about 8 quarts [8 liters]

¼ cup	cumin seeds	50 ml.
¼ cup	aniseed	50 ml.
¼ cup	dill seeds	50 ml.
¼ cup	angelica seeds	50 ml.
¼ cup	caraway seeds	50 ml.
¼ cup	coriander seeds	50 ml.
¼ cup	fennel seeds	50 ml.
7 quarts	eau de vie	7 liters
6 cups	sugar	1 ½ liters
2 cups	tepid water	½ liter

Pound all of the seeds together in a mortar until they are very finely crushed. Mix them in a large crock with the *eau de vie*, cover and allow to infuse for one month.

Dissolve the sugar in the tepid water; allow the mixture to cool. Strain the seeds from the infusion, add the sugar mixture and bottle the liqueur.

ROSALIE BLANQUET
LE PÂTISSIER DES MÉNAGES

Highland Bitters

Gentian is a classic herb grown for the alleged medicinal properties of its bitter-tasting root. The root is obtainable dried from herbalists.

In Scotland, bitters were traditionally drunk before a meal, especially breakfast, "for the purpose of strengthening the stomach, and by that means invigorating the general health." Any kind of spirit could be substituted for the Scotch and sometimes wine or ale.

To make about 1 ½ quarts [1 ½ liters]

¼ cup	dried camomile flowers	50 ml.
3 tbsp.	finely chopped dried gentian root	45 ml.
3 tbsp.	coriander seeds	45 ml.
2½ tbsp.	finely chopped bitter-orange peel	37 ml.
2 tbsp.	whole cloves	30 ml.
4-inch	cinnamon stick	10-cm.
1 ½ quarts	Scotch	1 ½ liters

Place the camomile flowers, gentian root, coriander seeds, orange peel, cloves and cinnamon in a mortar. Crush them together coarsely, place the mixture in an earthenware jar, pour in the whisky and cover the jar tightly. Leave for 10 days, then strain the bitters and bottle it.

WILMA PATERSON
A COUNTRY CUP

East Prussian Honey Cordial

Ostpreussischer Bärenfang

The author recommends a colorless eau de vie; flavorless vodka can be substituted.

To make about 1 quart [1 liter]

1 cup	water	¼ liter
¼	vanilla bean, split	¼
1	whole clove	1
1-inch	cinnamon stick	2½-cm.
⅔ cup	heather or acacia honey	150 ml.
2 cups	eau de vie	½ liter

Bring the water to a boil, add the spices, remove from the heat and let the spices infuse until the water is tepid. Strain out the spices, and dissolve the honey in the spiced water. Skim off any foam, stir in the *eau de vie*, pour into bottles and cork. Leave the mixture for at least a week before opening.

FRITZ BECKER
DAS KOCHBUCH AUS MECKLENBURG, POMMERN & OSTPREUSSEN

Usquebaugh, the Irish Cordial

Not a drop of water must be put to Irish cordial. It is sometimes tinged a fine green with the juice of spinach, instead of the saffron tint from which it takes the name (as we conjecture) of usquebœœ, or yellow water.

To make about 2 quarts [2 liters]

1 tbsp.	whole cloves	15 ml.
1 tbsp.	whole cardamoms	15 ml.
2 quarts	brandy or Irish whiskey	2 liters
1 lb.	raisins	½ kg.
3 tbsp.	grated nutmeg	45 ml.
4	sugar cubes, rubbed over the peel of an orange—preferably a Seville orange	4
¼ tsp.	powdered saffron, dissolved in ¼ cup [50 ml.] of boiling water	1 ml.
1 cup	brown sugar	¼ liter

Bruise the cloves and cardamoms in a mortar. Pour the brandy or whiskey into a large jar and stir in the raisins, nutmeg, cloves, cardamoms, sugar cubes, saffron and brown sugar. Cork the jar. Shake the infusion every day for two weeks. Strain out the raisins and spices before serving the cordial.

ANDRÉ L. SIMON
HOW TO MAKE WINES AND CORDIALS

Tea Cream

Crème de Thé

The author recommends a colorless eau de vie; flavorless vodka can be substituted. The technique of making sugar syrup is shown on page 26. To make a smaller quantity, reduce the ingredients proportionately.

To make 7 ¼ quarts [7 ¼ liters]

2½ cups	green tea leaves	625 ml.
1 cup	boiling water	¼ liter
4 quarts	*eau de vie*	4 liters
3 quarts	sugar syrup, made with 3 quarts [3 liters] water and 2 cups [½ liter] sugar	3 liters

Infuse the tea leaves in the boiling water for five minutes and pour the infusion with the tea leaves into the *eau de vie*. Leave for 24 hours, then strain the mixture, add the sugar syrup and bottle the liqueur.

C. DURANDEAU
GUIDE DE LA BONNE CUISINIÈRE

Orange Wine

Le Vin d'Orange

The author recommends using a colorless eau de vie; flavorless vodka can be substituted.

To make 5 cups [1 ¼ liters]

1 quart	red wine	1 liter
	thinly pared peel of 2 or 3 oranges	
1 cup	sugar	¼ liter
⅔ cup	*eau de vie*	150 ml.
1	vanilla bean	1

Combine the red wine, orange peel, sugar, *eau de vie* and vanilla bean. Cover, and let the mixture infuse for two months; then strain the liquid and bottle it.

RODOLPHE BRINGER
LES BONS VIEUX PLATS DU TRICASTIN

Georgette's Orange Wine Cordial

Vin à l'Orange de "Georgette"

To make a smaller quantity, reduce the ingredients proportionately. The author recommends using a colorless eau de vie; flavorless vodka can be substituted. Seville or bitter oranges have a tart flavor; they are obtainable at fruit specialty stores and Latin American markets in winter. If not available, they may be replaced by sweet oranges. Before the oranges and lemon are halved, they should be thoroughly cleaned by being blanched in boiling water.

To make about 7 quarts [7 liters]

5 quarts	white or rosé wine	5 liters
1 quart	*eau de vie*	1 liter
4 to 5 cups	sugar	1 to 1 ¼ liters
6	Seville oranges, halved, the juice strained	6
1	orange, halved, the juice strained	1
1	lemon, halved, the juice strained	1
1	vanilla bean	1

Put all of the ingredients, including the squeezed halves of the fruits, into a large crock. Cover and allow to macerate for 42 days. Strain and bottle the cordial; keep it in a cool place.

ALAIN CHAPEL
LA CUISINE C'EST BEAUCOUP PLUS QUE DES RECETTES

Punches

Mrs. Arnold's Rum Punch

To serve the punch, pour it into a punch bowl containing a block of ice, as demonstrated on pages 80-81. Before sweetening the punch, dissolve the sugar in a little hot water.

This is a famous old Virginia recipe that has come down through the generations. I can remember, when I was a child, watching my father make quite a ceremony of opening a bottle of rum punch put up by his grandfather on the latter's plantation long before the Civil War. I must admit that I omit the "strain through muslin"—the lemon peel goes to the bottom anyway.

To make about 8½ quarts [8½ liters]

18	lemons, the peel of 9 grated, the juice of all 18 strained	18
4 quarts	boiling water	4 liters
3 quarts	rum	3 liters
2 cups	brandy	½ liter
2 cups	green tea, strained	½ liter
	sugar	

To the juice and peel of the lemons, add the boiling water. When nearly cold, pour in the rum, brandy and tea. Strain through muslin or cheesecloth and sweeten to taste.

MRS. WALTER HUSTED (EDITOR)
VIRGINIA COOKERY—PAST AND PRESENT

Cold Duck
Kalte Ente

To make about 9 cups [2¼ liters]

¼ cup	sugar	50 ml.
3 tbsp.	water	45 ml.
1½ quarts	Moselle, chilled	1½ liters
1	lemon, the peel pared in a single strip	1
3 cups	sparkling white wine, chilled	¾ liter

Bring the sugar and water to a boil, cool it and mix this syrup with the Moselle in a punch bowl. Hang the lemon peel over a wooden spoon and place it in the punch bowl. After 20 minutes, remove the peel and spoon, and fill the bowl with the sparkling wine. Serve the punch immediately in chilled wine glasses.

ROTRAUD DEGNER
DAS SCHNELLKOCHBUCH FÜR FEINSCHMECKER

Creole Champagne Punch
Ponche au Vin de Champagne à la Créole

To make about 5½ quarts [5½ liters]

2 cups	sugar	½ liter
2 cups	fresh lemon juice	½ liter
1 quart	dry white wine	1 liter
1 quart	Champagne	1 liter
2 quarts	soda water	2 liters
¼ cup	Curaçao	50 ml.
1	pineapple, peeled, quartered and cored, half of the flesh grated, half sliced	1
	ice	
36	strawberries, hulled	36

In a large punch bowl, combine the sugar, lemon juice, white wine, Champagne, soda water, curaçao and the grated pineapple. Mix together well. Put in a large block of ice and decorate with the sliced pineapple and the strawberries. Let the mixture chill and serve in small glass cups.

THE PICAYUNE CREOLE COOK BOOK

Fairy Punch

To make about 2½ quarts [2½ liters]

1 quart	unsweetened grape juice	1 liter
3	oranges, juice strained	3
1 cup	cold tea	¼ liter
2 cups	sugar	½ liter
¼	pineapple, peeled, cored and diced	¼
1	lemon, sliced	1
½	banana, sliced	½
8	maraschino cherries	8
	ice	
1 quart	soda water	1 liter

In a large bowl, combine the grape juice, orange juice, tea and sugar. Stir well, then add the pieces of pineapple, lemon and banana and the cherries. Place a small block of ice in a punch bowl and pour the mixture into it. Let the mixture stand for up to 30 minutes, then add more ice and the soda water and serve at once.

MARTHA MEADE
RECIPES FROM THE OLD SOUTH

May Wine

Maiwein (Maitrank)

If possible, young sweet woodruff should be sought out before it blooms, and the lower leaves and stem removed. Orange pieces may be added to the drink. The wine will keep for several days, but you must take care that small pieces of woodruff do not get into the wine.

To make sweet woodruff-leaf extract, steep two sprigs of woodruff in a bottle of Moselle or Rhine wine for 10 to 15 minutes. Strain and bottle.

To make about 1 quart [1 liter]

4 tbsp.	sweet woodruff leaves	60 ml.
2 tsp.	sugar	10 ml.
1 quart	Moselle or Rhine wine	1 liter
⅔ cup	sweet woodruff extract (optional)	150 ml.

Put the woodruff leaves in a sieve over a punch bowl and sprinkle them with about 1 teaspoon [5 ml.] of sugar. Pour the wine through the sieve so that it takes on the flavor of the woodruff. Sweeten the wine to taste with the rest of the sugar and add the sweet woodruff extract, if used.

HENRIETTE DAVIDIS
PRAKTISCHES KOCHBUCH

Chablis Cup

Other white wines may be used, and a mixture of orange juice and lime juice may be substituted for the lemon juice.

To make about 2½ quarts [2½ liters]

½ cup	sugar	125 ml.
1 cup	water	¼ liter
2	lemons, the peel of 1 thinly pared, the juice of both strained	2
3 cups	Chablis	¾ liter
1	sprig fresh lemon verbena	1
5 cups	soda water	1¼ liters
	pineapple shreds or thin slices of lemon or other fruit	
½ cup	sherry (optional)	125 ml.
	crushed ice (optional)	

Put the sugar and water into a small saucepan with the lemon peel. Dissolve the sugar slowly and bring the water to a boil, then strain it into a jug or bowl and leave it to cool. Next, add the Chablis, lemon juice and lemon verbena, and stand the mixture in a cold place until it is required. Strain it into a pitcher, adding the soda water and the pieces of fruit. Add the sherry and crushed ice, if using.

FLORENCE B. JACK
ONE HUNDRED DRINKS & CUPS

Fish House Punch

To make about 7 quarts [7 liters]

3 quarts	water	3 liters
2 cups	brown sugar	½ liter
12 to 18	lemons, the peel grated and the juice strained	12 to 18
2 quarts	Jamaica rum	2 liters
1 quart	brandy	1 liter
⅔ cup	peach brandy	150 ml.
	crushed ice	

Make a syrup with the water and brown sugar and pour it hot over the peel and juice of the lemons. Cool. Add the rum and brandy, and dash well with peach brandy to make the punch mellow and extra-fine. Serve in a bowl of crushed ice.

MRS. HELEN BULLOCK
THE WILLIAMSBURG ART OF COOKERY

Sangría

This exquisite "edible" drink can contain nearly all types of fruit. The longer it is prepared beforehand, the more aroma and flavor it will have. Add the banana only 30 minutes before serving, lest it get mushy.

To make about 4 quarts [4 liters]

1 quart	dry red wine	1 liter
3	lemons, the juice of 2 strained, 1 cut into thin wedges	3
1	orange, cut into thin wedges	1
2	peaches, peeled, halved, pitted and diced	2
1	apple, peeled, cored and diced	1
1	pear, peeled, cored and diced	1
1	banana, sliced	1
¼ cup	sugar	50 ml.
¼ cup	brandy	50 ml.
18 to 20	ice cubes	18 to 20
	ground cinnamon (optional)	

Pour the wine into a 4-quart [4-liter] pitcher. Add the lemon juice and all of the cut fruit. With a wooden spoon, stir in the sugar and brandy. Add the ice and a pinch of cinnamon, if you wish. Taste and add more sugar if necessary. The mixture should be allowed to stand for at least 30 minutes before serving, although it can be left for several hours. Serve the fruit with the liquid, or in a separate glass with a spoon when the liquid has been drunk.

LA COCINA PASO A PASO

Red Cucumber Bowl

Rode Komkommerbowl

To make about 7 cups [1¾ liters]

1	cucumber, unpeeled, thinly sliced	1
1½ quarts	dry red wine	1½ liters
1	small cinnamon stick	1
3	whole cloves	3
½ cup	maraschino liqueur	125 ml.

Place the cucumber in a glass or ceramic bowl, and pour in 1½ cups [375 ml.] of the wine. Tie the spices in a piece of cheesecloth and add them to the bowl. Let the mixture stand for one hour. Remove the spices, add the remaining wine and the maraschino, and refrigerate the punch until it is well chilled—two to three hours—before serving it.

ROLAND GÖÖCK (EDITOR)
ELSEVIERS GROTE KOOKBOEK

Admiral Gannon

To make about 2 quarts [2 liters]

3¾ cups	bourbon	925 ml.
2½ cups	light rum	625 ml.
1¼ cups	fresh lemon juice	300 ml.
⅔ cup	maple syrup	150 ml.

About three hours before serving, combine all the ingredients in a punch bowl containing a 5-pound [2½-kg.] block of ice. Serve in cocktail glasses or in punch cups.

MICHAEL ROY
MIKE ROY'S AMERICAN KITCHEN

Coffee Punch

If you prefer, coffee ice cream may be used instead of the vanilla ice cream.

To make about 3½ quarts [3½ liters]

2 quarts	cold strong coffee	2 liters
2 cups	milk	½ liter
1 tsp.	vanilla extract	5 ml.
½ cup	sugar	125 ml.
1 quart	vanilla ice cream (recipe, page 165), softened slightly	1 liter
1 cup	heavy cream, whipped	¼ liter

Whisk the coffee, milk, vanilla extract, sugar and ice cream together. Float the whipped cream on top.

LADYFOOD: A COLLECTION OF RECIPES ENJOYED
BY LADIES & GENTLEMEN

Brown Betty

To make 2 quarts [2 liters]

⅔ cup	brown sugar	150 ml.
2½ cups	hot water	625 ml.
1	lemon, sliced	1
½ tsp.	ground cloves	2 ml.
½ tsp.	ground cinnamon	2 ml.
1¼ cups	brandy	300 ml.
5 cups	ale	1¼ liters
2	slices homemade-style white bread with the crusts removed, toasted and cubed	2
	freshly grated nutmeg	
	fresh ginger	

Dissolve the sugar in the water, add the lemon and let the mixture stand for 15 minutes. Then add the cloves, cinnamon, brandy and ale; stir well, put in the toasted bread, sprinkle some nutmeg and ginger over the toast, and the drink is fit for use. Ice it well and it will prove a good summer drink; warm it and it will become an equally pleasant winter beverage.

OXFORD NIGHT CAPS

Cider Cup

Vanilla extract may be substituted for the pineapple extract.

To make about 2 quarts [2 liters]

1 quart	sweet (nonalcoholic) cider	1 liter
½ cup	sherry	125 ml.
¼ cup	brandy	50 ml.
1 quart	soda water	1 liter
½	lemon, half of the peel pared off in a thin strip, the juice strained	½
	sugar	
	grated nutmeg	
	pineapple extract	
1	sprig fresh verbena (optional)	1
2	sprigs fresh borage (optional)	2

Put the cider, sherry, brandy, soda water, lemon juice and peel into a bowl. Add sugar and nutmeg to taste and a dash of pineapple extract. Add verbena and borage, if desired. Strain and chill well.

FREDERICK DAVIES AND SEYMOUR DAVIES
DRINKS OF ALL KINDS

Claret Cup

To make about 7 cups [1¾ liters]

3 cups	red Bordeaux	¾ liter
2 tbsp.	maraschino liqueur	30 ml.
3 cups	soda water	¾ liter
1½ cups	crushed ice	375 ml.
¼ cup	superfine sugar	50 ml.
¼ tsp.	grated nutmeg	1 ml.
1	sprig fresh borage	1

Put the liquid ingredients, the ice and the sugar into a very large silver cup. Mix them well and top with the nutmeg and borage sprig. Hand the cup around with a clean napkin passed through one of the handles, that the edge of the cup may be wiped after each guest has partaken of the contents.

HOPE ANDREWS AND FRANCES KELLY
MARYLAND'S WAY

Imperial Punch

To make about 2 quarts [2 liters]

3 cups	red Bordeaux	¾ liter
1 quart	soda water	1 liter
¼ cup	sugar	50 ml.
2 tbsp.	maraschino liqueur	30 ml.
¼ tsp.	grated nutmeg	1 ml.
3 or 4	slices cucumber rind	3 or 4
	ice block	

Mix the ingredients in a punch bowl and add a block of ice.

N. E. BEVERIDGE
CUPS OF VALOR

Old-fashioned Tea Punch

To make about 1½ quarts [1½ liters]

4 tbsp.	black tea leaves	60 ml.
1 quart	boiling water	1 liter
1 cup	honey	¼ liter
½ cup	fresh lemon juice	125 ml.
1 cup	sparkling mineral water	¼ liter
	cracked ice	
	mint sprigs	

Make the tea in the usual way with the boiling water, then add the honey and lemon juice. Cool the tea and strain it into a punch bowl partly filled with cracked ice. Add the mineral water and strew a handful of mint sprigs over the surface just before serving.

HAZEL BERTO
COOKING WITH HONEY

Fruit and Mint Tea Punch

To make about 5 cups [1¼ liters]

2½ cups	hot black tea	625 ml.
¾ cup	sugar	175 ml.
1¼ cups	fresh orange juice	300 ml.
⅔ cup	fresh lemon juice	150 ml.
1	orange, sliced	1
1	lemon, sliced	1
6	strawberries, hulled and sliced	6
8	fresh mint leaves	8
	ice cubes	

Strain the hot tea onto the sugar, and add the orange and lemon juices. When the liquid is cold, add it to the sliced fruit, mint leaves and ice cubes.

SERENA HARDY
THE TEA BOOK

Tea Nog

To make about 6 quarts [6 liters]

four 4-inch	cinnamon sticks	four 10-cm.
1 tbsp.	whole cloves	15 ml.
¼ cup	honey	50 ml.
2 tbsp.	grated orange peel	30 ml.
2 tsp.	grated lemon peel	10 ml.
2 cups	water	½ liter
1 cup	fresh orange juice	¼ liter
1 cup	fresh lemon juice	¼ liter
¾ cup	black tea leaves	175 ml.

Cook the cinnamon, cloves, honey, and orange and lemon peels in the water over medium heat for 10 minutes. Let the mixture stand for one hour, then strain it into a large bowl. Add the orange and lemon juices. Brew the tea in 5 quarts [5 liters] of boiling water and strain it into the bowl. Serve hot.

MARTHA MEADE
RECIPES FROM THE OLD SOUTH

Hot Spiced Wine

Vin Chaud aux Épices

If you wish to serve the spiced wine very hot, strain it into a bowl before adding the spirits, then return it to the pan and heat it again together with the rum or brandy. This technique is demonstrated on pages 82-83.

To make about 1 quart [1 liter]

3	dried figs, halved	3
1	apple, quartered	1
1	orange, quartered	1
⅔ cup	sugar	150 ml.
6	almonds	6
1	cinnamon stick	1
3	whole cloves	3
1 quart	red wine	1 liter
½ cup	rum or brandy	125 ml.

Put the fruits, sugar, almonds, cinnamon and cloves in a nonreactive saucepan. Pour in the wine and cook over high heat for 12 minutes to reduce the liquid. Take the pan from the heat; cover it and let the mixture infuse for five minutes. Add the rum or brandy, strain and serve hot in cups.

LUCETTE REY-BILLETON
LES BONNES RECETTES DU SOLEIL

Swedish Glögg

The burning sugar is the secret for the flavor of this drink.

To make about 1 quart [1 liter]

1½ cups	dry red wine	375 ml.
2 cups	brandy	½ liter
6	whole cloves	6
3	whole cardamoms, the pods slightly crushed	3
2-inch	cinnamon stick	5-cm.
⅓ cup	seedless raisins	75 ml.
10 to 12	almonds, blanched and peeled	10 to 12
¾ cup	sugar	175 ml.

Into a large, nonreactive pan, combine all of the ingredients except 1 teaspoon [5 ml.] of the sugar. Bring the mixture slowly to the boiling point, then pass a match over the surface of the liquid to ignite it, immediately sprinkling the reserved sugar into the burning liquid. Extinguish the flame by covering the pan after 15 seconds. Serve hot in small glasses, adding a few of the raisins or almonds to each glass.

ANN ROE ROBBINS
TREADWAY INNS COOK BOOK

Mulled Wine

Le Vin Chaud

To make 1 quart [1 liter]

1 tbsp.	sugar	15 ml.
1 quart	red wine	1 liter
2-inch	cinnamon stick	5-cm.
2 tsp.	grated lemon peel	10 ml.
1 tbsp.	Curaçao	15 ml.

In a nonreactive saucepan, combine the sugar and wine. Add the cinnamon stick and lemon peel. Heat the mixture, without boiling, until a gray scum appears on the surface. Remove the pan from the heat and skim off the scum. Add the Curaçao and let the mixture infuse for several minutes. Strain the wine and serve it while still hot.

GASTON DERYS
LES PLATS AU VIN

Christmas Wine

Julglögg

Tart-flavored Seville or bitter oranges are obtainable at fruit stores and Latin American markets during the winter. If not available, they may be replaced by sweet oranges.

To make about 2 quarts [2 liters]

1 quart	aquavit	1 liter
3 cups	red Bordeaux or other red wine	¾ liter
10	cardamom seeds	10
5	whole cloves	5
3	Seville oranges, the peel thinly pared	3
4	dried figs	4
1 cup	almonds, blanched and peeled	¼ liter
1 cup	raisins	¼ liter
1½-inch	cinnamon stick	4-cm.
½ lb.	sugar tablets	¼ kg.

For the glögg, first pour the aquavit into a heavy, nonreactive saucepan. Add the wine, cardamom, cloves, orange peel, figs, almonds, raisins and cinnamon. Cover and heat slowly to the boiling point, then remove the glögg from the heat. Place a fine-meshed wire rack over a second nonreactive saucepan and lay the sugar tablets on the rack. Ignite the glögg, and ladle it—while burning—over the sugar to melt the tablets. Cool the glögg. Keep it in tightly covered or corked bottles. Heat it before serving, but do not boil it. Serve hot in wine glasses; garnish it, if you like, with additional raisins and almonds.

SAM WIDENFELT (EDITOR)
FAVORITE SWEDISH RECIPES

Spiced Wine

Hipocras de Vin Rouge

The author of this 17th Century recipe suggests tying small quantities of musk and ambergris in a cloth and placing them in the bag through which the wine is strained. Modern cooks do not add perfume to food or drink.

To make about 1 quart [1 liter]

1 quart	red wine	1 liter
1½ cups	sugar	375 ml.
2	fresh hot chilies, lightly crushed	2
1-inch	cinnamon stick	2½-cm.
12	whole cloves	12
2	blades mace	2
2-inch	piece fresh ginger, sliced	5-cm.
1	tart apple, peeled and sliced	1
12	almonds, crushed to a paste	12

Place the wine in a bowl with the sugar, chilies, spices and apple. Cover the bowl and let the mixture infuse for 30 minutes, or until the sugar is completely dissolved.

Place the almonds in a jelly bag or a sieve lined with a double layer of cheesecloth. Pour the wine into the cloth, stir it and leave it to drip through into a large bowl. Bottle the wine. If the wine is to be stored, cork it well; otherwise it can be drunk immediately.

L'ESCOLE PARFAITE DES OFFICIERS DE BOUCHE

Singaree, Hot or Cold

Sangarée, Chaud ou Froid

This winter drink can be served cold in summer by mixing the wine and water and sugar, and adding the juice of a lemon or orange, a little lemon peel and grated nutmeg.

To make about 2 cups [½ liter]

1 cup	boiling water	¼ liter
6	whole cloves	6
12	whole allspice	12
2-inch	cinnamon stick	5-cm.
3 tbsp.	sugar	45 ml.
1 cup	red wine	¼ liter
	grated nutmeg	

Boil the water and the spices together for 15 minutes, until the water is thoroughly flavored with the spices. Remove from the heat and dissolve the sugar in the mixture. Put the wine in a heatproof pitcher and strain the water and sugar into it. Flavor with grated nutmeg and add more sugar, if necessary, to taste. Serve hot immediately.

THE PICAYUNE CREOLE COOK BOOK

Mulled Ale

To make about 2 cups [½ liter]

1¼ cups	ale	300 ml.
1	whole clove	1
1-inch	piece fresh ginger, lightly crushed	2½-cm.
1 tsp.	butter	5 ml.
1 tsp.	sugar	5 ml.
2	eggs, beaten with 1 tbsp. [15 ml.] ale	2

Put the ale, clove, ginger, butter and sugar into a nonreactive saucepan and bring the mixture to the boiling point. Stirring constantly, gradually pour the boiling mixture into the beaten eggs and then into a large jug. Pass the mixture from one jug to another for some minutes, and at a good height, until very frothy. Return it to the pan and reheat it, but do not let it boil. Remove the ginger before serving.

VICTORIAN CUPS AND PUNCHES AND OTHER CONCOCTIONS

Lambs Wool

Formerly, the first day of November was dedicated to the angel presiding over fruits, seeds, etc., and was therefore named *la mas ubal*, that is, "the day of the apple fruit," and being pronounced *lamasool*, our country people have corrupted it to Lambs Wool. This mixture is sometimes served up in a bowl, with sweet cakes floating in it.

To make about 1½ quarts [1½ liters]

6	apples, roasted or baked until soft, peeled, halved and cored	6
	brown sugar	
1	nutmeg, grated	1
	ground ginger	
5 cups	ale, heated	1¼ liters

Mix the pulp of the apples with brown sugar to taste, the nutmeg and a small quantity of ginger. Add the ale, made moderately warm. Stir the whole well together and, if sweet enough, it is fit for use.

OXFORD NIGHT CAPS

Toast and Ale

This is a winter drink, which is served at the end of dinner at the same time as the cheese.

To make 1 quart [1 liter]

1 tsp.	ground ginger	5 ml.
1 quart	ale	1 liter
1	thick slice homemade-style white bread with the crust removed, toasted and torn into small pieces	1

Add the ginger to the ale and bring to a boil. Place the toasted bread in a jug with a metal lid and pour the nearly boiling liquid into the jug. Let it cool slightly before serving it.

ALFRED SUZANNE
LA CUISINE ANGLAISE ET LA PÂTISSERIE

Oxford Receipt for Bishop

Bishop is frequently made with a Seville orange stuck with cloves and slowly roasted, and its flavor to many tastes is infinitely finer than when made with raw lemons.

To make about 1 quart [1 liter]

2	lemons	2
12	whole cloves	12
½-inch	cinnamon stick	1-cm.
½-inch	blade mace	1-cm.
6	whole allspice	6
½-inch	piece fresh ginger	1-cm.
1¼ cups	water	300 ml.
3 cups	port	¾ liter
4	sugar cubes	4
	freshly grated nutmeg	
	sugar	

Make several incisions in the peel of one of the lemons and stick six cloves into these. Roast the lemon by a slow fire or under a broiler—turning it often until it softens and begins to color, about 10 minutes. Put the cinnamon, mace, allspice and ginger into a small saucepan with the water; let it boil until it is reduced by one half.

In a large, nonreactive pan, bring the port to a boil and burn a portion of the spirit out of it by applying a lighted paper or a match to the surface. Put the roasted lemon and the spices and water into the port; stir it up well and let it stand near the fire, or over very low heat, for 10 minutes. Rub the sugar cubes on the peel of the remaining lemon and put the sugar into a bowl or jug with the juice of half of the lemon. Pour in the port, add some grated nutmeg, sweeten the mixture to taste, and serve it up with the lemon and spices floating in it.

ELIZA ACTON
MODERN COOKERY

Yuletide Wassail

To make about 7 cups [1¾ liters]

6	apples, peeled and cored	6
	sugar	
½ tsp.	ground cinnamon	2 ml.
½ tsp.	ground ginger	2 ml.
¼ tsp.	grated nutmeg	1 ml.
1½ quarts	ale or beer	1½ liters
2 tsp.	grated lemon peel	10 ml.
¾ cup	sherry, or any sweet red or white wine	175 ml.

Place the apples in a buttered baking dish, and fill the center of each apple with about 2 teaspoons [10 ml.] of sugar. Bake the apples in a preheated 350° F. [180° C.] oven until tender—about 30 minutes. Let the apples cool. Add the cinnamon, nutmeg, ginger and ¾ cup [175 ml.] of sugar to 2 cups [½ liter] of the ale or beer and let it stand where it will get hot, but not boil. Stir occasionally. When the mixture is hot, add the lemon peel, the remaining ale or beer and the wine. Stir the wassail occasionally again until it is very hot; add the baked apples and serve the drink from a big bowl.

IDA BAILEY ALLEN
BEST LOVED RECIPES OF THE AMERICAN PEOPLE

Panada

This is an early-19th Century recipe.

To make about 1 quart [1 liter]

1 cup	fresh white bread crumbs	¼ liter
¼ cup	wine or 1 tbsp. [15 ml.] rum or vinegar	50 ml.
	grated nutmeg	
4 tbsp.	butter	60 ml.
½ cup	sugar	125 ml.
about 1 tsp.	ground mixed spices	about 5 ml.
3 cups	boiling water	¾ liter

Put the bread crumbs in a bowl. Add the wine or rum or vinegar, as may suit best, grated nutmeg to taste, the butter, sugar and mixed spices. Pour the water on boiling hot.

HELEN BULLOCK
THE WILLIAMSBURG ART OF COOKERY

Mecklenburg Punch

Mecklenburger Punsch

To make about 3 quarts [3 liters]

1½ quarts	Rhine wine	1½ liters
1½ cups	brandy	375 ml.
1½ cups	Madeira	375 ml.
3 cups	strong tea, strained	¾ liter
1 cup	sugar	¼ liter
4 tsp.	grated lemon peel	20 ml.

Put all the ingredients into a saucepan and heat to the simmering point, but do not boil. Strain and serve in glasses.

LILO AUREDEN
WAS MÄNNERN SO GUT SCHMECKT

Mulled Orange Tea

To make about 3¾ quarts [3¾ liters]

3 quarts	strong black tea	3 liters
1 tbsp.	whole cloves	15 ml.
6	cinnamon sticks	6
1½ cups	fresh orange juice	375 ml.
⅓ cup	fresh lemon juice	75 ml.
1 cup	honey	¼ liter
	orange or lemon slices	

Steep the tea and spices for five minutes over low heat; strain. Add the juices and honey. Stir well and heat the tea through. Serve in mugs. Garnish with citrus slices.

JAN BLEXRUD
A TOAST TO SOBER SPIRITS AND JOYOUS JUICES

Apple Toddy, Kentucky-Style

To make about 1½ quarts [1½ liters]

6	apples, peeled and cored	6
	sugar syrup *(recipe, page 164)*, made from 1 cup [¼ liter] sugar and 1 cup water	
	ground cinnamon	
2 cups	boiling water	½ liter
	sugar	
2 cups	bourbon	½ liter
	grated nutmeg	

Place the apples in a baking dish and pour the syrup over them. Dust the apples with cinnamon and bake in a preheated 325° F. [160° C.] oven until soft, basting frequently. This takes about one hour. Remove the apples and juice from the oven and mash in the bottom of a silver or china punch bowl. Pour in the boiling water, stir in sugar to taste and add the bourbon. Grate nutmeg over the toddy and ladle into cups. Serve at once with little cookies.

MARION FLEXNER
OUT OF KENTUCKY KITCHENS

Coffee Rum Punch

Cremat

To make about 2½ quarts [2½ liters]

1¾ cups	light rum	425 ml.
1¼ cups	dark rum	300 ml.
⅔ cup	brandy	150 ml.
	sugar	
	thinly pared peel of 1 lemon	
2	cinnamon sticks	2
½ tsp.	grated nutmeg (optional)	2 ml.
1½ quarts	hot coffee	1½ liters

Mix the light rum, dark rum and brandy together in a nonreactive container. Stir in sugar to taste, the lemon peel, cinnamon and the nutmeg, if you are using it. Heat the mixture, set it alight, and let it flame for a few minutes; then add the coffee a little at a time, making sure that the liquid goes on flaming by stirring it with a spoon or ladle. When the flame dies, serve the coffee rum punch immediately in heavy earthenware cups.

ENCICLOPEDIA SALVAT DE LA COCINA: TOMO 3

Ginger Posset

Possets of various kinds were very popular with the Victorians. The basic ingredients were milk or cream heated with ale or wine, and flavored with spices.

To make about 5 cups [1¼ liters]

2½ cups	milk	625 ml.
1-inch	piece fresh ginger, bruised	2½-cm.
1	slice toast, broken into pieces	1
1	egg yolk	1
¼ cup	sugar	50 ml.
1 tbsp.	butter	15 ml.
2½ cups	brown ale	625 ml.

Bring the milk to a boil, then remove it from the heat. Put the ginger and the toast pieces into the pan with the hot milk. Let the milk stand for 30 minutes. Remove the ginger.

Stir the egg yolk, sugar, butter and ale into the milk. Bring almost to the boiling point and simmer for five minutes—the surface should become frothy. Ladle into heatproof glasses and serve immediately.

ANNE AGER
THE GINGER COOKBOOK

To Make a Sack Posset at a Wedding

This is a 17th Century recipe. Sack, or sherris sack, is the old name for sherry. The author suggests that this recipe can be made with cream instead of milk, in which case only 10 eggs should be used.

To make about 9 cups [2¼ liters]

2 cups	medium-dry sherry	½ liter
15	eggs, beaten	15
5 cups	milk	1¼ liters

Stir the sherry into the beaten eggs and set aside. Heat the milk gently over low heat until it is almost boiling. Take the milk from the heat and pour it from a height into the sherry-and-egg mixture, stirring all the time. Let the posset stand in a warm place for half an hour.

MRS. ANN BLENCOWE
THE RECEIPT BOOK OF MRS. ANN BLENCOWE

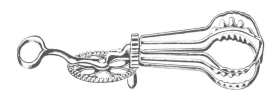

Advocate

Advocaat

To make about 1½ quarts [1½ liters]

12	eggs	12
2 cups	sugar	½ liter
2 tsp.	vanilla extract	10 ml.
1 quart	brandy	1 liter
	heavy cream, whipped	
	grated nutmeg	

Beat the eggs with the sugar and vanilla until light and fluffy. Put the mixture in the top of a double boiler and add the brandy very slowly, stirring constantly with a wire whisk. Remove from the heat and allow it to cool.

Serve this drink in glasses with a dollop of whipped cream and a little grated nutmeg on top.

C. COUNTESS VAN LIMBURG STIRUM
THE ART OF DUTCH COOKING

Egg Punch

Eier-Punsch

To make about 3 quarts [3 liters]

1½ quarts	dry red wine	1½ liters
1 tsp.	black tea leaves, infused in 3 cups [¾ liter] boiling water and strained	5 ml.
3 cups	sugar	¾ liter
2 tsp.	grated lemon peel	10 ml.
⅓ to ½ cup	fresh lemon juice	75 to 125 ml.
4	eggs	4
8	egg yolks	8
1½ cups	arrack	375 ml.

In a large, nonreactive pan, combine the red wine with the strained tea. Whisk in first the sugar, lemon peel and lemon juice, then the whole eggs and egg yolks. Set the mixture over low heat and whisk it until it comes to a boil, then stir in the arrack.

SOPHIE WILHELMINE SCHEIBLER
ALLGEMEINES DEUTSCHES KOCHBUCH FÜR ALLE STÄNDE

The Counselor's Cup

When this recipe was first published in 1845, white sugar was sold in solid loaves from which cooks cut off the required amount in chunk form. For this reason, the original version of The Counselor's Cup specifies a 4-ounce [125-g.] piece of sugar and calls for rubbing the sugar over oranges to flavor it. Adding grated orange peel to granulated sugar is simpler, and produces similar results.

To make about 1½ quarts [1½ liters]

½ cup	sugar	125 ml.
½ tsp.	grated orange peel	2 ml.
2½ cups	water	625 ml.
2 to 2½ cups	fresh orange juice	500 to 625 ml.
3 tbsp.	fresh lemon juice	45 ml.
1¼ cups	Cognac	300 ml.

Combine the sugar and orange peel in a nonreactive saucepan and pour in the water; boil gently for two to three minutes. Mix the orange and lemon juices and pour them into the pan. The moment the mixture begins to boil, pour it into a hot jug and stir into it the Cognac. Serve it immediately.

ELIZA ACTON
MODERN COOKERY

151

Caudle

Kandeel

In the Netherlands, caudle is the drink traditionally served to guests visiting the mother of a new baby.

To make about 5 cups [1 1/4 liters]

6	whole cloves	6
4-inch	cinnamon stick	10-cm.
1/2	lemon, the peel thinly pared	1/2
1/3 cup	water	75 ml.
2/3 cup	sugar	150 ml.
12	egg yolks	12
3 cups	Rhine wine	3/4 liter

Put the spices and lemon peel into the water and place over low heat to infuse for about 30 minutes; do not let the liquid boil. Strain the liquid. Put the sugar in a heavy nonreactive pan and stir in the egg yolks. Slowly mix in the wine and the spiced water. Put the pan in a larger pan partly filled with almost boiling water and set over low heat, or place it on a heat-diffusing pad over low heat. Stir the mixture constantly until it is creamy. Serve warm in cups or glasses.

F. M. STOLL AND W. H. DE GROOT
HET HAAGSE KOOKBOEK

A Fine Caudle

To make about 3 cups [750 ml.]

2 cups	milk	1/2 liter
2 tbsp.	medium-dry sherry	30 ml.
	ground mace	
	grated nutmeg	
2	slices white bread with the crusts removed, torn into pieces	2
2	eggs	2
2 or 3	egg yolks	2 or 3
	sugar	

Warm the milk and add the sherry so that the milk separates. Then strain the mixture and let it cool. When it is cold, put it into a heavy pan with a pinch each of mace and nutmeg and the white bread. Bring to a boil, then remove from the heat. Beat the eggs and egg yolks together and pour the hot milk onto them slowly, stirring all the time so that the mixture does not curdle. Pour the mixture into the pan and place over gentle heat; stir until the mixture thickens. Remove from the heat and sweeten to taste.

HELEN BULLOCK
THE WILLIAMSBURG ART OF COOKERY

Hoppel-Poppel

To make about 3 cups [3/4 liter]

4	egg yolks	4
1/2 cup	sugar	125 ml.
1 cup	rum or arrack	1/4 liter
1/4 tsp.	grated nutmeg	1 ml.
1 cup	heavy cream, whipped	1/4 liter

Beat the egg yolks with the sugar until light and fluffy. Beat in the rum or arrack and the nutmeg. Fold in the whipped cream. Chill well.

C. COUNTESS VAN LIMBURG STIRUM
THE ART OF DUTCH COOKING

Rumfustian

To make 3 quarts [3 liters]

5 cups	beer	1 1/4 liters
3 cups	red wine	3/4 liter
2 1/2 cups	gin	625 ml.
12	egg yolks	12
3/4 cup	sugar	175 ml.
1 tsp.	ground cinnamon	5 ml.
1 tsp.	ground ginger	5 ml.
1 tsp.	grated nutmeg	5 ml.

Beat and warm all the ingredients over low heat—but on no account boil, as that would curdle the egg yolks. The rumfustian should be opaque and rather thick.

DOROTHY HARTLEY
FOOD IN ENGLAND

Egg Punch with Kirsch

Eierpunch met Kirsch

To make 1 quart [1 liter]

1 1/2 cups	water	375 ml.
2/3 cup	sugar	150 ml.
1 1/2 cups	kirsch	375 ml.
6	egg yolks	6

Stirring constantly, bring the water and sugar to a boil in a heavy saucepan, and cook until the sugar dissolves. Let this syrup cool for a moment and then mix in the kirsch. Whisk the egg yolks until frothy. Stirring constantly, add the whisked egg yolks to the liquid. Place the punch mixture over low heat or pan of simmering water. Whisk the punch vigorously until it is thick and foamy. Do not allow it to boil.

ROLAND GÖÖCK (EDITOR)
ELSEVIERS GROTE KOOKBOEK

Cambridge Milk Punch

To make about 3½ quarts [3½ liters]

2	eggs, well beaten	2
2½ quarts	milk	2½ liters
	thinly pared peel of 1 lemon	
1 cup	sugar	¼ liter
2½ cups	rum	625 ml.
1¼ cups	brandy	300 ml.

Mix the beaten eggs with ⅔ cup [150 ml.] of the milk and strain the mixture through a sieve. Throw into the remaining milk the lemon peel and sugar; bring it slowly to a boil, take out the lemon peel, remove from the heat and quickly stir in the mixture of eggs and milk; the milk must not of course be allowed to boil after this is added. Add gradually the rum and brandy; whip the punch to a froth and serve it immediately in warm glasses.

ELIZA ACTON
MODERN COOKERY

Raleigh Eggnog

To make about 4 quarts [4 liters]

12	eggs, the yolks separated from the whites	12
2 cups	superfine sugar	½ liter
1 cup	Jamaica rum	¼ liter
1 quart	rye whiskey	1 liter
2 quarts	milk	2 liters
2 cups	cream	½ liter
	grated nutmeg	

Beat the egg yolks until lemon-colored, then gradually add the sugar. Slowly beat in the rum and rye. Stir in the milk and cream. Beat the egg whites until they are stiff and fold them into the mixture. Sprinkle with the nutmeg.

MRS. WALTER HUSTED (EDITOR)
VIRGINIA COOKERY—PAST AND PRESENT

Marion Green's Eggnog Superb

All those who are lucky enough to sample this eggnog describe it as "the best and richest eggnog in the world." If you want the eggnog to go further, take the 12 unused egg whites, beat them to a stiff froth and fold into the mixed eggnog. This also makes the brew a little less rich.

To make about 2½ quarts [2½ liters]

12	egg yolks	12
2½ cups	sugar	625 ml.
1 quart	bourbon	1 liter
1 quart	heavy cream, beaten until thick but not buttery	1 liter
	nutmeg	

Beat the yolks very, very lightly with the sugar—an electric mixer helps. They should be spongy and lemon-colored. Add the bourbon very, very slowly (about 1 tablespoon [15 ml.] at a time), beating after each addition. Fold the cream into the batter mixture and pour into a crystal or silver bowl. The bowl should be placed in a larger one filled partway with chipped ice to keep the eggnog thoroughly chilled. Grate nutmeg over the top, or put a little over each serving.

MARION FLEXNER
OUT OF KENTUCKY KITCHENS

Egg Nog of the Commonwealth Club, Richmond, Virginia

To make about 10 quarts [10 liters]

24	eggs, the yolks separated from the whites, the whites stiffly beaten	24
3 cups	sugar	¾ liter
2 quarts	whiskey	2 liters
½ cup	rum	125 ml.
½ cup	brandy	125 ml.
2 quarts	light cream	2 liters
1 quart	heavy cream, whipped	1 liter

In a large bowl beat thoroughly the yolks of the eggs, then gradually beat in the sugar. Pour the egg mixture into a saucepan, and stir and heat the mixture well. Stir in well the whiskey, rum and brandy. Pour the mixture into a large punch bowl. Add the light cream slowly and mix thoroughly. Fold in the beaten egg whites, then the whipped cream.

ALICE B. TOKLAS
THE ALICE B. TOKLAS COOKBOOK

Mixed Drinks

Churchill Downs Mint Julep

A silver julep cup is preferable for making this famous old drink, although it is by no means essential. If you are lucky enough to own such heirlooms, chill the cups thoroughly before mixing the juleps. If highball glasses are substituted for silver cups, they will not frost.

	To make 1 tall drink	
	sugar	
1 tbsp.	chopped fresh mint leaves, plus 1 or 2 small sprigs mint	15 ml.
1 tbsp.	water	15 ml.
	finely crushed ice	
1 to 2 oz.	bourbon	30 to 60 ml.

Place a teaspoonful of sugar (or more, to taste) and the chopped mint leaves in a small crockery bowl. Bruise the leaves well with a pestle or the back of a wooden spoon, until the mixture forms a paste. Add the water and stir. There should be a thick green syrup by this time. Fill a chilled julep cup or 8-ounce [250-ml.] highball glass half-full with very finely crushed ice. Add the mint syrup and the bourbon. Fill up the cup or glass with more crushed ice. Slip the mint sprigs into the ice and add two straws, cut short; the straws should be no taller than the mint. If you are using a julep cup, lift it onto a tray, being careful not to touch the sides with your fingers, and put it into the freezer to frost. This will take from 30 minutes to one hour.

MARION FLEXNER
OUT OF KENTUCKY KITCHENS

Modi's Mint Julep

	To make 1 tall drink	
12	sprigs fresh mint	12
2 tsp.	sugar	10 ml.
	finely crushed ice	
6 oz.	bourbon	180 ml.
2	pieces pineapple (optional)	2
2 tsp.	white crème de menthe (optional)	10 ml.

In a 14-ounce [425-ml.] Tom Collins glass, put six sprigs of mint and muddle these gently with the sugar; hard muddling gives off a bitter taste. Stir this up once so that it coats

the inside of the glass. Put crushed ice in the glass up to the halfway mark; pour in a third of the bourbon. Put the half-filled glass in the freezer and freeze the contents solid: You can keep it there until doomsday without harm.

When needed, fill the glass with more crushed ice, pour in the rest of the bourbon and stir this upper unfrozen layer. Cut short the stems of the remaining mint and stand them in the glass. Garnish as you wish, but two pieces of sun-ripened pineapple go best. Float crème de menthe on the top, if you wish. Now watch the frost form on the outside of the glass— the frozen ice-mint-bourbon foundation in the glass is what does the trick.

CHARLES H. BAKER JR.
THE SOUTH AMERICAN GENTLEMAN'S COMPANION

Whiskey Sour

	To make 1 cocktail	
1½ oz.	bourbon or rye	45 ml.
½	lemon, the juice strained	½
1 tsp.	sugar	5 ml.
	crushed ice	
1	maraschino cherry	1

Combine the whiskey, lemon juice, sugar and ice in a cocktail shaker, and shake. Strain the mixture into a chilled 5-ounce [150-ml.] whiskey-sour glass and add the cherry.

FANNIE MERRITT FARMER
THE FANNIE FARMER COOKBOOK

Sazerac

The technique of making a Sazerac is shown on page 88.

	To make 1 cocktail	
	Pernod or Ricard	
1	sugar cube	1
1 tsp.	water	5 ml.
	Angostura bitters	
	Peychaud bitters	
3 or 4	ice cubes	3 or 4
2 oz.	bourbon	60 ml.
1	strip thinly pared lemon peel	1

Coat the inside of a chilled 8-ounce [250-ml.] old-fashioned glass with two dashes of the Pernod or Ricard. Discard any excess. Muddle the cube of sugar with the teaspoon [5 ml.] of water and a dash each of the two bitters. Add the ice cubes. Pour in the bourbon and top with the twist of lemon.

HAROLD J. GROSSMAN
GROSSMAN'S GUIDE TO WINES, BEERS, AND SPIRITS

Gimlet

You may, if you wish, substitute fresh lime juice for the bottled juice. In that case, add ½ teaspoon [2 ml.] of super-fine sugar to the gin or vodka in the glass and stir with a bar spoon to dissolve the sugar before adding the ice cubes.

	To make 1 cocktail	
3 oz.	gin or vodka	90 ml.
2	ice cubes	2
2 oz.	Rose's sweetened lime juice	60 ml.
1	lime slice	1

Pour the gin or vodka into a chilled 6-ounce [180-ml.] old-fashioned or cocktail glass and add the ice cubes. Top with lime juice and garnish with the lime slice.

WINES AND SPIRITS
FOODS OF THE WORLD

Dry Martini

The proportion of vermouth to gin is entirely according to taste; some martini lovers deem it enough to rinse out the pitcher with a little vermouth. The technique of making a martini cocktail is demonstrated on page 88.

	To make 1 cocktail	
	ice cubes	
2 oz.	gin	60 ml.
½ oz.	dry vermouth	15 ml.
	thinly pared lemon peel	

Half-fill a chilled pitcher with ice cubes and pour in the gin and vermouth. Use a long spoon to stir the mixture well. Hold the ice back with the spoon and pour the cocktail into a chilled 3-ounce [90-ml.] cocktail glass. Serve garnished with a piece of the lemon peel.

THE SAVOY COCKTAIL BOOK

Pink Gin

	To make 1 cocktail	
	Angostura bitters	
1 oz.	gin	30 ml.
	ice water or soda water	

Swirl several dashes of Angostura bitters in a chilled, 4-ounce [125-ml.] cocktail glass and discard the bitters. Add the gin, and water or soda water to taste.

UNITED KINGDOM BARTENDERS' GUILD
INTERNATIONAL GUIDE TO DRINKS

Silver Fizz

	To make 1 tall drink	
½	lemon, plus 1 thinly pared strip of lemon peel	½
1 ½ oz.	gin	45 ml.
1 tsp.	sugar	5 ml.
1	egg white	1
	ice cubes	
	soda water, chilled	

Squeeze the lemon into a cocktail shaker. Add the gin, sugar and egg white, and shake together. Pour over ice cubes into an 8-ounce [250-ml.] highball glass containing three or four ice cubes. Fill the glass with soda water and twist the lemon peel as you add it to the glass.

HAROLD J. GROSSMAN
GROSSMAN'S GUIDE TO WINES, BEERS, AND SPIRITS

Major Bailey

	To make 1 tall drink	
1 tsp.	superfine sugar	5 ml.
	fresh lime juice	
6	mint leaves	6
1 cup	crushed ice	¼ liter
1 oz.	gin	30 ml.

Muddle the sugar, a few dashes of lime juice and the mint leaves in a chilled tall goblet or 8-ounce [250-ml.] highball glass. Fill with crushed ice, then add the gin. Stir until the outside of the glass is frosted.

THE EDITORS OF AMERICAN HERITAGE
THE AMERICAN HERITAGE COOKBOOK

Peach Apéritif

Pfirsich Apéritif

	To make 4 cocktails	
4	ripe peaches, peeled, halved and pitted	4
½ cup	gin	125 ml.
	ice cubes	
	soda water, chilled	

Rub the peaches through a nylon or stainless-steel sieve or purée them in an electric blender. Combine the purée with the gin. Chill. Place ice cubes in four chilled 6-ounce [175-ml.] wine glasses, pour in the peach mixture and top up the glasses with soda water to taste.

URSULA GRÜNIGER
COOKING WITH FRUIT

Singapore Sling

The Singapore Sling is said to have originated in the Raffles Hotel in Singapore, and some claim that the original drink also contained a few drops of Benedictine and Brandy, a slice of orange and a sprig of fresh mint. Many recipes substitute soda water for the ice water; although tasty, this would then be called a Singapore Rickey and not a Singapore Sling.

	To make 1 tall drink	
2	ice cubes, whole or cracked	2
½ oz.	Cherry Heering or cherry brandy	15 ml.
½ oz.	fresh lemon juice	15 ml.
3 oz.	gin	90 ml.
2 to 4 oz.	ice water	60 to 125 ml.

Combine the ice, Cherry Heering or brandy, lemon juice and gin in a chilled 8-ounce [250-ml.] highball glass. Fill the glass with ice water and stir.

WINES AND SPIRITS
FOODS OF THE WORLD

Ramos Gin Fizz

Henry C. Ramos arrived in New Orleans in 1888 and purchased the Imperial Cabinet saloon, where this famous drink was served. The drink requires such a great deal of shaking—at least five minutes—that one of the distinctive features of Ramos' establishment was its corps of young boys who did nothing but stand behind the bar to attend to shaking Gin Fizzes. During the Mardi Gras of 1915, the corps reached the prodigious size of 35.

	To make 1 tall drink	
1½ oz.	dry gin	45 ml.
1 tbsp.	superfine sugar	15 ml.
3 or 4 drops	orange-flower water	3 or 4 drops
½ oz.	fresh lime juice	15 ml.
1 oz.	fresh lemon juice	30 ml.
1	egg white	1
1½ oz.	light cream	45 ml.
	soda water	
2 drops	vanilla extract (optional)	2 drops
	crushed ice	

Put the gin, sugar, three or four drops of orange-flower water, the lime juice, lemon juice, egg white, cream, a dash of soda water and two drops of vanilla—if you are using it—in a cocktail shaker. Fill the shaker with crushed ice (the ice should not be too fine since lumps are needed to whip the egg white and cream to a froth). Shake long and steadily until the mixture thickens. Strain into a chilled 12-ounce [375-ml.] highball glass.

THE EDITORS OF AMERICAN HERITAGE
THE AMERICAN HERITAGE COOKBOOK

Tom Collins

	To make 1 tall drink	
2 tbsp.	fresh lemon juice	30 ml.
1 tsp.	superfine sugar	5 ml.
1½ oz.	gin	45 ml.
	ice cubes	
	soda water, chilled	

Shake the juice, sugar and gin together. Pour the mixture into a chilled 10- to 14-ounce [300- to 425-ml.] glass containing three or four ice cubes. Fill the glass with soda water.

HAROLD J. GROSSMAN
GROSSMAN'S GUIDE TO WINES, BEERS, AND SPIRITS

Gin and Tonic

Your hardy Britisher out in the fever-ridden areas of the East gravitated to gin and tonics quite naturally, for sparkling quinine soda tasted better than quinine and plain water, as a blood-cooler, fever warder-offer and general tonic. This drink can be acid or not, to suit your whim; but no sugar at all, ever. Note that it is not at its best unless served very, very cold indeed.

To make 1 tall drink

2 oz.	dry gin	60 ml.
¼	lemon or 1 small lime, juice strained and shell reserved	¼
	ice cubes	
1	paper-thin slice lemon or lime	1
3 oz.	tonic water, chilled	90 ml.
3 drops	Angostura bitters (optional)	3 drops

In a shaker, combine the gin and the lemon or lime juice. Rub the flesh of the lemon or lime shell around the inside of a 10-ounce [300-ml.] Tom Collins glass about 1 inch [2½ cm.] down from the lip of the glass. Then toss the shell into the shaker with some ice cubes. Shake hard to chill the mixture, strain it into the Collins glass and add three ice cubes and the slice of lemon or lime. Fill the glass with the chilled tonic water. Stir gently to blend and top with the bitters, if using.

CHARLES H. BAKER JR.
THE SOUTH AMERICAN GENTLEMAN'S COMPANION

Pink Lady

To make 1 cocktail

1 to 1½ oz.	gin	30 to 45 ml.
1 to 1½ oz.	Calvados or applejack	30 to 45 ml.
1½ oz.	fresh lemon juice	45 ml.
½ oz.	grenadine	15 ml.
1	egg white	1
3 or 4	ice cubes	3 or 4

Combine all of the ingredients in a cocktail shaker and shake vigorously. Strain into a chilled 6-ounce [180-ml.] cocktail glass.

COLLETTE RICHARDSON (EDITOR)
HOUSE & GARDEN'S DRINK GUIDE

Raspberry Fizz

To make 1 tall drink

½ cup	raspberries	125 ml.
1½ oz.	gin	45 ml.
1½ to 2 oz.	fresh orange juice	45 to 60 ml.
1 tsp.	superfine sugar	5 ml.
	crushed ice	
	soda water, chilled	
	fresh mint sprigs	

Crush the raspberries and work through a fine sieve into a cocktail shaker. Add the gin, orange juice and sugar. Cover the shaker and shake well. Pour into a chilled 8-ounce [250-ml.] glass partly filled with crushed ice. Fill the glass with soda water and garnish with fresh mint.

MARGARET WOOLFOLK
COOKING WITH BERRIES

Planter's Punch

To make 1 tall drink

1½ oz.	fresh lime juice	45 ml.
1 tsp.	brown sugar	5 ml.
4 oz.	Jamaica rum	125 ml.
1 to 1½ cups	finely crushed ice	250 to 375 ml.
2	lime slices	2
1	maraschino cherry	1
1	sprig fresh mint (optional)	1

Combine the lime juice and brown sugar in a chilled 10- to 14-ounce [300- to 425-ml.] Tom Collins glass. Stir with a muddler or bar spoon to dissolve the sugar, then add the rum. Fill the glass three quarters full with crushed ice and stir again. Decorate with the slices of lime and the cherry and, if you wish, the fresh mint. Serve with a straw.

WINES AND SPIRITS
FOODS OF THE WORLD

Piña Colada

To make 1 tall drink

2 oz.	golden Puerto Rican rum	60 ml.
3 oz.	unsweetened pineapple juice	90 ml.
½ cup	crushed ice	125 ml.
3 or 4	ice cubes	3 or 4
1	pineapple slice (optional)	1

Combine the rum, pineapple juice and crushed ice in the jar of an electric drink mixer or blender and blend for 10 to 20 seconds. Pour into a chilled 10- to 14-ounce [300- to 425-ml.] Tom Collins glass containing the ice cubes. Garnish with the pineapple slice, if desired, and serve with a straw.

TRADER VIC
TRADER VIC'S BARTENDER'S GUIDE, REVISED

Frozen Avocado Daiquiris

To make 8 cocktails

2	avocados, halved, pitted, peeled and cut into chunks	2
2 cups	light rum	½ liter
⅔ cup	fresh lime juice	150 ml.
½ cup	sugar	125 ml.
	ice cubes	

Combine the avocados, rum, lime juice and sugar in a bowl. Place half of the mixture at a time in the container of a blender. Fill the container with ice cubes and blend the ingredients until the mixture is fairly smooth. Pour into chilled cocktail glasses and serve with short straws.

JOE CARCIONE
THE GREENGROCER COOKBOOK

Manhattan

To make 1 cocktail

2 oz.	rye	60 ml.
½ oz.	dry vermouth	15 ml.
½ oz.	sweet vermouth	15 ml.
3 or 4	ice cubes	3 or 4

Combine the rye, dry vermouth, sweet vermouth and ice cubes in a mixing glass or pitcher. With a bar spoon, stir gently lest you cloud the drink. Strain the mixture into a chilled 4-ounce [125-ml.] cocktail glass.

ANTHONY HOGG
COCKTAILS AND MIXED DRINKS

Frozen Daiquiri

To make a fruit daiquiri, add about ½ cup [125 ml.] of coarsely cubed, peeled banana, peach, apricot or melon to the rum mixture and blend until the fruit is puréed. Serve the drink in a chilled 8- to 10-ounce [250- to 300-ml.] glass.

To make 1 cocktail

2 oz.	light rum	60 ml.
	maraschino liqueur	
½	lime, the juice strained	½
1 tsp.	superfine sugar	5 ml.
2 or 3	ice cubes	2 or 3
1	maraschino cherry	1

Blend the rum, a dash of maraschino, the lime juice, superfine sugar and ice cubes in a blender, and pour the mixture into a chilled 4-ounce [125-ml.] cocktail glass. Add the cherry and serve with straws.

THE SAVOY COCKTAIL BOOK

Old-fashioned

Add fruit if you like—a cherry, a slice of lemon or orange, or a piece of pineapple.

To make 1 cocktail

2 drops	Angostura bitters	2 drops
1	sugar tablet	1
1 tbsp.	boiling water	15 ml.
2	ice cubes, crushed	2
1½ oz.	rye or bourbon	45 ml.
	soda water, chilled	

Put the bitters, sugar and boiling water in a 6-ounce [180-ml.] old-fashioned glass and stir the mixture until the sugar melts. Put in the ice cubes. Add the rye or bourbon, stir and add a dash of soda water.

FANNIE MERRITT FARMER
THE FANNIE FARMER COOKBOOK

Tequila Sunrise

To make 1 tall drink

6	ice cubes, 3 crushed	6
2 oz.	tequila	60 ml.
1 oz.	grenadine	30 ml.
1 oz.	fresh lemon juice	30 ml.
	soda water, chilled	
1	slice lime	1

Combine the tequila, grenadine, lemon juice and crushed ice in a cocktail shaker. Shake well and strain into a chilled, 8-ounce [250-ml.] highball glass. Add the ice cubes, top up the drink with soda water and fix the lime slice onto the rim of the glass. Serve with a straw.

A TO Z OF COCKTAILS

Margarita

Triple Sec is a sweet, white, orange-flavored Curaçao. Any other Curaçao could be used instead. The technique of making a Margarita is demonstrated on page 86.

To make 1 cocktail

1½ oz.	tequila	45 ml.
½ oz.	Triple Sec	15 ml.
1 oz.	fresh lime or lemon juice	30 ml.
	crushed ice	
1	piece lemon peel, or 1 lemon half	1
	salt	

Shake the tequila, Triple Sec, and lime or lemon juice with ice. Moisten the rim of a chilled 4-ounce [125-ml.] stemmed cocktail glass by rubbing it with the lemon peel or lemon half, then dip the moistened rim in salt. Pour the tequila mixture into the glass. Sip the cocktail over the salted edge.

UNITED KINGDOM BARTENDERS' GUILD
INTERNATIONAL GUIDE TO DRINKS

Black Russian

To make 1 cocktail

3 or 4	ice cubes	3 or 4
2 oz.	vodka	60 ml.
1 oz.	Kahlúa or other coffee-flavored liqueur	30 ml.

Put the ice cubes in a chilled 6-ounce [180-ml.] old-fashioned glass. Pour in the vodka and Kahlúa and stir well.

INA C. BOYD
COCKTAILS & HORS D'OEUVRES

Ninotchka Cocktail

To make 1 cocktail

1½ oz.	vodka	45 ml.
½ oz.	crème de cacao	15 ml.
½	lemon, juice strained	½
	crushed ice	

Pour all the ingredients into a cocktail shaker, shake well and strain into a chilled 3-ounce [90-ml.] cocktail glass.

THE DINERS' CLUB, INC.
THE DINERS' CLUB DRINK BOOK

Spicy Bloody Mary

Professional bartenders shake drinks in a 16-ounce [½-liter] mixing glass with a matching 32-ounce [1-liter] metal shaker inverted over the top as a cover, and use a flat round metal strainer to strain them.

To make 1 cocktail

8 to 12	ice cubes	8 to 12
½ cup	tomato juice	125 ml.
3 oz.	vodka	90 ml.
2 tsp.	fresh lemon juice	10 ml.
	Worcestershire sauce	
	Tabasco sauce	
	freshly ground black pepper	

Fill a mixing glass with ice cubes and add the tomato juice, vodka, lemon juice and two drops each of Worcestershire sauce and Tabasco sauce. Season with a few grindings of black pepper. Place a shaker on top of the mixing glass and, grasping them firmly together with both hands, shake vigorously. Remove the shaker, place a strainer on top of the mixing glass and strain the drink into a chilled 8-ounce [250-ml.] glass.

WINES AND SPIRITS
FOODS OF THE WORLD

Screwdriver

	To make 1 cocktail	
2 oz.	vodka	60 ml.
1 oz.	fresh orange juice	30 ml.
2 tbsp.	superfine sugar	30 ml.

Combine the vodka, orange juice and superfine sugar in a cocktail shaker. Shake well and pour into a chilled 4-ounce [125-ml.] cocktail glass.

ANTHONY HOGG
COCKTAILS AND MIXED DRINKS

Bullshot

The technique of making beef tea is shown on pages 62-63.

	To make 1 cocktail	
2 or 3	ice cubes	2 or 3
1½ oz.	vodka	45 ml.
¼ cup	cold strong beef consommé or beef tea *(recipe, page 128)*	50 ml.
	salt and pepper	

Put the ice cubes in a cocktail shaker with the vodka and consommé, add salt and pepper to taste, shake and strain into a chilled 4-ounce [125-ml.] cocktail glass.

A TO Z OF COCKTAILS

Honeybee Special

	To make 1 cocktail	
1 tsp.	honey	5 ml.
1 tbsp.	fresh lemon juice	15 ml.
1½ oz.	applejack	45 ml.

Warm the honey until it runs freely. Warm a 3-ounce [90-ml.] cocktail glass by rinsing it in hot water. Mix the honey and lemon juice in the glass and add the applejack.

ANN ROE ROBBINS
TREADWAY INNS COOK BOOK

Brandy Alexander

	To make 1 cocktail	
1 oz.	brandy	30 ml.
½ oz.	crème de cacao	15 ml.
1 oz.	heavy cream	30 ml.
	ice cubes	
	grated nutmeg	

Shake the brandy, crème de cacao and cream with two or three ice cubes. Strain the mixture into a chilled Champagne glass. Dust the surface of the drink with nutmeg.

TRADER VIC
TRADER VIC'S BARTENDER'S GUIDE, REVISED

Horse's Neck Highball

During Prohibition, the American version of this highball lost its alcoholic content.

	To make 1 tall drink	
	ice cubes	
1½ oz.	brandy	45 ml.
	Angostura bitters	
	ginger ale	
1	lemon, the peel pared in one continuous strip	1

Place the ice cubes in a 10-ounce [300-ml.] highball glass. Add the brandy and two dashes of Angostura bitters. Fill the glass with ginger ale. Place one end of the lemon peel over the edge of the glass and let the rest curl inside the glass.

THE SAVOY COCKTAIL BOOK

Angel's Delight

The technique of layering liqueurs is shown on page 90. A pousse-café glass is a small, narrow liqueur glass.

	To make 1 after-dinner drink	
½ tbsp.	grenadine	7 ml.
½ tbsp.	Triple Sec	7 ml.
½ tbsp.	Crème Yvette	7 ml.
½ tbsp.	heavy cream	7 ml.

Carefully pour the four ingredients, in the order given, into a pousse-café glass so that each ingredient floats on top of the preceding one.

THE DINERS' CLUB, INC.
THE DINERS' CLUB DRINK BOOK

Chartreuse in Orange Cup

Chartreuse en Copa de Naranja

A variety of other liqueurs can be served in this orange-peel cup: orange Curaçao, Cointreau, Grand Marnier, Drambuie.

	To make 1 after-dinner drink	
1	very small orange	1
1 to 2 tsp.	brandy	5 to 10 ml.
	finely crushed ice	
2 oz.	chartreuse, yellow or green	60 ml.

Cut about ½ inch [1 cm.] off the top of the orange so that it will fit up to the rim of a large, widemouthed goblet. Scoop out the orange pulp. Turn the orange shell inside out and force it down into the goblet. Pour in the brandy and set it alight to bring out the aroma of the peel. Now fill the orange shell with finely crushed ice, and then pour in the chartreuse—the strong green is preferred. Stir once. Use no garnish, but serve with an orange-colored straw, cut quite short.

CHARLES H. BAKER JR.
THE SOUTH AMERICAN GENTLEMAN'S COMPANION

Classic Pousse-Café

Le Pousse-Café Classique

For instructions on how to measure density and layer liqueurs in the glass, see page 90.

	To make 1 after-dinner drink	
¼ oz.	grenadine or raspberry syrup	7 ml.
¼ oz.	crème de cacao	7 ml.
¼ oz.	maraschino liqueur	7 ml.
¼ oz.	orange Curaçao	7 ml.
¼ oz.	green crème de menthe	7 ml.
¼ oz.	*parfait amour*	7 ml.
¼ oz.	Cognac or brandy	7 ml.

Use a tall, narrow liqueur glass. Pour in the ingredients in their order of density.

NINETTE LYON
LE GUIDE MARABOUT DES COCKTAILS ET BOISSONS ALCOOLISÉES

Rusty Nail

	To make 1 cocktail	
1½ oz.	Drambuie	45 ml.
1½ oz.	Scotch	45 ml.
2 or 3	ice cubes	2 or 3

Pour the Drambuie and Scotch over the ice cubes in a chilled 6-ounce [180-ml.] old-fashioned glass. Stir and serve.

INA C. BOYD
COCKTAILS & HORS D'OEUVRES

Shandygaff

	To make 1 tall drink	
½ cup	chilled beer	125 ml.
½ cup	chilled ginger beer or bitter lemon	125 ml.

Mix the beer and ginger beer or bitter lemon in a chilled 12-ounce [375-ml.] glass.

ELEANOR GRAVES
GREAT DINNERS FROM LIFE

Wine Cobbler

The technique of making wine cobbler is shown on page 89.
   The cobbler is a drink of American origin, now an established favorite, particularly in warm climates.

	To make 1 cocktail	
	crushed ice	
3 oz.	red Burgundy or Bordeaux, Rhine wine, port or sherry	90 ml.
	orange Curaçao	
1 tsp.	superfine sugar	5 ml.
1	sprig fresh mint (optional)	1
	fresh fruit such as whole berries, pineapple or papaya cubes, peach or orange slices	

Half-fill a chilled 6-ounce [180-ml.] wine glass with crushed ice. Pour the wine or fortified wine over the ice. Add four dashes of Curaçao and the superfine sugar. Stir the drink well, garnish it with the mint, if you wish, and with fruit of your choice. Serve with straws.

UNITED KINGDOM BARTENDERS' GUILD
INTERNATIONAL GUIDE TO DRINKS

Ale Sangaree

To make 1 tall drink

1 tsp.	superfine sugar	5 ml.
1 tbsp.	water	15 ml.
1 or 2	ice cubes	1 or 2
⅔ cup	ale	150 ml.
	grated nutmeg	

Put the confectioners' sugar into a chilled 8-ounce [250-ml.] highball glass and dissolve it in the water; put in the ice cube and fill up the glass with the ale. Dust with nutmeg to taste.

FREDERICK DAVIES AND SEYMOUR DAVIES
DRINKS OF ALL KINDS HOT AND COLD

Black Velvet

Stout is a heavy, dark ale brewed from roasted malt. The technique of making Black Velvet is shown on page 89.

To make 1 tall drink

4 oz.	stout, chilled	125 ml.
4 oz.	Champagne, chilled	125 ml.

Tilt a chilled, tall, narrow, 10-ounce [300-ml.] glass and pour the stout slowly in a thin stream down the side of the glass to prevent the formation of too much froth. Fill the glass with the Champagne.

THE SAVOY COCKTAIL BOOK

Sherry Cobbler

To make 1 tall drink

4 oz.	sherry	125 ml.
1 tbsp.	superfine sugar	15 ml.
2 or 3	orange slices	2 or 3
	finely crushed ice	
	fresh berries	

Put the sherry, sugar and orange slices in a chilled 12-ounce [360-ml.] Tom Collins glass and fill the glass with finely crushed ice. Mix well, and ornament the cobbler with whatever berries are in season.

FREDERICK DAVIES AND SEYMOUR DAVIES
DRINKS OF ALL KINDS HOT AND COLD

Champagne Cocktail

The technique of making Champagne Cocktail is demonstrated on page 89.

To make 1 cocktail

1	sugar cube	1
	Angostura bitters	
1 oz.	brandy	30 ml.
5 oz.	Champagne, chilled	150 ml.
1	slice orange	1

Chill an 8-ounce [250-ml.] wineglass. Put the sugar cube in the bottom of the glass and saturate the sugar with a dash of Angostura bitters. Add the brandy, then fill the glass with the Champagne. Serve garnished with a slice of orange.

UNITED KINGDOM BARTENDERS' GUILD
INTERNATIONAL GUIDE TO DRINKS

Kir

Crème de cassis is a black currant cordial.

It was Canon Kir, later deputy-mayor of Dijon, who, while a parish priest at Nolay, first thought of sweetening white Burgundy with a little crème de cassis, a Burgundian liqueur specialty.

To make 1 after-dinner drink

½ oz.	crème de cassis	15 ml.
2½ oz.	white Burgundy	75 ml.

Pour the crème de cassis and the white Burgundy into a small cocktail glass.

NINETTE LYON
LE GUIDE MARABOUT DES COCKTAILS ET BOISSONS ALCOOLISÉES

Mimosa

In England, this drink is known as Buck's Fizz.

To make 1 cocktail

⅓ cup	fresh orange juice	75 ml.
about ⅔ cup	Champagne, chilled	about 150 ml.

Pour the orange juice into a chilled 10-ounce [300-ml.] wine glass, then fill the glass with the Champagne.

ANTHONY HOGG
COCKTAILS AND MIXED DRINKS

Americano

To make 1 cocktail

1 oz.	sweet vermouth	30 ml.
1 oz.	Campari	30 ml.
3	ice cubes	3
	soda water, chilled	
½-inch	strip lemon peel	1-cm.

Put the vermouth and Campari in a chilled 6-ounce [180-ml.] old-fashioned glass. Stir, add the ice cubes and top up the drink with soda water. Twist the lemon peel over the glass to release its oil and drop the peel into the drink.

A TO Z OF COCKTAILS

Vermouth Cassis

To make 1 tall drink

2 oz.	French vermouth	60 ml.
1 oz.	crème de cassis	30 ml.
2 or 3	ice cubes	2 or 3
	soda water, chilled	

Stir the vermouth and crème de cassis with the ice cubes in a chilled 8-ounce [250-ml.] highball glass. Fill the glass with soda and stir lightly.

TRADER VIC
TRADER VIC'S BARTENDER'S GUIDE, REVISED

Hot Toddy for Cold Night

This is the recipe of the 18th Century *Auberge du Vieux Puits* at Pont Audemer in Normandy. The recipe is attributed to Gustave Flaubert.

To make 1 toddy

3 oz.	Calvados	90 ml.
1½ oz.	apricot brandy	45 ml.
1½ oz.	heavy cream	45 ml.

Warm the Calvados and the apricot brandy over low heat. Pour the mixture into a glass. Slowly pour in the cream. Do not stir. Pour into a warmed 8-ounce [250-ml.] glass or mug. Serve at once.

ALICE B. TOKLAS
THE ALICE B. TOKLAS COOK BOOK

Hot Buttered Rum

To make 1 drink

2 to 3 oz.	dark rum	60 to 90 ml.
	twist of lemon peel	
	cinnamon stick	
2	whole cloves	2
1	sugar cube (optional)	1
1 cup	boiling sweet cider or water	¼ liter
1 tbsp.	unsalted butter	15 ml.
	freshly grated nutmeg	

Put the rum, lemon peel, cinnamon and cloves in a 12-ounce [375-ml.] pewter tankard or heavy mug that has been rinsed out in very hot water to warm it. Add a sugar cube if you wish. Pour the boiling cider or water into the spiced rum. Add the butter and stir well. Top with nutmeg.

COLLETTE RICHARDSON (EDITOR)
HOUSE & GARDEN'S DRINK GUIDE

Tom and Jerry

The secret of a Tom and Jerry is to have a stiff batter and a warm mug to make it in.

To make 1 hot drink

¾ cup	hot milk	175 ml.
1¾ oz.	rum	50 ml.
½ oz.	brandy	15 ml.
	freshly grated nutmeg	
Egg batter		
1	egg, the yolk separated from the white, both beaten thoroughly	1
2 tbsp.	superfine sugar	30 ml.
	baking soda	
½ tbsp.	rum	7 ml.

To make the batter, combine the beaten egg yolk and white in a bowl, add 1 tablespoon [15 ml.] of the sugar and whisk until the mixture is stiff. Add a pinch of baking soda and the rum to preserve the batter, then add the remaining sugar to stiffen the mixture.

Warm a 10-ounce [300-ml.] mug and in it dissolve the batter in 3 tablespoons [45 ml.] of the hot milk. Add the rum. Fill the mug to within ¼ inch [6 mm.] of the top with the rest of the milk; stir gently. Top with the brandy and the nutmeg.

THE DINERS' CLUB, INC.
THE DINERS' CLUB DRINK BOOK

Standard Preparations

Sugar Syrup

This recipe will yield a light sugar syrup. For a medium sugar syrup, use 1½ cups [375 ml.] of sugar; for a heavy syrup, use 2 cups [½ liter] of sugar.

To make about 3 cups [¾ liter] syrup

1 cup	sugar	¼ liter
2½ cups	water	625 ml.

Place the sugar and water in a saucepan and cook over medium heat, stirring continuously until the sugar dissolves. Dip a pastry brush in hot water and use it to wipe down the sides of the pan to dissolve any clinging sugar crystals. Increase the heat, bring the syrup to a boil without stirring, and boil it for one minute before removing the pan from the heat.

Basic Fruit Syrup

This recipe will make a medium-strength syrup; the addition of more or less sugar will produce a heavier or lighter syrup. Any ripe, soft fruit can be used—apricots, berries, cherries, currants, grapes and plums among them.

To make about 2½ cups [625 ml.] syrup

2 lb.	soft fruit, pitted if necessary	1 kg.
about 4 cups	sugar	about 1 liter

Put the fruit in a bowl and crush it with a wide pestle until it forms a thick purée. Cover the bowl and leave it in a cool place overnight. Line a sieve with a layer of muslin or cheesecloth and place the sieve over a bowl. Strain the fruit purée through the sieve, stirring it with a wooden spoon. Pick up the four corners of the cloth and twist the cloth tightly to extract as much juice as possible.

Measure the juice and add 2 cups [½ liter] of sugar to every cup [¼ liter] of juice. Pour the mixture into a non-reactive pan and place the pan over low heat. Stir the mixture gently until the sugar dissolves. Dip a pastry brush in hot water and use it to brush down the sides of the pan to dissolve any crystals that may have formed. Increase the heat and bring the mixture to a boil. Then reduce the heat to low and set the pan half off the heat. Skim off the scum that forms on the cooler side of the pan and keep skimming until no more scum forms—about 10 minutes. Remove the pan from the heat and leave the syrup until it is cold.

Set a funnel in a clean, dry bottle and pour the cold syrup through the funnel, leaving just enough space for the cork. Cork the bottle tightly. Store the syrup in the refrigerator; it will keep safely for about four weeks.

Basic Chicken Broth

To make about 2 quarts [2 liters]

5 lb.	stewing chicken, trussed, heart and gizzard reserved	2½ kg.
1 lb.	chicken necks and wing tips	½ kg.
about 3 quarts	water	about 3 liters
3	carrots, peeled	3
2	onions	2
1	bouquet garni	1
1	garlic bulb	1
	salt and pepper	

Place a metal rack in the bottom of a pot and put the trussed chicken on the rack. Add the heart, gizzard and chicken trimmings and enough cold water to cover the chicken by about ½ inch [1 cm.]. Bring slowly to a boil over medium heat—about 30 minutes. Remove the scum repeatedly until no more scum forms. Add the carrots, onions, bouquet garni and garlic bulb. Place the lid slightly ajar on the pot and simmer the broth over low heat for two to three hours, removing the trussed chicken from the pot when it is tender.

Line a large sieve with several thicknesses of dampened muslin or cheesecloth, and set the sieve over a clean pan. Strain the broth through the sieve. Boil the broth, uncovered, over high heat until it is reduced by about a quarter. Skim off any remaining fat from the surface of the broth. Season the broth to taste and serve it hot in warmed cups.

Basic Meat Broth

This broth is made with lamb. You can also make a basic meat broth by using 2 pounds [1 kg.] of boneless beef or veal shoulder instead of the lamb and by substituting carrots for the turnips.

To make about 1½ quarts [1½ liters]

2 lb.	boneless lamb neck or shoulder	1 kg.
about 2 quarts	water	about 2 liters
1	onion, stuck with 2 whole cloves	1
2	turnips, peeled	2
1	bouquet garni	1
	salt and pepper	

Trim all the surface fat away from the lamb and cut the meat into small pieces. Put a metal rack into a large pot and place the pieces of meat on the rack. Pour enough cold water into the pot to cover the meat by about 2 inches [5 cm.]. Bring slowly to a boil, skimming off the scum that rises. Keep skimming, occasionally adding a glass of cold water, until no more scum rises—about 10 to 15 minutes. Be careful not to stir the liquid, lest the scum disperse and cloud the broth. Add the onion, turnips and bouquet garni to the pot. Cover the pot, leaving the lid partially ajar, and simmer the broth over low heat for two and one half hours.

Line a large sieve with several thicknesses of dampened muslin or cheesecloth and set the sieve over a clean pan. Strain the broth through the sieve. Skim all of the remaining fat from the surface of the broth and boil the broth rapidly for 10 to 15 minutes, until it is reduced by about a quarter. Season the broth and serve it very hot in warmed cups.

Coconut Milk

To make about 1 cup [¼ liter] coconut milk

1	coconut	1
about 1 cup	hot water	about ¼ liter

If the coconut is still encased in its husk, pull or cut the husk away. Use a skewer to pierce the three indentations at the tip of the coconut. Turn the coconut upside down over a bowl and let the juice drain out through the holes.Taste the juice and, if it has a sweet flavor, reserve it. Place the coconut on a hard surface, grasp it firmly at one end and tap around it sharply with the dull side of a cleaver until a crack encircles the shell. Strike the crack sharply to split the coconut in half. Break the halves into smaller pieces, then use a sharp knife to remove the coconut flesh from the shell and peel off the brown skin. Grate the coconut pieces coarse, either with a grater or in a food processor. Place the grated coconut in a bowl and add the coconut juice if you reserved it. Pour in enough hot water to cover the grated coconut, and leave the mixture for one hour.

Line a sieve with dampened cheesecloth and set it over a clean bowl. Pour the grated coconut and liquid into the sieve, a little at a time, making sure that all the liquid has drained through the sieve before adding more. Once all the liquid has passed through the sieve, pick up the four edges of the cheesecloth and twist the cheesecloth tightly to release as much coconut milk as possible. Discard the flesh.

Yogurt

To make 1 quart [1 liter]

1 quart	milk	1 liter
3 tbsp.	yogurt	45 ml.

Pour the milk into a heavy pan and bring it to a boil over medium heat, stirring occasionally. Remove the pan from the heat. Warm a dairy, candy or deep-frying thermometer in tepid water and put it into the pan of milk. Let the milk cool to 110° F. [43° C.]. Remove any skin that has formed on the surface of the milk. In a large bowl, whisk the yogurt until it is smooth. Pour the milk onto the yogurt and blend the mixture by whisking it well.

Ladle the mixture into heatproof jars. Place the jars side by side in a deep pot. Pour enough tepid water into the pot to reach halfway up the sides of the jars. Cover the jars; set the lid on the pot and wrap it in a blanket or towels. Set the pot in a warm, draft-free place and let the yogurt incubate for at least four hours—preferably overnight. When the yogurt is firmly set, transfer the jars to the refrigerator; the yogurt will become firmer as it chills and can be kept for a week.

Basic Ice Cream

The technique of freezing ice cream in an ice-cream maker is demonstrated on page 52.

To make about 4 quarts [4 liters] ice cream

2½ quarts	heavy cream	2½ liters
2 cups	sugar	½ liter
1	vanilla bean	1
¼ tsp.	salt	1 ml.

In a heavy saucepan, mix 1 quart [1 liter] of the cream with the sugar, vanilla bean and salt. Stir over medium heat until the sugar dissolves and the mixture is scalded, but not boiling. Remove the pan from the heat, cover it and let the cream cool to room temperature. Take out the vanilla bean, and wash and dry it to reserve it for another use. Stir the remaining 1½ quarts [1½ liters] of cream into the mixture. Cover the pan and refrigerate the mixture for one hour, or until well chilled. Pour the mixture into the canister of an ice-cream maker and freeze it.

Philadelphia vanilla ice cream. As soon as the cream mixture is removed from the heat, take out the vanilla bean and split it lengthwise. Scrape the vanilla-bean seeds into the pan and discard the pod.

Chocolate ice cream. Melt 4 ounces [125 g.] of semisweet chocolate in 1 cup [¼ liter] of the cream and stir it into the sweetened mixture after removing the vanilla bean.

Chocolate chip ice cream. Grate 14 ounces [420 g.] of semisweet chocolate and stir it into the frozen ice cream while it is still soft.

Fruit ice cream. While the frozen ice cream is still soft, stir in 3 cups [¾ liter] of crushed or sliced, peeled and pitted peaches; 3 cups of crushed or sliced strawberries; 3 cups of crushed raspberries; or 12 mashed and sieved bananas.

Nut ice cream. Stir 1 cup [¼ liter] of chopped or coarsely ground pecans or walnuts and 1½ tablespoons [22 ml.] of vanilla extract into the frozen ice cream while it is still soft.

Basic Custard Ice Cream

The technique of freezing ice cream in an ice-cream maker is demonstrated on page 52.

To make about 5 cups [1 ¼ liters] ice cream

8	egg yolks	8
⅔ cup	sugar	150 ml.
2½ cups	milk, scalded	625 ml.

Beat the egg yolks and sugar until they are thick and pale. Beating constantly, gradually add the scalded milk to the yolks and sugar. Pour the mixture into a heavy pan. Over low heat, stir the mixture with a wooden spoon until it is thick enough to coat the spoon; do not let it simmer or boil. Strain the custard through a sieve into a metal bowl.

Fill a large bowl with ice cubes and set the metal bowl containing the custard over the ice. Stir the custard continuously until it has cooled—about 20 minutes. Pour the custard into the canister of an ice-cream maker and freeze it. If you do not have an ice-cream maker, you can pour it into ice trays and freeze it until firm—about three hours; to ensure a smooth consistency, remove the trays from the freezer every 30 minutes and beat the custard in a bowl.

Vanilla ice cream. Combine a split vanilla bean and 2½ cups [625 ml.] of cold milk in a heavy pan and bring the milk to a boil. Set the milk aside to cool and infuse for about 20 minutes. Add the milk and vanilla bean to the beaten egg yolks and sugar; the vanilla bean is strained out when the custard has been cooked.

Chocolate ice cream. Melt 2 ounces [60 g.] of semisweet chocolate in ¼ cup [50 ml.] of water in a heavy pan over very low heat. Stir continuously until the mixture forms a smooth paste. Stir the paste into the strained, cooked custard.

Coffee ice cream. Add ⅓ cup [75 ml.] of very strong coffee to the strained, cooked custard.

Berry or soft-fruit ice cream. Purée or crush 1 cup [¼ liter] of raspberries, strawberries or peeled and chopped soft fruit such as peaches, apricots, mangoes or bananas; if using raspberries, pass them through a fine sieve to remove the seeds. Stir the purée into the strained, cooked custard.

Ice-Cream Soda

To make about 1 ½ cups [375 ml.]

2 to 3 tbsp.	flavored syrup	30 to 45 ml.
	soda water	
2 scoops	vanilla ice cream (recipe, page 165)	2 scoops
	heavy cream, whipped	
	fresh fruit, chopped nuts or grated sweet chocolate (optional)	

Pour the syrup into a tall glass. Add a dash of soda water and stir to dilute the syrup slightly. Add the ice cream and fill the glass to the top with soda water. Spoon the whipped cream on top and garnish, if you like, with fruit, nuts or chocolate.

Basic Beer

The technique of making beer is shown on pages 70-71.

To make about forty-eight 12-ounce [375-ml.] bottles beer

20 quarts	water, 12 quarts [12 liters] boiled and cooled, plus 1 cup [¼ liter] tepid water	20 liters
3½ lb.	can unhopped malt extract	1¾ kg.
4¼ cups	corn sugar	1,050 ml.
1 oz.	package hop pellets	30 g.
2 tsp.	water-treatment crystals	10 ml.
¼ oz.	package all-purpose beer yeast	7 g.

In a large, nonreactive stockpot, bring 8 quarts [8 liters] of water to a boil. Add the malt extract and 3 cups [¾ liter] of the corn sugar, stirring until they dissolve. Add three quarters of the hop pellets, and the water-treatment crystals. Stir well and bring the mixture to a boil. Reduce the heat to low and let the mixture simmer uncovered for 30 minutes, then stir in the remaining hops. Simmer for 15 minutes longer.

Strain the mixture through a cheesecloth-lined strainer set over a 30-quart [30-liter] single-stage fermentation tank. Add the cooled boiled water to the tank. Let the liquid cool to 80° F. [25° C.], testing the temperature with a deep-frying, candy or instant-response thermometer. Combine the beer yeast with the cup [¼ liter] of tepid water, stir well and let the mixture stand for 10 minutes. Add the yeast mixture to the fermentation tank, stirring well to incorporate it fully. Cover the tank with its lid and fill the air lock halfway with water before fitting it into the lid. Set the tank in a 60° to 80° F. [15° to 25° C.] place and allow the beer mixture to ferment for 12 to 14 days.

When fermentation has ceased, use a hydrometer to test the specific gravity of the beer. If the hydrometer registers 1.004, the beer is ready; siphon it into a large stockpot. Otherwise, cover the tank again and let the beer ferment for another day or two. Test it again before siphoning it.

Ladle 1 cup of the siphoned beer into a small saucepan. Add the remaining 1¼ cups [300 ml.] of corn sugar and bring the mixture to a boil, stirring until the sugar dissolves. Boil for one minute, then remove the syrup mixture from the heat. When the syrup mixture has cooled, stir it into the beer. Siphon the beer into bottles, cap the bottles and store them upright in a cool (60° to 65° F. [15° to 18° C.]), dark place for six weeks. Chill the beer before serving it.

Basic Dry Wine

This recipe can be used for any soft ripe fruit—berries, grapes, currants, cherries, peaches, apricots, plums, bananas and the like. Of these, strawberries, peaches, apricots, plums and bananas are deficient in tannin: Add ½ teaspoon [2 ml.] of powdered grape tannin or ½ cup [125 ml.] of strong black tea at the same time you add the pectic enzyme.

The techniques of making wine and conducting the acid and sugar tests are shown on pages 72-73.

	To make 4 quarts [4 liters] wine	
3 lb.	soft ripe fruit, cut up if large and pits—if any—removed	1½ kg.
about 3 quarts	water, boiled and cooled	about 3 liters
	acid blend	
	sugar	
2	Campden tablets, each dissolved in 1 tsp. [5 ml.] water as needed	2
½ tsp.	pectic enzyme	2 ml.
½ tsp.	powdered grape tannin or ½ cup [125 ml.] strong black tea (optional)	2 ml.
	yeast nutrient	
⅙ oz.	package all-purpose wine yeast, mixed with 1 cup [¼ liter] tepid water and left to stand for 10 minutes	5 g.

Wash the fruit thoroughly and place it in an 8-quart [8-liter] primary fermentation bucket. Crush the fruit and add 3 quarts [3 liters] of cooled boiled water. Remove and strain about 1 cup [¼ liter] of the liquid mixture and use it to make the acid and sugar tests. Then add the appropriate amounts

of acid blend and sugar to the mixture in the bucket and stir to dissolve the sugar.

Add one dissolved Campden tablet to the mixture along with the pectic enzyme, the tannin or tea, if you are using it, and the yeast nutrient. Cover the bucket with plastic wrap and set it aside overnight.

Stir in the yeast. Cover the bucket securely with plastic wrap and set it aside in a warm—70° F. [20° C.]—place for about seven days, stirring the mixture thoroughly each day. When the foam subsides, strain the fermented mixture through a cheesecloth-lined strainer set over a large bowl. Gather up the corners of the cheesecloth and squeeze it tightly to extract the juice from the fruit. Discard the pulp.

Ladle the strained liquid through a funnel into a 4-quart [4-liter] secondary fermentation jug. Fill the jug to within 1 inch [2½ cm.] of the top; add cooled boiled water, if necessary. Fill a fermentation lock halfway with water and fit the lock in the neck of the jug. Set the jug in the 70° F. place and let the wine ferment for about four weeks.

When fermentation has ceased, siphon the wine into a clean jug; add cooled boiled water if necessary to fill the jug. Replace the lock and let the wine stand in a 60° F. [15° C.] place for about four weeks, or until it clears. At this stage the wine may be siphoned into bottles and the bottles corked; for clearer wine, however, you may prefer to siphon it into a clean jar and let it rest for four weeks longer. To ensure that the fermented wine remains free from contamination during the siphoning process, add one dissolved Campden tablet.

Store the bottled wine in a cool—55° to 60° F. [12° to 15° C.]—dark place for at least six months before drinking it.

Apple or pear wine. Thoroughly wash 6 pounds [3 kg.] of fruit. (For the apple wine, use equal parts of sweet and tart apples, using up to 1 pound [½ kg.] of crab apples if available.) Cut the fruit into small pieces, then crush the fruit coarse and add 2 quarts [2 liters] of cooled boiled water. Add 5 cups [1¼ liters] of sugar to the mixture. The sugar test is not used for apple or pear wine; the acid test is conducted after the primary fermentation. Add the other ingredients to the fruit mixture, doubling the amount of pectic enzyme. Crush the fruit twice daily during the primary fermentation period to help reduce it to a pulp. Press the pulp through a fruit press to extract the maximum amount of juice. Place the juice in a container and proceed with the acid test, adding the acid blend to the juice before ladling it into the secondary fermentation jug.

Citrus wine. Pare the colored peel from six oranges or three grapefruits, taking care to leave behind the bitter white pith. Squeeze the pared fruit and enough additional oranges or grapefruits to yield 1 quart [1 liter] of juice; refrigerate the juice. Place the peel in a bowl and pour 1 quart of boiling water over the peel. Cover the bowl and let the peel stand at room temperature overnight. Strain the liquid and combine it with the juice. Add enough cooled boiled water to make 4 quarts [4 liters] of liquid. Make the acid and sugar tests and follow the procedure explained above, using the additional tannin or the tea.

Recipe Index

All recipes in the index that follows are listed by the English title except in cases where beverages of foreign origin, such as cassis, are widely recognized by their source name. Entries are organized in separate categories by major ingredients specified in the recipe titles. Foreign recipes are listed under the country or region of origin. Recipe credits appear on pages 173-176.

General Index/ Glossary

Included in this index to the cooking demonstrations are definitions, in italics, of special culinary terms not explained elsewhere in this volume. The Recipe Index begins on page 168.

Acid: in fruit, and use of nonreactive metals, 31
Alcoholic drinks (fermented): beer, 65, 70-71; cider, 65, 72-73; equipment, 65; ginger beer, 68-69; mead, 76-77; wine, 65, 74-75. *See also* Cocktails; Liqueur
Ale: in Black Velvet, 89; mulling, 82
Almonds: blanching and peeling, 42; infusing, 38, 43; in mulled wine, 82-83; preparing a syrup from, 42-43
Angelica: *a native European herb cultivated mostly for its roots, which are used in producing cordials and liqueurs, and for its stalks, which are candied in sugar syrup when they are green.*
Apples: infusing to make juice, 32-33; making hard cider, 72-73; in mulled wine, 82-83; preparing for a punch, 80; varieties for cider, 72
Apricots: blanching, 66; in daiquiri, 87; preserving in spirits, 66-67
Arrack: *a Middle Eastern or Indonesian alcoholic beverage distilled from dates, or rice and sugar, or coconut palm sap.*
Assam tea, 12, 13
Bananas: in daiquiri, 87; puréed, in combination with coconut milk, 38
Barley: infusing, 33; use in beer, 70

Beef: cuts for broth, 60; cuts for tea, 62
Beer: ale or stout to make a Black Velvet, 89; bottling, 8, 71; brewing at home, 70-71. *See also* Ginger beer
Berries: preparing for punch, 80; puréeing, 32, 37; syrup made from, 40
Bitter orange: *a tart-flavored orange, also called a sour or Seville orange. Sold at fruit stores and Latin American markets in winter;* 14
Bitter orange: tisane prepared from, 14
Black teas, 6, 12, 18, 19
Blackberry wine, 74-75
Black Velvet, 89
Blanch: *to plunge food into boiling water for up to one minute. Done to facilitate the removal of skins or shells, or to soften vegetables or fruits before further cooking;* 42, 66
Bloody Mary, 88
Blue Mountain coffee, Jamaican, 17
Boldo: tisane prepared from, 14, 15
Borage: *an herb whose flavor is reminiscent of cucumber;* 81
Bottling: alcoholic beverages, 8; capping and corking bottles, 8-9; cleaning and sterilizing bottles, 8; syrups, 8
Bouquet garni: *a bunch of mixed herbs — the classic three being parsley, thyme and bay leaf — tied together or wrapped in cheesecloth and used for flavoring stocks, sauces, braises and stews;* 60, 61, 63
Bourbon: in mint julep, 89; in Sazerac, 88

Brandy: in café brûlot, 28-29; in Champagne cocktail, 89; in a fruit punch, 80-81; in mulled wine, 82; in pousse-café, 90; in a punch with rum and tea, 80-81
Broth, 7, 55; adding lemon juice, 56; adding peppercorns, 56, 57; chicken, 60-61; garlic, 58-59; meat, 60-61; mixing *pommade* with, 58; skimming, 55, 57; spices and herbs in, 56; straining, 57; vegetable, 54, 56-57
Burdock: infusing leaves to make a small beer, 68
Cabbage: in vegetable broth, 56
Cacao bean: processing of, 46
Café brûlot, 28-29
Café au lait, 24
Calvados: *a French apple brandy named for the district in Normandy where it is produced. It is similar to American applejack.*
Camomile: tisane prepared from, 14, 15
Campari: *an Italian bitters with a pungent flavor, distilled from a blend of herbs.*
Campden tablets (sodium metabisulphite): as sterilizing agent, 8, 65, 72, 74, 76
Capping bottles, 8
Cappuccino, 24
Cardamom: *an East Indian spice consisting of a fibrous oval pod containing hard, brownish black seeds with a faintly lemon-like flavor. When dried in kilns, the pod remains green; when sun-dried, the pod bleaches to a cream color. Obtainable where fine spices are sold;* 18, 19, 24, 56, 82
Carrots: in beef tea, 62-63; in

chicken broth, 61; infusing, 32; juicing, 35; in meat broth, 60-61; in vegetable broth, 56-57
Caudle, 84-85
Celeriac, in vegetable broth, 56
Celery: in beef tea, 62-63; stewing and sieving to make juice, 32; in vegetable broth, 56-57
Ceylon tea, 12, 13
Champagne cocktail, 89
Chartreuse: *a green, yellow or white liqueur, made from a blend of herbs and spices. Chartreuse is produced only in France and Spain by the Carthusian monks.*
Cheese: Parmesan, in a *pommade,* 58
Cherries: crushing and sieving to make juice, 32; preparing for a punch, 80
Cherry Heering: *a cherry-flavored liqueur from Denmark.*
Chervil: flavoring in tomato juice, 36
Chicken broth: cooking, 60-61
Chocolate: hot, 46-47; syrup, 53
Cider (hard): apple varieties, 72; bottling, 8; brewing, 72-73; mulling, 82
Cinnamon: in Mexican coffee, 25; in mulled wine, 82
Citrus fruit: in combination with coconut milk, 38; extracting juice from, 32; orange and carrot juice, 35; peel, in café brûlot, 28-29
Cocktails, 86-89; Black Velvet, 89; Bloody Mary, 88; Champagne, 89; combining liquids of varying densities, 86; daiquiri, 87; Margarita, 88; martini, 88; mint julep, 89; mixing, 86; proper glasses, 86; Sazerac, 88; Silver

Sarsaparilla: infusing roots, 68
Sazerac, 88
Scald: *a cooking term — usually applied to milk — that means to heat liquid to just below the boiling point, or until small bubbles appear around the edge of the pan.*
Scented orange pekoe tea, 13
Semolina: *coarse cream-colored granules, milled from the hearts of durum-wheat berries. It is similar to farina, which is made from the hearts of other hard-wheat berries.*
Sherry: in eggnog, 84; in wine cobbler, 89
Shrub: *a beverage made of vinegar and fruit juice.*
Silver Fizz, 88
Small beer, 68
Soda water: in ice-cream soda, 53
Spices: in coffee, 24; in mulled wine, 82; in tea, 18; in vegetable broth, 56; in yogurt-based drinks, 50
Spinach: in vegetable broth, 56
Strawberries: in fruit punch, 80-81; puréeing into a juice, 37; syrup, made into ice-cream soda, 53
Sugar: in fruit syrup, 40, 41;

piloncillo, 24, 25; superfine, in mixed drinks, 86, 88, 89; syrup, 26
Syrup: from almonds, 42-43; from black currants, 40-41; chocolate, in milk shake, 53; fruit, uses, 40; in ice-cream drinks, 53; from mint, 43; from nuts, flowers and herbs, 42-43; sugar, 26
Tamarind: *the tart, brown fruit of the tamarind tree. The dried pulp from the pod is obtainable at gourmet food stores and at Asian and Latin American markets.*
Tea: amount to use, 18; ceremonial aspects, 5-6; cultivation, 5, 6; flavorings, 18, 19; iced, 18, 19; in mead, 76; pot for, 18; processing leaves, 6, 11, 12-13; in punch, 80-81; storing, 13; varieties, 12-13
Tea, beef: preparing, 62-63
Tequila: in Margarita, 86
Thyme: preparing tisane from, 14, 15
Tisanes, 6; drying herbs, 15; iced, 18, 19; infusing, 18-19; varieties, 14-15
Tomatoes: cooking in vegetable broth, 56-57; juice, in Bloody Mary,

88; puréeing in food mill to make juice, 32, 36; seeding, 56
Tom Collins, 86-87
Triple Sec: *a colorless, orange-flavored liqueur, the name for which means "thrice dry." The liqueur was originally three times as dry as other orange liqueurs, but Triple Sec today is often quite sweet.*
Turkish coffee, 6, 24, 25
Turnips: in beef tea, 62-63; in meat broth, 60-61; in vegetable broth, 56-57
Vanilla bean: flavoring for ice cream, 52; flavoring for liqueur, 66
Vanilla sugar: *a flavoring made by leaving a whole vanilla bean in a closed canister of sugar for about a week.*
Veal: in broth, 60
Vegetables: in beef tea, 62, 63; broth made from, 54, 56-57; carrot and orange juice, 35; in chicken broth, 61; in meat broth, 60-61; preparing juice, 32; tomato juice, 36
Vermouth: in dry martini, 88
Vervain: tisane prepared from, 15
Vodka: in Bloody Mary, 88;

in liqueur, 66-67
Walnuts: infusing, 38
Water, 5, 70
Watermelon: making juice from, 32
Whiskey: in Irish coffee, 28, 29
Wine: blackberry, 74-75; bottling, 8, 75; cobbler, 89; in fruit liqueur, 66-67; making, 74-75; mulled, 82-83; sparkling, with beer in a Black Velvet, 89; sparkling, in punch, 80, 81; sugar in, 74, 75; testing for acidity, 74; white, in a caudle, 84-85
Wine press, 65, 72
Woodruff: *a sweet, aromatic herb, traditionally used to flavor wine;* 82
Yeast: beer, 70-71; in hard cider, 72; in mead, 77; role during fermentation, 7, 65, 68; in wine, 74
Yerba maté: tisane prepared from, 14, 15
Yogurt: bacteria in, 45; flavoring with cumin seeds and mint leaves, 51; flavoring with honey and mango, 51; history, 7; homemade, 50; spices and herbs for, 50; starter, 50; thinning to prepare a drink, 50
Yunnan tea, 13
Zucchini: in vegetable broth, 56

Recipe Credits

The sources for the recipes in this volume are shown below. Page references in parentheses indicate where the recipes appear in the anthology.

A to Z of Cocktails. © Ward Lock Limited 1980. Published by Ward Lock Limited, London. By permission of Ward Lock Limited(158, 160, 163).
Ace, Donald L. and James H. Eakin Jr., *Winemaking as a Hobby.* Copyright © 1977 Pennsylvania State University, College of Agriculture. By permission of the publisher, Pennsylvania State University, University Park(131, 132, 134).
Acton, Eliza, *Modern Cookery.* Published by Longman, Brown, Green, and Longmans, London 1856(149, 151, 153).
Ager, Anne, *The Ginger Cookbook.* © Anne Ager 1976. Published by Vantage Books, Bourne End. By permission of the author(150).
Allen, Ida Bailey, *Best Loved Recipes of the American People.* Copyright © 1973 by Ruth Allen Castelli. By permission of the publisher, Doubleday & Company, Inc., New York(123, 149).
American Heritage, the editors of, *The American Heritage Cookbook.* Copyright © 1980 by American Heritage Publishing Co., Inc. Published by American Heritage Publishing Co., Inc., New York. By permission of American Heritage Publishing Co., Inc.(155, 156).
Andrews, Hope and Frances Kelly, *Maryland's Way.* Copyright, 1966—The Hammond-Harwood House Association. Published by The Hammond-Harwood House Association, Annapolis. By permission of The Hammond-

Harwood House Association(146).
Aureden, Lilo, *Was Männern So Gut Schmeckt.* Copyright 1953 by Paul List Verlag München. Published by Paul List Verlag, Munich. Translated by permission of Paul List Verlag(150).
Aylett, Mary, *Country Wines.* Published by Odhams Press Ltd., London 1953. By permission of David Higham Associates Ltd., London(128, 132).
Baker, Charles H., Jr., *The South American Gentleman's Companion.* Copyright, 1951, by Crown Publishers, Inc. Published by Crown Publishers, Inc., New York. By permission of Crown Publishers, Inc.(154, 157, 161).
Becker, Fritz, *Das Kochbuch aus Mecklenburg, Pommern & Ostpreussen.* © copyright 1976 by Verlagsteam Wolfgang Hölker. Published by Verlag Wolfgang Hölker, Münster. Translated by permission of Verlag Wolfgang Hölker(141).
Beech, F. W. (Editor), *Home-Made Wines, Syrups and Cordials.* Published by the National Federation of Women's Institutes, London 1954. By permission of WI Books Ltd., London(113, 114, 134).
Belorechki, Alexander Dimitrov and Nikolay Angelov Dzhelepov, *Obodritelnite Pitieta v Nashiya Dom.* Published by Tehnika, Sofia 1976. Translated by permission of Jusautor Copyright Agency, Sofia(92, 96, 98).
Bennani-Smires, Latifa, *Moroccan Cooking.* Published by Societe d'Edition et de Diffusion, Al Madariss—Casablanca(118).
Bernhard, William, *The Book of One Hundred Beverages.* Published by Houlston and Stoneman, London 1850(102, 112).
Berto, Hazel, *Cooking with Honey.* Copyright © 1972 by Hazel Berto. By permission of the publisher, Gramercy Publishing Company, a division of Crown Publishers, Inc.(93, 124, 146).
Beveridge, N. E., *Cups of Valor.* Copyright © 1968 by The Stackpole Company. By permission of the publisher,

Stackpole Books, Harrisburg, Pennsylvania(146).
Blanquet, Rosalie, *Le Pâtissier des Ménages.* Published by Librairie de Théodore Lefèvre et Cie: Émile Guérin, Éditeur, Paris 1878(139, 141).
Blencowe, Ann, *The Receipt Book of Mrs. Ann Blencowe (A.D. 1694).* Published by Guy Chapman, The Adelphi, London, 1925(151).
Blexrud, Jan, *A Toast to Sober Spirits & Joyous Juices.* © 1976 by Janet C. Blexrud. Published by CompCare Publications, Minneapolis, Minnesota. By permission of CompCare Publications(96, 106, 150).
Boeglin, C. H., *Sundaes, Ices and Ice Cream Sodas, How to Make Them.* Published by Herbert Jenkins, 1928. By permission of Hutchinson Publishing Group, London(124).
Boni, Ada, *The Talisman Italian Cook Book.* Translated and augmented by Matilde La Rosa. Copyright 1950, 1977 by Crown Publishers Inc. Published by Crown Publishers Inc., New York. By permission of Crown Publishers Inc.(99).
Boyd, Ina C., *Cocktails & Hors d'Oeuvres.* Copyright 1978 by Nitty Gritty Cookbooks. By permission of the publisher, Nitty Gritty Productions, Concord, California(159, 161).
Bravery, H. E., *The Complete Book of Home Winemaking.* © H. E. Bravery 1970. Published by Pan Books Ltd., London. By permission of Granada Publishing Ltd., St. Albans(131, 133).
Bringer, Rodolphe, *Les Bons Vieux Plats du Tricastin.* Published by Éditions Daniel Morcrette, Luzarches, France. Translated by permission of Éditions Daniel Morcrette(142).
Brown, Cora, Rose and Bob, *The South American Cook Book.* Originally published by Doubleday, Doran & Company, Inc., 1939. Republished by Dover Publications Inc., New York 1971(109, 110, 118).
The Buckeye Cookbook: Traditional American Recipes. As published by The Buckeye Publishing

Company in 1883. Republished by Dover Publications, Inc., New York 1975(106).

Bullock, Helen, *The Williamsburg Art of Cookery.* Copyright 1938, © 1966 by The Colonial Williamsburg Foundation. Published by Colonial Williamsburg. Reprinted by permission of Holt, Rinehart and Winston, Publishers, New York(136, 144, 149, 152).

Buonassisi, Vincenzo, *Il Caffè.* © Copyright 1980 Centro Luigi Lavazza per Gli Studi e le Ricerche sul Caffè. Published by Publirel, Milan, on behalf of Centro Luigi Lavazza per Gli Studi e le Ricerche sul Caffè. Translated by permission of Publirel(97, 99).

Cabanillas, Berta and Carmen Ginorio, *Puerto-Rican Dishes.* Copyright 1956 by Berta Cabanillas and Carmen Ginorio. Published by Editorial Universitaria, Universidad de Puerto Rico. By permission of University of Puerto Rico(105, 109).

Carcione, Joe, *The Greengrocer Cookbook.* Copyright © 1975 by Joe Carcione. Published by Celestial Arts, Millbrae, California. By permission of Celestial Arts(103, 105, 158).

Catalunya Llaminera. © Editorial Millà—1979. Published by Editorial Millà, Barcelona. Translated by permission of Editorial Millà(112).

Chapel, Alain, *La Cuisine C'est Beaucoup Plus que des Recettes.* © Éditions Robert Laffont, S.A., Paris, 1980. Published by Éditions Robert Laffont, S.A. Translated by permission of Éditions Robert Laffont, S.A.(142).

Child, Mrs., *The American Frugal Housewife.* Published by Carter, Hendee, and Co., Boston 1832(113).

Chow, Dolly, *Chow!* Published in 1963 by the Kin Ma Publishing Company, Taiwan(93).

Cifnentes, Rosario, *Cocina Practica.* Copyright by Editorial Everest—León. Published by Editorial Everest, S.A., León-España. Translated by permission of Editorial Everest, S.A.(98).

La Cocina Paso a Paso (Gran Enciclopedia Sarpe: 1). © Marshall Cavendish Limited, 1977. © SARPE 1979. Published by SARPE, Madrid. Translated by permission of Marshall Cavendish Limited, London(144).

Contini, Mila, *Fatto in Casa.* Longanesi & C., © 1976. Published by Longanesi & C., Milan. Translated by permission of Longanesi & C.(100, 107, 108, 112).

Corey, Helen, *The Art of Syrian Cookery.* Copyright © 1962 by Helen Corey. Published by Doubleday & Company, Inc., New York. By permission of Doubleday & Company, Inc.(93).

Il Cuoco Milanese e la Cuciniera Piemontese. Published by Francesco Pagnoni, tipografo-editore, Milan 1863. Translated by permission of Anastasia Pagnoni, Milan(112).

Cutler, Carol, *The Woman's Day Low-Calorie Dessert Cookbook.* Copyright © 1980 by CBS Consumer Publications, a Division of CBS Inc. By permission of the publisher, Houghton-Mifflin Company, Boston(100).

Czerny, Zofia and Maria Strasburger, *Zywienie Rodziny.* Copyright by Zofia Czerny and Maria Strasburger. Published by Czytelnik Spoldzielnia Wydawnicza 1948. Translated by permission of Angencia Autorska, Warsaw, for the heiress to the authors(107, 111).

Dannenbaum, Julie, *Fast & Fresh.* Copyright © 1981 by Julie Dannenbaum. Published by Harper & Row, Publishers, Inc., New York. By permission of Edward J. Acton Inc., New York(137, 139, 140).

Darden, Norma Jean and Carole, *Spoonbread and Strawberry Wine.* Copyright © 1978 by Norma Jean Darden and Carole Darden. Published by Anchor Press/Doubleday & Company, Garden City, New York. By permission of Doubleday & Company, Inc.(135).

Daughters of the American Revolution, Timothy Bigelow Chapter, *A Book of Beverages.* Published in 1904 for the Daughters of the American Revolution, Worcester, Massachusetts(101).

David, Elizabeth, *Italian Food.* Copyright © Elizabeth David, 1954, 1963, 1969, 1977. Published by Penguin Books Ltd., London. By permission of Penguin Books Ltd.(106).

Davidis, Henriette, *Praktisches Kochbuch.* Newly revised by Luise Holle. Published in Bielefeld and Leipzig, 1898(144).

Davies, Frederick and Seymour Davies, *Drinks of all Kinds.* Published by Sir Isaac Pitman & Sons, Ltd., London. By permission of Pitman Publishing Ltd., London(145, 162).

De Croze, Austin, *Les Plats Régionaux de France.* Published by Éditions Daniel Morcrette, BP26,95270 Luzarches, France. Translated by permission of Éditions Daniel Morcrette(138).

Degner, Rotraud, *Das Schnellkochbuch für Feinschmecker.* © Copyright by Südwest Verlag Neumann & Co. KG, München. Published by Bastei-Verlag, Bergisch Gladbach. Translated by permission of the author, Munich(143).

De Gouy, Louis P., *The Gold Cook Book.* Copyright © 1947, 1948, 1964 by Louis P. De Gouy. Published by Chilton Book Company, Radnor, Pennsylvania. By permission of Chilton Book Company(122, 123).

Delineator Home Institute, *Beverages for Parties.* Copyright 1929 by the Butterick Publishing Co.(104, 124).

Derys, Gaston, *Les Plats au Vin.* Copyright 1937 by Albin Michel. Published by Éditions Albin Michel, Paris. Translated by permission of Éditions Albin Michel(147).

Detskoe Pitanie. Published by Gostorgizdat, Moscow 1958. Translated by permission of VAAP—The Copyright Agency of the U.S.S.R., Moscow(100).

The Diners' Club Drink Book. Copyright © 1961, by The Diners' Club, Inc. Published by Regents American Publishing Corporation, New York. By permission of Matty Simmons, Beverly Hills(159, 160, 163).

Dissanayake, Chandra, *Ceylon Cookery.* Printed by Metro Printers Limited, Ceylon, Sri Lanka. By permission of the author, Ceylon(93).

Dumont, Émile, *La Bonne Cuisine Française.* Published by Victorion Frères et Cie., Éditeurs, Paris 1889(113).

Durandeau, C., *Guide de la Bonne Cuisinière.* © 1979 by Éditions Baudouin, Paris. Published by Éditions Baudouin. Translated by permission of Société Nouvelle René Baudouin, Paris(114, 138, 142).

Edmonds, Anna G. (Editor), *An American Cook in Turkey.* Published by Redhouse Press, Istanbul 1978. By permission of Redhouse Press(92, 94, 95, 111).

Enciclopedia Salvat de la Cocina: Tomo 3. © 1972. Salvat, S.A. de Ediciones, Pamplona y S.A. Femmes d'Aujourd'hui—EDIPER, S.A. Published by Salvat S.A. de Ediciones, Pamplona. Translated by permission of Salvat S.A. de Ediciones(150).

L'Escole Parfaite des Officiers de Bouche. Published by Jean Ribou, Paris 1662(140, 148).

Farmer, Fannie Merritt, *The Fannie Farmer Cookbook.* Eleventh edition, revised by Wilma Lord Perkins. Copyright 1896, 1900, 1901, 1902, 1903, 1904, 1905, 1906, 1912, 1914 by Fannie Merritt Farmer. Copyright 1915, 1918, 1923, 1924, 1928, 1929 by Cora D. Perkins. Copyright 1930, 1931, 1932, 1933, 1934, 1936, 1940, 1941, 1942, 1943, 1946, 1951, © 1959, 1964, 1965 by Dexter Perkins Corp. Published by Little, Brown and Company, Boston. By permission of The Fannie Farmer Cookbook Corporation, Bedford(115, 123, 154, 158).

Favorite Island Cookery: Book II. Published by the Honpa Hongwanji Buddhist Temple, Honolulu, Hawaii 1975. By permission of the Honpa Hongwanji Buddhist Temple(102).

Feest: Tips en Recepten vor Partijtjes Thuis en Buiten. Published by Meijer Pers n.v., Amsterdam 1968. Translated by permission of Meijer Pers n.v.(123, 124).

Fitchett, Laura S. (Editor), *Beverages and Sauces of Colonial Virginia.* Copyright 1906 by Laura S. Fitchett. Published by The William Byrd Press, Inc., Richmond, Virginia 1938(105).

Flexner, Marion, *Out of Kentucky Kitchens.* © Copyright, 1949 by Marion Flexner. Published by Bramhall House, a division of Clarkson N. Potter, Inc., by arrangement with Franklin Watts, Inc. By permission of Franklin Watts, Inc., New York(150, 153, 154).

Foods of the World, *Wines and Spirits.* Copyright © 1968 Time Inc. Published by Time-Life Books, Alexandria, Virginia(155, 156, 157, 159).

Francatelli, Charles Elmé, *The Modern Cook.* Published by Richard Bentley, London 1862(127, 128).

Fuller, Richard R., *Tea for the Connoisseur.* Copyright © 1977 Richard R. Fuller. Published by United Writers Publications, St. Ives. By permission of the author(93).

Garrett, Blanche Pownall, *Canadian Country Preserves & Wines.* Copyright © 1974 by Blanche Pownall Garrett. Published by James Lewis & Samuel, Publishers, Toronto. By permission of James Lorimer & Co. Ltd., Toronto(130, 132).

Gaspero, Josh (Editor), *Hershey's 1934 Cookbook.* © Copyright 1971 by Hershey Foods Corporation. Designed and produced in the U.S.A. by Western Publishing Company, Inc. Published by Hershey Foods Corporation, Hershey, Pennsylvania. By permission of Hershey Foods Corporation(123).

Georgievsky, N. I., M. E. Melman, E. A. Shadura and A. S. Shemjakinsky, *Ukrainian Cuisine.* © English translation, Technika Publishers, 1975. Published by Technika Publishers, Kiev. By permission of the AAP, Copyright Agency of the U.S.S.R., Moscow(102, 129, 137, 139).

Gööck, Roland (Editor), *Elseviers Grote Kookboek.* © N. V. Uitgeversmaatschappij Elsevier, Amsterdam-Brussel. Published by Elsevier, Amsterdam-Brussel 1965. Translated by permission of Verlagsgruppe Bertelsmann International GmbH, Munich(145, 152).

Graves, Eleanor, *Great Dinners from Life.* Copyright © 1969 Time Inc. Published by Time-Life Books, Alexandria, Virginia(161).

Grigson, Jane, *Food with the Famous.* Copyright © 1979 by Jane Grigson. Published by Michael Joseph, London. By permission of David Higham Associates Limited for the author(99).

Grossman, Harold J., *Grossman's Guide to Wines, Beer and Spirits.* Sixth revised edition, edited by Harriet Lembeck. Copyright © 1974, 1977 by Charles Scribner's Sons. By permission of Charles Scribner's Sons, New York(154, 155, 156).

Grüninger, Ursula, *Cooking with Fruit.* © George Allen & Unwin Ltd., 1971. Published by George Allen & Unwin Ltd., London. By permission of George Allen & Unwin Ltd.(101, 156).

Hardy, Serena, *The Tea Book.* © 1979 by Serena Hardy. Published by Whittet Books Ltd., Weybridge. By permission of Whittet Books Ltd.(146).

Harland, Marion and Christine Terhune Herrick, *The National Cook Book.* Copyright 1896, by Charles Scribner's Sons for the United States of America. Published by T. Fisher Unwin, London 1896. By permission of Charles Scribner's Sons, New York(95, 106, 119, 137).

Hartley, Dorothy, *Food in England.* Published by Macdonald and Jane's (Macdonald & Co. (Publishers) Ltd.) London 1954. By permission of Macdonald Futura Publishers Ltd., London(137, 152).

Hazelton, Nika, *The Regional Italian Kitchen.* Copyright © 1978 by Nika Hazelton. Published by M. Evans and Company, Inc., New York. By permission of Curtis Brown Ltd., New York(126). *The Swiss Cookbook.* Copyright © 1967 by Nika Standen Hazelton. Published by Atheneum Publishers, Inc., New York(116).

Het Volkomen Zuivelboek. © 1973 Meijer Pers b.v., Amsterdam. Published by Meijer Pers b.v. Translated by permission of Meijer Pers b.v.(117, 118, 119, 120).

Hogg, Anthony, *Cocktails and Mixed Drinks.* © Copyright The Hamlyn Publishing Group Limited 1979. Published by The Hamlyn Publishing Group Limited, London. By permission of The Hamlyn Publishing Group Limited(158, 160, 162).

Hopkins, Albert A., *Home Made Beverages.* Copyright 1919, by The Scientific American Publishing Co. All rights reserved. Published by The Scientific American Publishing Company, New York. By permission of The Scientific American Publishing Company(111).

Husted, Mrs. Walter (Editor), *Virginia Cookery—Past and Present.* Copyright, 1957, by The Woman's Auxiliary of Olivet Episcopal Church, Franconia, Virginia. Published by The Woman's Auxiliary of Olivet Episcopal Church. By permission of The Woman's Auxiliary of Olivet Episcopal Church(142, 153).

Jack, Florence B., *Cookery for Every Household.* Published by Thomas Nelson and Sons, Ltd., London 1934. By permission of Thomas Nelson & Sons Ltd.(128). *One Hundred Drinks & Cups.* Published by Country Life Ltd., London 1927. By permission of The Hamlyn Publishing Group Limited, London(110, 117, 144).

Jarrin, G. A., *The Italian Confectioner.* Published by E. S. Ebers and Co., London 1841(103).

Katrandzhiev, K., *Bulgarskoto Kiselo Mlyako.* Published by the Bulgarian Academy of Sciences, Sofia 1962. Translated by permission of Jusautor Copyright Agency, Sofia(122).

Kennedy, Diana, *Cuisines of Mexico.* Copyright © 1972 by Diana Kennedy. By permission of the publisher, Harper & Row, Publishers, Inc., New York(97, 110, 116).

Kolpas, Norman, *The Chocolate Lovers' Companion.* Copyright © 1977 The Felix Gluck Press Ltd. Twickenham, England. Published by Quick Fox, New York and Tokyo. By permission of the author(115, 117).

Ladyfood: A Collection of Recipes Enjoyed by Ladies & Gentlemen. Copyright 1979. Printed by Specialty Publications/Taylor Publishing Company, Dallas, Texas. By permission of the Ladyfood Cookbook, Plano, Texas(145).

Lal, Premila, *Premila Lal's Indian Recipes.* Copyright © 1968 by Premila Lal. Published by Rupa & Co., Calcutta(95, 103, 105).

Lamb, Venice, *The Home Book of Turkish Cookery.* © Venice Lamb, 1969, 1973. Published by Faber and Faber Limited, London. By permission of Faber and Faber Ltd.(119).

Leslie, Mrs., *The American Family Cook Book.* Published by Higgins, Bradley, & Dayton, 1858(130).

Lewis, Edna, *The Taste of Country Cooking.* Copyright © 1976 by Edna Lewis. By permission of the publisher, Alfred A. Knopf, Inc.(115).

Leyel, Mrs. C. F. and Miss Olga Hartley, *The Gentle Art of Cookery.* Copyright by the Executors of Mrs. C. F. Leyel, 1925. Published by Chatto and Windus, London. By permission of Chatto and Windus Ltd.(95, 111).

Lincoln, Mrs. Mary J., *Mrs. Lincoln's Boston Cook Book.* Copyright, 1883, 1900, by Mrs. D. A. Lincoln. Copyright, 1904, by Little, Brown and Company. Published by Little, Brown and Company, Boston(116).

Lyon, Ninette, *Le Guide Marabout des Cocktails et Boissons Alcoolisées.* © 1980 s.a. Les Nouvelles Éditions Marabout, Verviers, Belgique. Published by s.a. Les Nouvelles Éditions Marabout. Translated by permission of s.a. Les Nouvelles Éditions Marabout(161, 162).

Manual de Cocina. Published by Editorial Almena, Madrid. Translated by permission of Editorial Doncel, Madrid(100, 140).

Manuel Pratique de Cuisine Provençale. © Pierre Belfond, 1980. Published by Éditions Pierre Belfond, Paris(140).

Marković, Spasenija-Pata (Editor), *Veliki Narodni Kuvar.* Copyright by the author. First Edition "Politika," Belgrade, 1938. Published by Narodna Knjiga, Belgrade, 1979. Translated by permission of Jugoslovenska Autorska Agencija, Belgrade, for the heir to the author(129).

Marković, Spasenija-Pata, *Yugoslav Cookbook.* Copyright © by Izdavacki Zavod "Jugoslavija," Belgrade. Fourth edition 1977. Published by Publicisticko-Izdavacki Zavod "Jugoslavija," Belgrade. Original title in Serbo-Croatian *Jugoslovenska Kuhinja.* By permission of Jugoslovenska Autorska Agencija, Belgrade, for the heir to the author(96).

Meade, Martha, *Recipes from the Old South.* Copyright © 1961 by Martha Meade. Published by Bramhall House, a division of Clarkson N. Potter, Inc., New York. By permission of Holt, Rinehart and Winston, Publishers, New York(143, 146).

Mestayer de Echagüe, María (Marquesa de Parabere), *Confitería y Repostería. (Enciclopedia Culinaria).* Copyright © 1950 by Espasa-Calpe, S.A., Madrid. Translated by permission of Espasa-Calpe, S.A.(112).

Montagné, Prosper, *The New Larousse Gastronomique.* English text copyright © 1977 by The Hamlyn Publishing Group Limited, London. By permission of Crown Publishers, Inc. New York(94).

Montenero, Pasquale, Anna Baslini Rosselli and Massimo Alberini, *L'Arte di Saper Mangiare (Senza Rinunce).* Copyright © 1972 by G. C. Sansoni S.P.A., Firenze. Published by G. C. Sansoni S.P.A. Translated by permission of G. C. Sansoni Editore Nuova S.P.A.(94, 102).

Morris, Harriett, *The Art of Korean Cooking.* Copyright in Japan, 1959 by the Charles E. Tuttle Company, Inc. Published by the Charles E. Tuttle Company, Inc., Tokyo. By permission of the Charles E. Tuttle Company, Inc.(94).

Olney, Richard, *The French Menu Cookbook.* © 1975 Richard Olney. Published by William Collins Sons & Co. Ltd., Glasgow and London. By permission of the author, Solliès-Pont(127).

Ortiz, Elisabeth Lambert, *Caribbean Cooking.* Copyright © Elisabeth Lambert Ortiz, 1973, 1975. Published by Penguin Books Ltd., London. By permission of Penguin Books Ltd.(103). *The Complete Book of Mexican Cooking.* Copyright © 1967 by Elisabeth Lambert Ortiz. Published by M. Evans and Company, Inc., New York. By permission of the author, London(104, 108).

Oxford Night Caps. Published by Slatter & Rose, Oxford 1860(145, 148).

Palay, Simin, *La Cuisine du Pays.* © 1970 Marrimpouey Jeune-Pau. Published by Éditions Marrimpouey Jeune et Cie, Pau. Translated by permission of Éditions Marrimpouey Jeune et Cie(113, 136, 138).

Paterson, Wilma, *A Country Cup.* Copyright © 1980 by Wilma Paterson. Published by Pelham Books Ltd., London(128, 135, 141).

Petits Propos Culinaires, October 1981. © Prospect Books 1981. Published by Prospect Books, London. By permission of the publisher(130, 136).

The Picayune Creole Cook Book. First published in 1901 as *The Original Picayune Creole Cook Book* by The Times-Picayune Publishing Co., New Orleans. Reprinted in 1971 by Dover Publications, Inc., New York(143, 148).

Pomiane, Édouard de, *Le Code de la Bonne Chère.* Published by Albin Michel, Éditeur, Paris. Translated by permission of Éditions Albin Michel, Paris(92).

Primlani, Kala, *Indian Cooking.* © Kala Primlani 1968. Published by IBH Publishing Company, Bombay. By permission of IBH Publishing Company(109, 125).

Reposteria Cocina Tipica. © Copyright 1972 Ediciones Naranco S.A. Published by Ediciones Naranco S.A., Oviedo. Translated by permission of Ediciones Naranco S.A.(117).

Rao, Shivaji and Shalini Devi Holkar, *Cooking of the Maharajas.* Copyright © 1975 by Shivaji Rao and Shalini Devi Holkar. Published by The Viking Press, New York. By permission of Shivaji Rao(118).

Rey-Billeton, Lucette, *Les Bonnes Recettes du Soleil.* © by Éditions Aubanel 1980. Published by Éditions Aubanel, Avignon. Translated by permission of Éditions Aubanel(141, 147).

Richardson, Collette (Editor), *House & Garden's Drink Guide.* Copyright © 1973 by The Condé Nast Publications, Inc., New York. Published by Simon and Schuster, New York. By permission of The Condé Nast Publications, Inc.(157, 163).

Richter, Gerda, *Wunderquelle Milch.* Copyright by Fackelträger-Verlag Schmidt-Küster GmbH. Published by Fackelträger-Verlag Schmidt-Küster GmbH., Hanover. Translated by permission of Fackelträger-Verlag Schmidt-Küster GmbH.(122).

Rinzler, Carol Ann, *The Signet Book of Yogurt.* Copyright © by Carol Ann Rinzler, 1979. Published by the New American Library, Inc., New York(121).

Robbins, Ann Roe, *Treadway Inns Cook Book.* Copyright © 1958 by Ann Roe Robbins. Published by Little, Brown and Company, Boston and Toronto. By permission of Little, Brown and Company, Boston(147, 160).

Roden, Claudia, *Coffee.* Copyright © Claudia Roden, 1977. Published by Penguin Books Ltd., London. By permission of the author, London(96, 99).

Rollin, Betty, *The Non-Drinker's Drink Book.* Copyright © 1965, 1966 by Betty Rollin and Lucy Rosenfeld. By permission of Doubleday & Company, Inc., New York(101, 102, 108).

Rombauer, Irma S. and Marion Rombauer Becker, *The Joy of Cooking.* Copyright © 1931, 1936, 1941, 1942, 1943, 1946, 1951, 1952, 1953, 1962, 1963, 1964, 1975, by Irma S. Rombauer and Marion Rombauer Becker. By permission of the publisher, The Bobbs-Merrill Company, Inc., New York(115, 116).

Roy, Michael, *Mike Roy's American Kitchen.* Copyright © 1974 by Michael Roy. Published by Harper's Magazine Press in association with Harper & Row, Publishers, Inc., New York. By permission of Harper & Row, Publishers, Inc.(145).

Rundell, Mrs., *Modern Domestic Cookery.* Published by Milner and Company, Limited, London(126).

Sahni, Julie, *Classic Indian Cooking.* Copyright © 1980 by Julie Sahni. By permission of the publisher, William Morrow & Company, Inc., New York(92, 121, 122, 127).

Santa Maria, Jack, *Indian Sweet Cookery.* © Jack Santa Maria 1979. Published by Rider and Company, London. By permission of Rider and Company(119, 121).

The Savoy Cocktail Book. © 1965 The Savoy Hotel Ltd. Published by Constable and Company Ltd., London. By permission of Constable and Company Ltd. and The Savoy Hotel, London(155, 158, 160, 162).

Schall, Sybille, *Cocina Rapida.* © Editorial Gräfe und Unzer. © by Editorial Everest. Published by Editorial Everest, S.A., León. Translated by permission of Gräfe und Unzer GmbH., Munich(116).

Schapira, Christiane, *La Cuisine Corse.* © Solar, 1979. Published by Solar, Paris. Translated by permission of Solar(137).

Schapira, Joel, David and Karl, *The Book of Coffee & Tea.* Copyright © 1975 by Joel Schapira and Karl Schapira. Published by St. Martin's Press Inc., New York. By permission of St. Martin's Press Inc.(114).

Scheibler, Sophie Wilhelmine, *Allgemeines Deutsches Kochbuch für alle Stände.* Published by C. F. Amelangs Verlag, Leipzig, 1896(151).

Schioler, Gail, *The Non-Drinker's Drink Book.* Copyright 1981 by Personal Library, Publishers, Toronto. By permission of the publisher, Personal Library, Publishers(107, 121, 122).

Serra Suñol, Victoria, *Sabores: Cocina del Hogar.* © Victoria Serra Suñol. Published by Editorial Luis Gili, Barcelona. By permission of John L. Gili, Oxford(114).

Simon, André L., *How to Make Wines and Cordials.* First published under the title *English Wines and Cordials* by Gramol Publications Ltd., London 1946. U.S. edition published by Dover Publications, Inc., 1972(142).

Shepard, Jean H., *The Fresh Fruits and Vegetables Cookbook.* Copyright © 1975 by Jean H. Shepard. Published by Little, Brown and Company, Boston. By permission of the author(104, 107).

Spagnol, Elena, *I Gelati Fatti in Casa con o Senza Macchina.* © 1975 Rizzoli Editore, Milano. Published by Rizzoli Editore. Translated by permission of Rizzoli Editore(107).

Stanforth, Deirdre (Editor), *Brennan's New Orleans Cookbook.* Copyright © 1961, 1964 Brennan's Restaurant and Hermann B. Deutsch. Published by Robert L. Crager & Company, Publishers, New Orleans. By permission of Robert L. Crager & Company(98).

Stevens, Karen Goldwach, *Dining In-Chicago.* Copyright © 1979 by Peanut Butter Publishing. By permission of the Publisher, Peanut Butter Publishing, Mercer Island, Washington(98).

Stirum, C. Countess von Limburg, *The Art of Dutch Cooking.* Copyright © 1961 by C. Countess von Limburg Stirum. By permission of the publisher, Doubleday & Company, Inc.(119, 120, 151, 152).

Stockbridge, Bertha E. L., *What to Drink.* Copyright, 1920, by D. Appleton and Company. Published by D. Appleton and Company, New York and London(110, 120, 124).

Stoll, F. M. and W. H. de Groot, *Het Haagse Kookboek.* © 1973 Van Goor Zonen. © 1979 Elsevier Nederland B.V., Amsterdam/Brussel. Published by Van Goor Zonen and de Gebroeders van Cleef, den Haag. Translated by permission of Elsevier Nederland B.V., Amsterdam(104, 152).

Suzanne, Alfred, *La Cuisine Anglaise et la Patisserie.* Privately published by the author, 1894(149).
Tante Marie, *La Véritable Cuisine de Famille.* © Éditions A. Taride, Paris, 1978. Published by Éditions A. Taride. Translated by permission of SARL Cartes Taride, Paris(140).
Tashev, Tasho, Zh. Stoyanova and Ya. Dzhambazova, *Dietichno Hranene.* Published by Meditsina i Fizkoultoura, Sofia 1976. Translated by permission of Jusautor Copyright Agency, Sofia(94, 111).
Tibbott, S. Minwel, *Welsh Fare.* © National Museum of Wales (Welsh Folk Museum). Published by National Museum of Wales (Welsh Folk Museum), Cardiff, 1976. By permission of National Museum of Wales (Welsh Folk Museum)(129).
Toklas, Alice B., *The Alice B. Toklas Cook Book.* Copyright, 1954, by Alice B. Toklas. Published by Anchor Books/Doubleday & Company, Inc., New York. By permission of Harper & Row, Publishers, Inc., New York(98, 153, 163).
Trader Vic, *Trader Vic's Bartender's Guide, Revised.* Copyright 1947, © 1972 by Victor Bergeron. By permission of the publisher, Doubleday & Company, Inc., New York(158, 160, 163).
Tritton, S. M., *Guide to Better Wine and Beer Making for Beginners.* Copyright 1969 by Dover Publications Inc., New York. By permission of the publisher, Dover Publications, Inc.(130, 133, 135).
Turner, Ben, *Winemaking & Brewing.* Copyright © 1971 by B.C.A. Turner. Published by Pelham Books Ltd., London(134).
United Kingdom Bartenders' Guild, *International Guide to Drinks.* © United Kingdom Bartenders' Guild 1980. Published by Hutchinson Benham, London. By permission of United Kingdom Bartenders' Guild, London(155, 159, 161, 162).
Urvater, Michèle and David Liederman, *Cooking the Nouvelle Cuisine in America.* Copyright © 1979 by Michèle Urvater and David Liederman. Published by Workman Publishing Co., Inc., New York. By permission of Workman Publishing Co., Inc.(126).
Van der Meer, Janny and Beatrice R. Mansur (Editors), *Tanzanian Food with Traditional and New Recipes.* Published by the Food and Agriculture Organization of the United Nations, Rome 1973(103, 104, 106).
Vera, *Si Fa Cosi.* © 1974 Rizzoli Editore, Milano. Published by Rizzoli Editore. Translated by permission of Rizzoli Editore S.p.A.(117).
Viard and Fouret, *Le Cuisinier Royal.* Paris, 1828(138).
Victorian Cups and Punches and other Concoctions. Copyright © Cassell and Co. 1974. Published by Cassell and Co. Ltd., London. By permission of Cassell Ltd.(148).
Voegeling, François, *La Gastronomie Alsacienne.* © Copyright by Éditions des Dernières Nouvelles de Strasbourg. Published by Éditions des Dernières Nouvelles d'Alsace-ISTRA, Strasbourg. Translated by permission of Librairie ISTRA, Strasbourg(139).
Widenfelt, Sam (Editor), *Favorite Swedish Recipes.* Published by Dover Publications, Inc., New York 1975. By permission of Dover Publications, Inc.(147).
Wilson, Ellen Gibson, *A West African Cook Book.* Copyright © 1971 by Ellen Gibson Wilson. Published by M. Evans and Company, Inc., New York. By permission of Shirley Burke Agency, New York(105, 109, 110, 125).
Witty, Helen and Elizabeth Schneider Colchie, *Better Than Store-Bought.* Copyright © 1979 by Helen Witty and Elizabeth Schneider Colchie. By permission of the publisher, Harper & Row, Publishers, Inc., New York(95, 100, 120, 125).
Wolfert, Paula, *Couscous and Other Good Food from Morocco.* Copyright © 1973 by Paula Wolfert. Published by Harper & Row, Publishers, Inc., New York. By permission of the author, New York(131).
Woolfolk, Margaret, *Cooking with Berries.* Copyright © 1979 by Margaret Woolfolk. Published by Clarkson N. Potter, Inc., New York. By permission of Crown Publishers, Inc.(137, 157).
Worth, Helen, *Damnyankee in a Southern Kitchen.* Copyright © 1973 by Helen Worth. Published by Westover Publishing Company, Richmond, Virginia. By permission of Helen Worth(100).
Young, Mala, *Drinks and Snacks.* Copyright © 1981 by David & Charles (Publishers), Ltd. By permission of the publisher, David & Charles (Publishers), Ltd., Newton Abbot, Devon, England(108).

Acknowledgments

The indexes for this book were prepared by Louise W. Hedberg. The editors are particularly indebted to Donald Ace, Pennsylvania State University, University Park; Norbert Bender, The Cellar, Fairfax, Virginia; Dr. F. William Cooler, Virginia Polytechnic Institute and State University, Blacksburg; Robert Dick, Food and Drug Administration, Brooklyn, New York; Gail Duff, Kent, England; Dr. James A. Duke, United States Department of Agriculture, Beltsville, Maryland; M. William Hirte, The Coffee Bean, Alexandria, Virginia; Vic Morris, Kent, England; Dr. G. Hamilton Mowbray, Westminster, Maryland; Ksai Nguyen, East Wind Restaurant, Alexandria, Virginia; Ann O'Sullivan, Majorca, Spain; Derek Pearman, W. R. Loftus Ltd., London; Claudia Roden, London; David Schwartz, London; Dr. R. H. Smith, Aberdeen, Scotland; Rex Talbert, Alexandria, Virginia; William Tayleur, Brew It Yourself Ltd., London; Tom Wolfe, Smile Herb Shop, College Park, Maryland.

The authors also wish to thank: John Adinolfi, National Coffee Association, New York; Markie Benet, London; Nicola Blount, London; Joseph W. Boling, Virginia Polytechnic Institute and State University, Blacksburg; Marisa Centis, London; Josephine Christian, Somerset, England; Lesley Coates, Essex, England; Emma Codrington, Surrey, England; Dr. William F. Collins, Virginia Polytechnic Institute and State University, Blacksburg; Cona Ltd., London; George Cook, University of California, Davis; Covent Garden Kitchen Supplies, London; Divertimenti Cooking and Tableware, London; June Dowding, Essex, England; Mimi Errington, Nottinghamshire, England; Fairfax Kitchen Shop, London; Jay Ferguson, London; Fortnum & Mason Ltd., London; Nayla Freeman, London; Gered, London; Scott Grønmark, London; Mary Harron, London; Maggi Heinz, London; H. R. Higgins (Coffee-man) Ltd., London; Household Articles, South Croydon, England; Maria Johnson, Kent, England; Aquila Kegan, London; Wanda Kemp-Welch, Nottingham, England; Bruce Kenney, The Cellar, Fairfax, Virginia;

J. McQuade, United Kingdom Bartenders Guild, London; John Man, Oxford, England; Everett Matthews, M. E. Swing Co., Washington, D.C.; Melita-Werke Bentz & Sohn, Dunstable, England; Philippa Millard, London; Sonya Mills, Oxford, England; Moka Express Ltd., London; Wendy Morris, London; Julia F. Morton, University of Miami, Coral Gables, Florida; Carolyn Myers, International Bartending Institute, Alexandria, Virginia; Dilys Naylor, Surrey, England; Winona O'Connor, London; Dr. Cornelius Ough, University of California, Davis; William Page and Co. Ltd., London; Helena Perry, Surrey, England; Neil Philip, London; Elizabeth Pickford, Long Ashton Research Station, Bristol, England; Sylvia Robertson, Surrey, England; Robert Schuck, London; Stephanie Thompson, London; Fiona Tillet, London; Majorie Vuylsteke, Oak Knoll Vineyards, Hillsboro, Oregon; Tina Walker, London; Beryl Walter, Tea Council of the U.S.A., Inc., New York; Rita Walters, Essex, England; Dr. A. D. Webb, University of California, Davis; Wine Institute, San Francisco.

Picture Credits

The sources for the pictures in this book are listed below. Credits for each of the photographers and illustrators are listed by page number in sequence with successive pages indicated by hyphens; where necessary, the locations of pictures within pages are also indicated—separated from page numbers by dashes.

Photographs by Bob Komar: Cover, 4, 8—bottom center and right, 9—bottom left and center, 15—top right and left, 18, 19—top left and center, bottom left and center, 20—bottom left and center, 21—top left and right, 30, 32—top, 33, 34—top center and right, 35, 36—top and bottom right, 37, 39—bottom right, 40—top, 41—top left, bottom, 42—bottom right, 43—bottom, 44, 48—bottom right, 49—bottom, 50—bottom left and center, 66—bottom, 67—bottom left and center, 68, 69—top left and center, bottom, 78, 80-81, 82—bottom, 83—top, 84-86, 87—top, bottom center and right, 88—top left, top center left, 89—top right, bottom left, bottom center left and right, 90—bottom left.

Other photographs (alphabetically): Tom Belshaw, 12-14, 15—except top right and left, 16, 17—except center, 34—top left, 39—bottom left, 51—top and bottom right, 53—bottom, 54, 56-57, 67—bottom right, 73—top center and right, bottom, 75—bottom center and right, 77—bottom, 82—top, 83—bottom, 88—bottom center right, bottom right, 89—top left, top center left, 90—top, bottom center and right. Alan Duns, 10, 23—bottom, 24—bottom, 25—top right, 27—top and bottom right, 28-29, 34—bottom, 40—bottom, 41—top center and right, 46-47, 48—top, bottom left, 49—top, 58-63, 67—top left and center, 72—top, bottom left, 73—top left, 74—bottom right, 75—bottom left, 76—top, 77—top, 87—bottom left, 89—top center right, bottom center right. John Elliott, 9—top left and center, 21—top center, bottom, 22—top, 23—top, 25—top left and center, 26, 27—top left and center, bottom left, 42—top, bottom left and center, 43—top, 50—top, bottom left, 51—top left and center, bottom left and center, 52, 53—top, 64, 66—top, 67—top right, 72—bottom right, 76—bottom. Fil Hunter, 19—top right, 20—bottom right, 25—bottom, 71—bottom right, 74—top, bottom left, 75—top, 88—top center right, top right,

bottom left, bottom center left. Louis Klein, 2. Aldo Tutino, 8—bottom left, 9—top and bottom right, 17—center, 19—bottom right, 22—bottom, 24—top, 32—bottom, 36—top left and center, bottom left and center, 38, 39—top, 69—top right, 70, 71—top, bottom left and center. Illustrations: From The Mary Evans Picture Library and private sources and *Food & Drink: A Pictorial Archive from Nineteenth Century Sources* by Jim Harter, published by Dover Publications, Inc., 1979, 93-167.

Library of Congress Cataloguing in Publication Data
Main entry under title:
Beverages.
(The Good cook, techniques & recipes)
Includes index.
1. Beverages. 2. Alcoholic beverages. I. Time-Life Books. II. Series.
TX815.B48 1983   641.8'7   82-19348
ISBN 0-8094-2946-2 (lib. bdg.)
ISBN 0-8094-2945-4 (retail ed.)

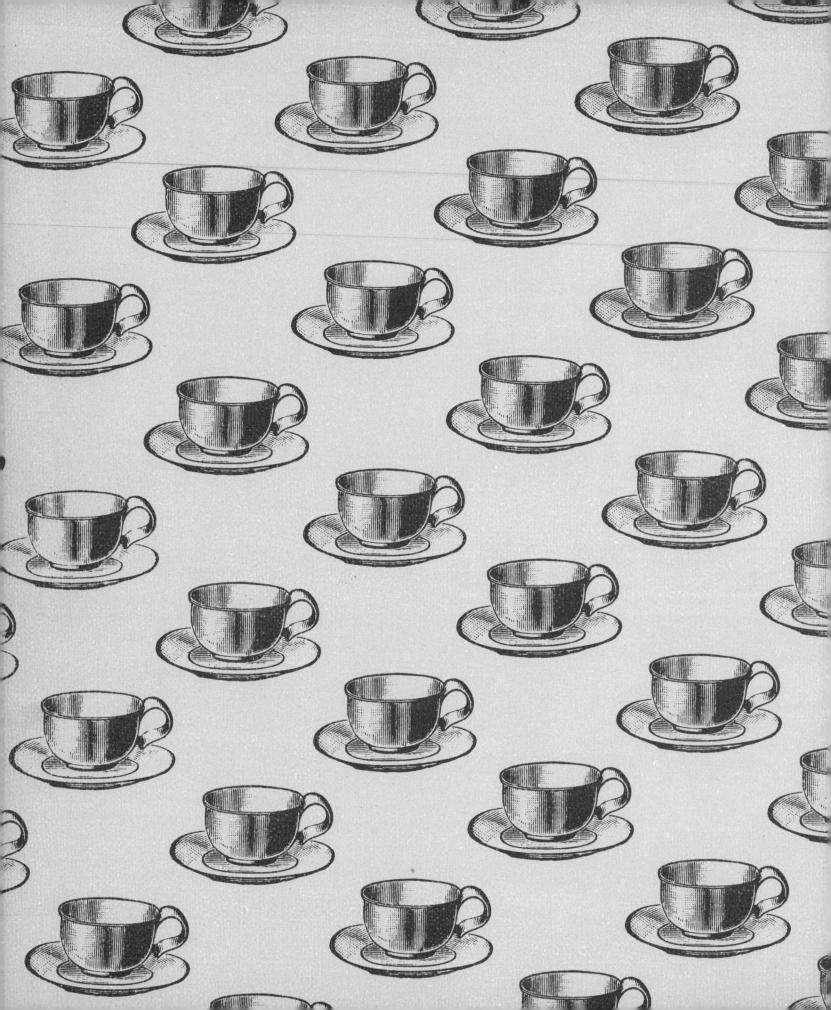